CHIC
made simple

....

ESTHER DEUTSCH

fresh. fast. fabulous.

KOSHER CUISINE

CHIC
made simple
ESTHER DEUTSCH

PHOTOGRAPHY John Uher, Menachem Adelman, Sam Freidman, Baila Gluck, Mark Thomas

EDITOR Suri Brand

FOOD STYLING Esther Deutsch, Melanie Dubberley: pp. 13, 45, 89, 175, 183, 195, 199
Aviv Mosovich: pp. 39, 79, 103, 125, 127, 349, AJ Schaller: pp. 43, 168, 186

GRAPHIC DESIGN CONCEPTS Anelis Design www.anelisdesign.com

PROOFREADERS Suri Brand, Jodi Newman, Dina Schreiber, Gill Hammersley

PRODUCTION ARTISTS Rochel Weller, Joy Yih

PUBLIC RELATIONS Stuart Schnee

PUBLISHED BY Manna 11 LLC. publisher@manna11.com

DISTRIBUTED BY Feldheim Publishers www.feldheim.com

© 2013 by Manna 11 LLC

First Printing: January 2013
Second Printing: June 2013
Third Printing: February 2014
Fourth Printing: April 2015
Fifth Printing: September 2019

ISBN 978-1-59826-021-2

Printed in China

THANK YOU

TO MY CHILDREN, who have taught me to serve both food and love—unconditionally—every day. You make it all worth it.

TO MY PARENTS, for their never-ending enthusiasm for this project and who make the best marketing and PR team!

TO RECHY FRANKFURTER, who encouraged me to share my kitchen with cooks everywhere within the pages of AMI magazine.

TO SURI BRAND, who went above and beyond the call of duty. You are the consummate professional and your reputation precedes you.

I WISH to express my appreciation to the following people who shared their unsurpassed talents, efforts, and grace in making this book a reality:

John Uher, Menachem Adelman, Sam Friedman, Baila Gluck, Esty Weiss, editor of AIM magazine, Elisheva Perlman of anelisdesign.com, Rochel Weller, Joy Yih, Dina Schreiber, Gill Hammersley, Jodi Newman, Eli M. Hollander, Yitzchak Feldheim and Feldheim Publishers, Max Lau, Stuart Schnee, Aviv Mosovich, Melanie Dubberley, Steve Wizel.

MANY THANKS to all those who tasted, tested, and shared their favorite recipes:

K. Bernstein, Avigail Braunstein, Shani Censor, Avigail Deutsch, Chany Deutsch, Michelle Deutsch, Ruthie Dombroff, Toby Eisenreich, Malky Goldzal, Esti Holcberg, Frumi Horowitz, Gabby Jimal, Yali Katz, Debbie Kazarnovsky, Joyce Khezrie, Tziporah Laub, Chanie Leiner, Esther Leiner, Karen Mause, Elisheva Perlman, Aviva Pifko, Debbie Richland, Lucy Rosenthal, Dini Roz, Chaya Rubin, Shoshana Rub, Malky Rabinowitz, Malky Safrin, Reb. Shoshana Safrin, Judy Schlanger, Dina Schreiber, Yocheved Schreiber, Ahuva Soibelman, Esther Soibelman, Rikki Wagh, Rivka Wassner, Mindy Weinberger, Esther C. and Tzali Weiss, Batsheva Weiss, Esty Weiss, Tammy Weiss, Tzila Elias

ABOVE ALL, I'm grateful to Hashem, the ultimate source of all our blessings.

CONTENTS

6 INTRODUCTION

8 APPETIZERS & SIDES

68 SOUPS

86 SALADS

122 POULTRY

150 MEAT

180 FISH

210 DAIRY

258 DESSERTS

363 INDEX

I couldn't have avoided the kitchen if I tried.

I come from a long line of stellar cooks, and good food—and plenty of it—was always central to family gatherings. My grandmother will always be remembered for her generous heart and quick wit, but it's her efforts at the stove top that have been immortalized in family lore. (We grandchildren still wax poetic about "kousala," her scrumptious signature dish that's impossible to replicate.)

The cooking gene was passed on to me, and when I was ten years old, I eagerly made my first attempt at eggplant parmesan—my absolute favorite food in those days. The abundance of traditional home-cooked foods that were part of my life while growing up were my comfort zone. I was a safe cook.

Then I got married. Cooking for someone who appreciated good food inspired in me a genuine interest, not just in cooking food, but in *creating*. It was perfect timing. America was undergoing a culinary renaissance that swept me right along. The more lavish the meal, the better. I reveled in setting my table days before a dinner party, with a luxurious attention to detail. No recipe was too labor intensive, no ingredient too esoteric. Buying store-bought pie crust was sacrilegious.

Then life happened. I had my babies, and suddenly the importance of pie-crust-from-scratch receded. I discovered that if I filled a ready-made pie crust with decadent ingredients, no one came knocking to accuse me of a culinary crime. On the contrary, they clamored for the recipe. I even abandoned recipes that called for separating eggs unless they specifically required a meringue topping. Why separate eggs when so many quicker chocolate cake recipes delivered the same—or even better—results?

So perfectionism was out, and fuss-free became the way to go. My essential criteria for good food hadn't lapsed—food still needed to be absolutely delicious and served with flair—but quick and easy now made the list, too.

I haven't looked back since. Though I have less time, cooking has remained exhilarating. I thrive on creating fabulously chic recipes that require barely any prep time but look elaborate and taste amazing. And I reap the ultimate reward of fuss-free cooking: as my time in the kitchen grows shorter, my time gathered around the table with the people I love grows longer. "You don't grow old at the table," they say, and it's where I spend my happiest hours.

After all the years of introducing new foods to my family, my efforts have paid off. My oldest has become a brave eater and my little ones have progressed far beyond the familiarity of macaroni and cheese. I can't help but feel a little triumphant when I get one of my fussy eaters to taste a lamb chop. As for the rare request for second helpings—well, being asked for doubles on anything is always music to my ears!

I also love the way food embraces all of our senses: the sight of a perfectly grilled steak, the smell of freshly baked apple cobbler, the velvety smooth texture of a melt-in-your-mouth cheesecake... The real secret of cooking isn't that it soothes the stomach; it's that it comforts and feeds our souls. For me, this strikes at the heart of why we cook: because it's another way to show we care.

As you flip through the pages of this cookbook, the photographs will make your mouth water and you will feel the urge to head over to your kitchen. Don't be surprised to find that you'll be done cooking much sooner than you expected.

Here, in CHIC MADE SIMPLE, I offer you my favorite dishes, brimming with a fusion of flavors prepared in luscious and enchanting ways. When you convene at your own table, I hope that my family favorites will become yours and that long after your meals with the people you care about most are over, the memories will linger.

I'm thrilled to share a cookbook that's about making your cooking more special—and your life easier. Sounds like an oxymoron? Turn the page.

Welcome to my kitchen. Life happens here.

Esther Deutsch

small bites, big flavor

APPETIZERS & SIDES

Scallion Quinoa Patties with Lemon Garlic Paprika Aioli

QUINOA PATTIES

2½ CUPS cooked quinoa

4 eggs

1 CUP flavored cornflake crumbs

1¼ TSP. kosher salt or sea salt

4 CLOVES garlic, minced

1 CUP scallions or chives, thinly sliced

- Fresh black pepper
- Oil, for frying

AIOLI

½ CUP mayonnaise

2 TBSP. fresh lemon juice

5 CLOVES garlic, minced

1 TBSP. water

½ TSP. paprika

CREATING THE *best recipe for quinoa presented a serious challenge. Quinoa is so healthy and good for you, and you know you should like it, but perhaps you've tried enough variations of quinoa to assume that it just doesn't do it for you.*

Not anymore. I was very demanding in my quest for the best quinoa recipe, and my efforts have paid off. This recipe will change how you feel about quinoa—guaranteed.

1. To prepare the aioli: In a small bowl, combine the aioli ingredients until mixed.

2. To prepare the patties: In a medium bowl, combine the quinoa, eggs, cornflake crumbs, salt, garlic, scallions or chives, and black pepper.

3. In a skillet, heat the oil over medium heat. Form the quinoa mixture into patties and fry in the oil until golden and crispy, about 5 minutes per side. Serve warm or at room temperature with the aioli spooned on top. **Yields 10–12 patties.**

Deli Roll Sushi with Dipping Sauce

⅓ CUP rice vinegar

¼ CUP sugar

1 TBSP. salt

3 CUPS sushi rice, washed and prepared according to package directions

16 SLICES smoked turkey roll, cut into ¼-inch strips

16 SLICES deli pastrami (or any deli meat of your choice), cut into ¼-inch strips

8 SHEETS nori seaweed

DIPPING SAUCE

1 CUP duck sauce

1 TBSP. Dijon mustard

2 TBSP. teriyaki sauce

GARNISH

• Baco Bits

• Chives, thinly sliced

• Black sesame seeds

DELI ROLL *has become one of the most ubiquitous foods served at Shabbos meals. Here is a fun, updated version that's full of great flavors to delight everyone—both sushi lovers and those who prefer deli. It will keep fresh in the fridge for up to a day, making it a great new item for your Shabbos lunch menu.*

The thought of making your own sushi can seem daunting, but this roll is no more complex than a puff pastry deli roll. With this easy-to-follow recipe, you'll soon be making sushi like a pro (a bamboo mat is not necessary). Once you get the hang of it, you'll only get better.

The rice is the most essential part of the sushi experience. After testing many sushi rice recipes, this one emerged the clear winner. Feel free to be heavy-handed with the Baco Bits— they add awesome flavor and texture.

note: If you plan to serve this appetizer for Shabbos lunch, bring the sushi to room temperature before serving.

1. To prepare the vinegar sushi rice: In a small bowl, combine the rice vinegar, sugar, and salt. Pour the vinegar mixture over the cooked rice and mix until evenly incorporated. (Be careful not to smash the grains of rice.)

2. Place a sheet of nori seaweed, shiny side down, on a flat surface. Gently spread about 1 cup of the rice on the seaweed to form a layer about ¼-inch thick—the rice layer should not be too thick. The rice should not be packed down, and some of the nori may be visible through the rice.

3. Arrange the strips of turkey and pastrami (or deli meat of your choice) evenly across the center of the rice, covering the full width of the sheet (and leaving uncovered rice above and below the meat). Each roll should include enough meat strips to equal about 4 slices of deli meat. Be careful not to overfill the roll.

4. Brush the top edge of the seaweed with water and roll the seaweed sheet jelly-roll style. Repeat with the remaining sheets of nori. If you are preparing the sushi rolls in advance, keep in mind that they will stay fresh in the refrigerator for no more than a day.

5. Slice just before serving: using a very sharp wet knife, trim the excess nori from the ends of the sushi rolls, and then slice the rolls into 6 bite-sized pieces.

6. To prepare the dipping sauce: In a small bowl, combine the duck sauce, mustard, and teriyaki sauce.

7. When ready to serve, garnish the sushi with the Baco Bits, chives, and sesame seeds. Serve with the dipping sauce on the side. **Serves 8.**

Asian Portobello Mushrooms

READING THIS *cookbook, you may notice that I'm partial to mushrooms—and with good reason. From the humble button mushroom to the prized truffle and all the varieties in between, they are extremely versatile, healthy, and packed with flavor. My personal favorites are portobello mushrooms with their dense, meaty texture and rich flavor.*

This recipe is great as a side dish or an appetizer. The mushrooms can also be grilled and added to your barbecue menu. Also try adding sliced eggplant, zucchini, and asparagus to this marinade and then grilling. Serve the portobello mushrooms whole or sliced— they're quite lovely sliced on salads.

6 large portobello caps

MARINADE

½ CUP oil

⅓ CUP lite soy sauce

1 TBSP. seasoned rice vinegar

1 TBSP. honey

5 CLOVES garlic, minced or sliced

• Kosher salt

• Fresh black pepper

OPTIONAL GARNISHES

• Radish sprouts

• Fresh parsley, chopped

1. To prepare the marinade: In a jar, combine all the marinade ingredients, shaking until well combined. Place the portobello caps in a large Ziploc bag and add the marinade. Seal the bag and refrigerate for at least 6 hours.

2. Preheat the oven to 425° F. Remove the mushrooms from the bag and roast, gill-side down, on a baking sheet until tender, 20 minutes. Serve warm, garnished with radish sprouts and fresh parsley, if desired. **Serves 6.**

Salmon Tartare

½ LB. sushi-grade salmon, finely chopped

2 TSP. chives, thinly sliced

1 TBSP. shallots, minced

1 TBSP. fresh dill, minced

1 TBSP. fresh lemon juice

1 TBSP. mayonnaise

½ TSP. kosher salt

¼ TSP. fresh black pepper

THIS SALMON *dish takes its cue from the classic tuna tartare, a combination of finely chopped raw tuna, sauce, and seasonings. Here the salmon is lightly cured by lemon juice, and the fresh dill, the essential ingredient in this recipe, lends a sweet and tangy note to the dish.*

Salmon tartare is the perfect instant appetizer that you can serve with your favorite crackers or bread, individually on endive leaves, tortilla chips, or wonton crisps (see page 54). You can prepare this tartare up to four hours in advance.

In a medium bowl, combine all the ingredients. Refrigerate until ready to serve. Bring to room temperature before serving. **Serves 6–8.**

Garlic Bread with Porcini-Onion Relish

1 LB. skirt steak or prepared hot pastrami

2 CLOVES garlic, minced

• Fresh black pepper

⅛ TSP. red pepper flakes

3 TBSP. oil

1 PKG. (8 oz.) frozen garlic bread

• Arugula, to garnish

• Hazelnuts, toasted and chopped, to garnish (optional)

RELISH

6 TBSP. oil

1 medium onion, diced

6 OZ. porcini mushrooms, thinly sliced

½ CUP chicken stock

• Kosher salt

• Fresh black pepper

¼ CUP dry white wine

IF **YOU** buy ready-made garlic bread (which is available in the freezer section of most supermarkets), these appetizers are nearly effortless. I used skirt steak for the dish in the photograph, but I've also prepared this appetizer with shredded hot pastrami (see note below). Alternatively, you can use chicken cutlets, shredded flanken, sliced London broil, or sliced rib steak.

Practically anything you put on garlic bread tastes great, but meat, onions, and mushrooms put it over the top. If you can't find fresh porcini mushrooms, you can use the dried variety; any other mushroom of your choice will also work.

To spruce up the presentation, I like to mix it up a bit with a mixture of sandwich-style and open-faced portions topped with arugula for a splash of color. Occasionally I sprinkle the tops of the sandwiches with chopped toasted hazelnuts to lend added interest and a slight dulcet flavor. Hazelnuts and porcini mushrooms are often paired together because of the nice flavor they produce when combined.

You may want to consider doubling the recipe—these go fast!

note: If you are using hot pastrami instead of skirt steak, bake a pastrami roast, covered very tightly, at 250° F, for a minimum of 6–8 hours, until it is super soft. Slice thinly against the grain.

1. Slice the skirt steak or pastrami into equal-size pieces. Coat the meat slices with the garlic, black pepper, and red pepper flakes. In a skillet, heat the 3 tablespoons of oil over high heat. When the oil is very hot, add the meat slices and sauté until medium rare, 2 minutes per side. Remove the meat from the skillet and allow to cool for 10 minutes.

2. Meanwhile, prepare the garlic bread according to the package directions.

3. To prepare the porcini-onion relish: In the skillet, heat 3 tablespoons of the oil. Add the onion and sauté in the oil over medium heat until translucent. Add the mushrooms and sauté until the mushrooms are soft, for several more minutes. Add the chicken stock, salt, and black pepper. Cook, stirring occasionally, until the chicken stock is reduced, several minutes. Raise the heat to high. Add the white wine to the skillet and cook for 3 minutes longer. Deglaze the pan by scraping off any bits stuck to the bottom and turn off the heat. Add additional salt and black pepper if needed.

4. To assemble the sandwiches: Slice open the garlic bread. Spread the bottom half with the porcini-onion relish and fill with slices of skirt steak or pastrami. Cut the sandwich into slices on the diagonal. To assemble open-faced sandwiches: Slice open the garlic bread. Top each half with porcini-onion relish and a slice of skirt steak or pastrami. Garnish with the arugula and toasted hazelnuts. **Serves 4-6.**

Tri-Color Garlic Mashed Potatoes with Caramelized Shallots

FOR A clever and easy way to prepare mashed potatoes, roast unpeeled potatoes in the oven, allowing them to steam in their skins. Roasting the potatoes in their skins maintains their crispiness and texture—and saves you lots of time—as opposed to boiling them in water, which reduces their flavor.

Once cooked, spear each spud with a fork and pull off the skin with a serrated knife, or cut each potato in half and scrape out the insides. The skin should come off easily with virtually no waste of potato flesh.

Prepare this recipe with your favorite potato, or triple the recipe and serve up a trio of colors using sweet, russet, and blue potatoes.

2 LB. potatoes (russet, sweet, or blue), peels intact

1 HEAD garlic

• Oil

1 CUP shallots, minced or finely diced

3 TBSP. trans-fat-free margarine

½ CUP chicken stock

2 TBSP. Tofutti sour cream

• Sea salt

• Fresh black pepper

1. Preheat the oven to 375° F. Roast the potatoes until cooked through, at least 1½ hours.

2. Meanwhile, drizzle the garlic head with the oil. Wrap the garlic in foil and bake for 1 hour (together with the potatoes).

3. In a large skillet, heat oil. Sauté the shallots in the oil until golden.

4. Remove the potatoes and garlic from the oven. Cut the potatoes in half and scoop out the flesh. In a large bowl, combine the potatoes, margarine, chicken stock, sour cream, salt, and black pepper.

5. Cut the garlic head in half and squeeze the softened cloves into the potatoes. Add the caramelized shallots. With a fork, mash the potato-cream mixture, garlic, and shallots or puree with a blender, depending on the desired consistency. Serve warm. **Serves 6.**

Wild Rice Pilaf with Cherries and Almonds

A SNEAK PEEK *into my freezer will tell you that I'm not much of a freezer person. I prefer to prepare meals fresh. But the one item I always keep frozen is chicken stock. It adds depth, flavor, and intensity to many side dishes—including this one.*

note: The recipe for the Cornish hen pictured here with the pilaf can be found on page 124.

3 TBSP. oil

⅓ CUP shallots, finely chopped

1 CUP wild rice

2 CLOVES garlic, minced

3 CUPS chicken stock

½ CUP almonds, sliced

½ CUP dried cherries or Craisins

3 TBSP. scallions, thinly sliced

- Sea salt

- Fresh black pepper

1. In a medium saucepan, heat the oil over medium heat. Add the shallots and cook, stirring occasionally, until tender, about 4 minutes. Add the rice and garlic and cook for 30 seconds. Add the chicken stock and bring to a boil. Reduce the heat to low and simmer, covered, until the rice is tender, about 50 minutes.

2. Meanwhile, toast the almonds: Preheat the oven to 350° F. Spread the sliced almonds on a baking sheet and toast until browned, about 10 minutes. Allow to cool.

3. Once the rice is cooked, add the toasted almonds, cherries or Craisins, and scallions. Season with the salt and black pepper. Serve warm or at room temperature. **Serves 6.**

Stuffed Eggplant Canapés with Veal

> **CANAPÉS ARE** *small-sized morsels or hors d'oeuvres that can be served either as an appetizer or a side dish. When scooping out the eggplants for these canapés, make sure to leave enough flesh that the skins hold their shape while baking. The stuffing for the eggplants can also be used to stuff a rack of veal, chicken, or turkey. Feel free to substitute chopped chuck beef for the veal.*

12 mini purple eggplants

4 TBSP. oil

1 large onion, finely diced

6 CLOVES garlic (fresh or frozen), minced

1 LB. chopped veal

1 TSP. liquid smoke

¼ CUP bread crumbs

2 TBSP. Worcestershire sauce

2 TBSP. fresh parsley, chopped

2 TBSP. fresh basil, chopped

¾ TSP. kosher salt

¼ TSP. fresh black pepper

1 red bell pepper, finely diced

• Chopped chives, to garnish

1. Preheat the oven to 350° F. Cut the mini eggplants in half, keeping the stems intact. Scoop out the eggplant flesh, reserving the skins, and dice finely.

2. In a skillet, heat the oil. Add the onion and garlic and sauté in the oil until cooked through. Add the diced eggplant and sauté until soft. Add the veal and sauté until all the liquid is evaporated and the meat begins to brown. Remove from the heat and break up the meat with a fork so that there are no large chunks.

3. Combine the meat and eggplant mixture with the liquid smoke, bread crumbs, Worcestershire sauce, parsley, basil, salt, and black pepper. Spoon the mixture into the eggplant skins and sprinkle with the diced red pepper. Transfer the stuffed eggplants to a greased baking dish and bake, covered, until the eggplants are completely soft and cooked through, at least 1½–2 hours. Before serving, garnish with the chopped chives. **Serves 12.**

Baked Sweet Potato Fries with Cajun Mayo and Garlic-Basil Mayo

4 sweet potatoes
- Sea salt
- Fresh black pepper

3 CLOVES garlic, minced

CAJUN MAYO

1 CUP mayonnaise

¼–½ TSP. cayenne pepper

3 CLOVES garlic, minced

½ TSP. Cajun seasoning

1 TSP. onion powder

⅛ TSP. fresh black pepper

¼ TSP. brown sugar

GARLIC-BASIL MAYO

1 CUP mayonnaise

5 CLOVES garlic, minced

4 frozen basil cubes

1 TBSP. lemon juice

¼ TSP. kosher salt or sea salt
- Fresh black pepper

TO PRODUCE *perfectly crisped baked sweet potatoes, the key is to bake them in a heavy nonstick baking sheet that was heated in the oven for 20 minutes before the sweet potatoes are added. A baking sheet retains more heat than disposable aluminum, allowing the potatoes to turn crispy. When you place the sweet potatoes on the baking sheet, you may even hear a faint sizzle, signaling that the baking sheet is piping hot.*

Coating the sweet potatoes with a beaten egg white also makes them crispier, but you may not particularly care for the taste of the egg white. You can try both methods and see which you prefer.

1. Preheat the oven to 400° F. Heat a large baking sheet or jelly-roll pan (13x18-inch) in the oven for 20 minutes.

2. In the meantime, peel the sweet potatoes and cut them into strips. Spray the heated pan with nonstick cooking spray. Spread the sweet potato strips on the bottom of the pan in a single layer and sprinkle them with the salt, black pepper, and garlic. Bake, uncovered, for 35–50 minutes until crispy.

3. Prepare the dips: In a bowl, combine all the ingredients for the Cajun mayonnaise. In another bowl, combine the ingredients for the garlic-basil mayonnaise. Serve the fries warm with the dips on the side. **Serves 4.**

Pastrami Potato Kugelettes

COOKS TEND *to be very loyal to their potato kugel recipes. It's either an inherited family favorite or the result of much trial and error. So when Rikki suggested I add a little sugar to my potato kugel, I was resistant. But I gave it a shot, and I've been doing it ever since.*

The effect of the sugar is so subtle that you'll barely detect any traces of sweetness, but it's enough to enhance the other flavors. With the addition of pastrami, this kugel can be a meal on its own. You can also try shredded flanken, kielbasa, thinly sliced hot dogs, or corned beef instead of the pastrami. Or, if you prefer the classic pareve potato kugel option, omit the pastrami altogether.

tip: *To cut the pastrami into thin strips, stack the slices and position them horizontally. With a sharp knife, cut through all the slices at once.*

alternative: *For a twist, add pastrami strips to your potato latkes.*

5 potatoes, peeled and grated

5 eggs, beaten

½ small onion, grated

1 TSP. sugar

1 SCANT TBSP. kosher salt

• Fresh black pepper

¼ CUP oil

½ LB. deli pastrami, cut into thin strips

1. Preheat the oven to 350° F. In a bowl, combine the grated potatoes, beaten eggs, grated onion, sugar, salt, and black pepper. Add the oil and pastrami strips and mix until well combined.

2. Pour into twelve 6-oz. greased ramekins or a greased 9-inch round Pyrex dish. Bake until the tops are crispy and golden, about 1½–2 hours. Cool for several minutes before removing from the ramekins. Serve warm. **Serves 8-12.**

Challah

THE AROMA *of this challah baking in the oven takes me on an evocative journey back to my childhood. For over thirty years, my mother and my aunt have been baking challah together. The heady scent permeates the air for most of Friday, hinting at the warm, fresh goodness awaiting us. And for many years, my mother used the same recipe; there was no challah recipe good enough that would sway her to change. Until this one came along. It's the best yet, and it looks like it's here to stay.*

You'll notice that this challah calls for Splenda. Replacing half the sugar with Splenda yields a lighter challah (and less calories). If you want a denser challah, omit the Splenda and use an entire cup of sugar instead.

The most essential ingredient of challah is fresh yeast: the fresher the yeast, the better tasting the challah. To ensure the freshest yeast possible, buy it fresh from a bakery.

note: Yeast doughs rise best in warm dry temperatures. If the air is too humid, it will rise poorly or not at all.

6 CUPS warm water

2½ OZ. fresh yeast

6 LB. all-purpose flour, sifted

½ CUP sugar

½ CUP Splenda

2 eggs

2 egg yolks

3 TBSP. kosher salt

5 OZ. oil

• Sesame seeds (optional)

EGG WASH

1 egg yolk, beaten with 2 drops water

1. Combine 1 cup of the warm water with the fresh yeast and let stand for several minutes until it bubbles. In the bowl of an electric mixer, beat the flour, sugar, Splenda, eggs, egg yolks, and salt on low speed for several minutes. Add the yeast mixture, being careful to keep it separate from the salt. Add the remaining 5 cups of water and the oil and continue to mix on low speed until just combined. Increase the speed to high and mix for 10 minutes longer.

2. Cover the bowl with plastic wrap and let the dough rise at room temperature until doubled in size, at least 45 minutes. Turn the dough onto a floured surface. Divide and shape according to preference. Spray baking pans with nonstick cooking spray and sprinkle them with flour. Transfer the shaped loaves to the pans and let the loaves rise at room temperature until doubled, 45 minutes.

3. Preheat the oven to 350° F. Brush the challah with the egg wash and sprinkle with sesame seeds, if desired. Bake until browned, about 1½ hours for large challahs and at least 1 hour for smaller ones. **Yields 5–8 challahs.**

Tongue Polonaise

1 LB. sliced prepared pickled tongue (from the deli counter)

SAUCE

2 TBSP. oil

1 TBSP. Dijon mustard

5 TBSP. ketchup

2 TBSP. distilled white vinegar

⅓–½ CUP brown sugar, to taste

SOME RECIPES *are sheer genius—they require no fuss and the results are absolutely sumptuous. These are the recipes you prepare in under five minutes, but your guests assume you slaved over the dish for hours.*

My mother-in-law's pickled tongue is just such a recipe. The secret is to buy presliced pickled tongue from the deli counter. Cooking tongue from scratch is a tedious process that requires hours of prep work. You can't have any qualms about peeling the skin, and then you have to tackle the task of slicing it. So this recipe, which calls for prepared tongue, will save you about four hours. Instead, think four minutes.

Pickled tongue has always been considered a delicacy and is especially popular during the holidays. My mother-in-law likes to serve this tongue as an appetizer, spooning it over a square slice of sweet noodle kugel. Regardless of how much she prepares, there are never any leftovers. It's so tender, it melts in your mouth and disappears even faster than it takes to prepare it.

1. Preheat the oven to 350° F. In a small saucepan, combine the sauce ingredients, adjusting the amount of brown sugar to the desired level of sweetness. Bring to a boil over medium–high heat, stirring continuously.

2. Transfer the tongue to a baking pan and pour the sauce over it. Bake, covered, for 20 minutes. Serve warm. **Serves 4.**

Potato Kugel and Sweet Potato Roulade

THIS ORIGINAL *Pesach creation is my mother's (she even graciously prepared the roll shown in the photograph). It's been given out to many, who have made it a year-round addition to their menus.*

For a savory variation, substitute the sweet potatoes with sautéed mushrooms and onions, or, for an innovative twist on shepherd's pie, with sautéed minced meat and onions.

SWEET POTATO MASH

3 sweet potatoes, peels intact

1 medium onion, diced

3 Tbsp. oil

• Kosher salt

KUGEL MIXTURE

5 large potatoes, peeled and grated

3 eggs

2 Tbsp. oil

1 Tbsp. kosher salt

• White pepper

1. To prepare the sweet potato mash: Preheat the oven to 350° F. Roast the sweet potatoes, uncovered, until soft, about 1½ hours.

2. Meanwhile, in a skillet, heat the 3 tablespoons of oil. Sauté the onion in the oil over medium heat, until soft and translucent, about 8 minutes. Remove the sweet potatoes from the oven and slice them in half. Scoop out the flesh, discard the peels, and mash. Combine the mashed sweet potatoes with the sautéed onions and season with the kosher salt.

3. To prepare the potato kugel mixture: In a bowl, combine the grated potatoes, eggs, oil, salt, and white pepper. Line a cookie sheet with parchment paper, and spread the potato mixture evenly over the parchment paper. Bake, uncovered, until the top of the mixture is firm, about 30 minutes. Remove from the oven and allow to cool for 5 minutes. Roll the potato kugel, jelly-roll style, together with the parchment paper. Allow to cool completely.

4. To assemble, unroll the potato kugel. Spread the mashed sweet potato evenly over the kugel. Roll again, this time pulling away the parchment paper to form a potato kugel roll (unrolling and rerolling is essential—it helps to maintain the shape of the roll). Serve warm. **Serves 8.**

Roasted Fingerlings and Brussels Sprouts with Sage Brown Butter

THIS RECIPE *will sway even the toughest of brussels sprout skeptics. With the right flavors and the pairing of brussels sprouts with fingerling potatoes, this dish is both hearty and satisfying—even your kids will agree!*

The brussels sprouts should be green with little black spots on the outside. I like to halve the brussels sprouts; this prevents the centers from getting mushy. And if you can't find fingerlings, you can use baby red potatoes.

1 LB. fingerling potatoes, washed and halved

2 TBSP. oil

1 TBSP. sesame oil

4 TBSP. trans-fat-free margarine

2 TBSP. MSG-free onion soup mix

2 TBSP. sage leaves, chopped

1 LB. brussels sprouts, washed and halved, with the outer yellow leaves removed

• Kosher salt

• Fresh black pepper

1. Preheat the oven to 400° F. Arrange the potatoes in a 9x13–inch baking pan. Add the oils, margarine, onion soup mix, and sage. Roast, covered, for 45 minutes.

2. Add the brussels sprouts to the pan, mix well, and continue to roast, uncovered, until the potatoes are cooked through and crispy on the outside, about 45–55 minutes.

3. Season with kosher salt and black pepper to taste. Serve warm. **Serves 4–6.**

Orzo Salad with Garbanzos, Peppers, and Dill

THIS IS *one of my most popular go-to side dishes that's good with just about any main dish. I prefer it warm or at room temperature, but it's even nice eaten cold, straight from the refrigerator. The addition of the garbanzo beans makes this dish satisfying and brimming with protein and nutritional benefits.*

note: The recipe for the salmon that accompanies this dish in the photo can be found on page 182.

2 CUPS orzo, prepared according to package directions

1 CAN garbanzo beans, drained

1 small red pepper, diced

1 small orange or yellow pepper, diced

½ CUP sliced black olives

1 small red onion, diced

1 TBSP. fresh lemon juice

4 TBSP. oil

⅓ CUP fresh dill, chopped

2 CLOVES garlic, minced

2–3 TSP. kosher salt

⅛ TSP. fresh black pepper

In a bowl, combine all the salad ingredients. Serve warm or at room temperature. **Serves 4.**

Mexican Chicken-Filled Crepes with Shallot Sauce

THIS IS *fusion cooking at its best, merging Mexican, Jewish, and French cooking. You may be skeptical about the grated eggs in the recipe, but they're essential for creating the perfect taste and texture for the chicken filling.*

Besides the chicken filling, warm liver sauté and mashed potatoes with onions are just some of the endless options you can choose from to fill these crepes. The chicken stock and the accompanying shallot sauce greatly enrich the flavor of the chicken filling. If you don't have shallots on hand, feel free to substitute with onions or, even if you do, try a combination of both. Shallots have a slightly milder and sweeter taste than onions with a slight hint of garlic.

note: To use the scallions as a tie, blanch the green leaves in hot boiling water for 2 minutes. Remove from the boiling water and immediately rinse with cold water to maintain its brightness. Fill each crepe with the chicken filling, being careful not to overfill. Gather the ends of the crepe together and tie with the scallion.

passover option: Substitute the flour in the crepes for potato starch.

CHICKEN FILLING

4 chicken bottoms

4 Tbsp. oil

2 onions, diced

4 tomatoes, peeled and diced

2 hard-boiled eggs, grated

1 cup chicken stock

1 Tbsp. all-purpose flour

5 cloves garlic, minced

¼ tsp. cayenne pepper

¼ tsp. chili powder

¼ tsp. cumin

• Kosher salt

• Fresh black pepper

CREPES

8 large eggs

1 cup water

1 cup all-purpose flour

⅓ cup oil, plus extra for frying

SHALLOT SAUCE

2 Tbsp. oil

1 cup shallots or onions, diced

2 cups chicken stock

1½ tsp. kosher salt

¼ tsp. fresh black pepper

3 Tbsp. cornstarch, dissolved in ½ cup water

3 Tbsp. good-quality dry dark red wine

1. Preheat the oven to 350° F. Bake the chicken bottoms, covered, for 1½ hours. Remove the skin, debone, and dice the meat.

2. In a skillet, heat the oil over medium heat. Add the diced onions and sauté in the oil until golden. Add the tomatoes, eggs, and diced chicken and sauté for 2 minutes longer. Add the chicken stock, flour, and garlic and cook until most of the chicken stock is absorbed. Add the cayenne pepper, chili powder, and cumin, and season with the salt and black pepper to taste. Remove from the heat.

3. To prepare the crepes: In a large bowl, beat the eggs. Beat in the water, flour, and oil until mixed. Coat the surface of a nonstick skillet with oil and heat over medium heat. Pour ¼ cup of the batter into the skillet. Fry until cooked through, about 1–2 minutes per side.

4. To prepare the shallot sauce: In a deep skillet, heat the 2 tablespoons of oil. Add the shallots or onions and sauté in the oil until golden brown. Add the chicken stock, salt, and black pepper. Raise the heat and bring to a boil. Stir in the cornstarch dissolved in water and the dry red wine. Reduce the heat and simmer for 10 minutes until the sauce thickens.

5. To serve, spoon the filling into the center of each crepe, roll, and drizzle with the sauce. Or gather the ends of the crepe and tie with a scallion. Serve over a spoonful of sauce. **Yields 18–22 crepes.**

Tuna Tartare

FOR THOSE *who dare to be more adventurous in the kitchen and possess a fearless palate, this tuna tartare will give you an urge to diverge.*

This recipe is the culmination of many different tartare recipes that I've experimented with. Now tuna tartare has become a staple in all of my holiday and Shabbos lunches. At first my family was a bit skeptical about eating raw fish, but after bravely tasting my tuna tartare more than a few times, they now thoroughly enjoy it, and it's become a desired substitute for tuna fish salad in my home.

If you prefer not to eat raw fish, sear the tuna for twenty seconds per side. For best results, tuna tartare should be prepared no more than four hours in advance.

½ LB. sushi-grade tuna, finely diced

1 jalapeno pepper, seeded and minced

2 TSP. shallots, minced

1 TSP. chives, minced

1 TSP. lite soy sauce

1 TSP. Dijon mustard

1 TSP. lime juice

1 TSP. kosher salt

1 TBSP. oil or mayonnaise

1 TSP. seasoned rice vinegar

In a bowl, combine all of the ingredients until mixed. Refrigerate, covered, until ready to serve. Serve on your favorite crackers or bread. **Serves 6–8.**

Skirt Steak Spring Rolls with Corn off the Cob

3 ears fresh corn

2 TBSP. oil

1 LB. skirt steak, cut into thin strips

1 large onion, diced

• Peanut oil, for frying

8 OZ. mushrooms of your choice, diced

2 TBSP. soy sauce

1 TSP. brown sugar

1 TSP. chili powder or 1 frozen chili cube

⅓ CUP good-quality barbecue sauce, plus extra for dipping

2 TBSP. fresh parsley, chopped

1 TSP. kosher salt

• Fresh black pepper

1 PKG. egg roll wrappers (6 inches)

HERE IS *a refreshing change from the usual spring roll, and it's so easy to prepare. The filling can be made in one pan in minutes, and no marinating is necessary.*

Skirt steak, the featured ingredient in this appetizer, is one of the most flavorful cuts of meat. There's no need to add salt—the steak is already salty enough. For a perfect complement, use your favorite barbecue sauce for dipping the rolls. Don't count on any leftovers.

1. Preheat the oven to 350° F. Remove the husks and silks from the corn. Roast the corn on oven racks until softened, about 35 minutes. Allow to cool. To cut the kernels off the cob: Hold the corn upright on a large cutting board. With a large, sharp knife, slice down the length of the ear between the kernels and the cob. Rotate the cob and repeat until all the kernels are cut.

2. To prepare the filling: In a skillet, heat the oil over medium heat. Sear the skirt steak in the oil until medium rare, 3 minutes. Remove the meat from the pan.

3. Add the onion, garlic, and 2 tablespoons of the peanut oil to the skillet and sauté until the onion begins to soften. Add the mushrooms and the corn kernels and cook for 2 minutes longer. Stir in the soy sauce, brown sugar, and chili. Remove from the heat. Add the skirt steak and barbecue sauce and season with the parsley, salt, and black pepper.

4. To wrap, place an egg roll wrapper on a flat surface. Spoon 3 tablespoons of filling onto the bottom third of the wrapper, leaving a small border along the sides and bottom edge. Brush water around the edges of the wrapper. Fold the bottom edge over the filling and begin rolling. About halfway up, fold the left and right edges toward the center and continue to roll tightly until it is closed. Press to seal.

5. Pour enough peanut oil into the skillet to reach a depth of ½ inch. Fry the egg rolls, starting with the seam side down, until golden, 2–3 minutes per side. When ready to serve, cut the spring rolls in half and serve with small dipping bowls filled with your favorite barbecue sauce, or drizzle the sauce on the side. **Yields 15–17 spring rolls.**

No-Grease Everything Knots

2 LB. pizza or challah dough

1 egg yolk, beaten with a drop of water

• Minced dried garlic

• Dried basil

• Dried parsley

• Dried chives

• Red pepper flakes

• Paprika

• Kosher salt or sea salt

• Sesame seeds

THESE KNOTS *are super addictive, so when you keep reaching for one after another, you'll be pleased that they won't leave a greasy residue on your hands. That's because these garlic knots are not coated with oil. Instead they're washed with egg yolk for maximum crispiness.*

It was my daughter's idea to call these knots "everything" instead of "garlic" knots. She reasoned that even though these knots are seasoned with minced garlic, they're also topped with various other spices and herbs, so the name is well deserved.

note: For the challah dough recipe, see page 27.

1. Preheat the oven to 350° F. Grease two large baking sheets and set aside.

2. Prepare the dough and allow to rise for ½ hour before shaping. Divide the dough in half. Wrap one half of the dough in plastic wrap. On a lightly floured surface, with a lightly floured rolling pin, roll the other half of the dough into a 10-inch square. (If the dough is sticky, add a little bit of flour.) With a pizza wheel or a sharp knife, cut the square in half, then cut each half crosswise into 15 strips, ¾ inch wide. Cover the strips with plastic wrap.

3. While keeping the other strips covered, gently tie each strip into a knot, pulling the ends tightly to secure. Arrange the knots 1 inch apart in rows on the first baking sheet. Cover the knots with plastic wrap while you prepare the rest of the knots.

4. Roll out and cut the remaining dough in the same way, form into knots, and arrange on the second baking sheet. Let the knots rise until doubled in size.

5. Brush all the knots with the beaten egg yolk. Sprinkle with the minced garlic, then sprinkle with the herbs, seasonings, and sesame seeds, as desired. Bake until light brown and golden, 35–40 minutes. Serve warm or at room temperature. **Yields 60 knots.**

Bell Pepper Mushroom Crostini

CROSTINI IS *the Italian word for "toast." Bruschetta, another type of Italian bread, and crostini are very similar in meaning—the difference between the two is that bruschetta is prepared with larger slices of bread and crostini is usually prepared from baguettes, yielding smaller "toasts." So depending on which bread you use, you can name this recipe accordingly.*

Adding roasted peppers and roasted portobello mushrooms, with their meaty, satisfying flavor, to a classic crostini imparts an appealing earthy quality to the taste.

8 SLICES crusty French or ciabatta bread

4 CLOVES garlic

4 TBSP. oil

3 portobello mushroom caps

2 bell peppers (assorted colors), sliced

¼ CUP shallots, minced

• Sea salt or kosher salt

• Fresh black pepper

¼ CUP fresh basil or oregano, shredded, plus extra to garnish

1 TBSP. balsamic or red wine vinegar

1. Preheat the oven to 350° F. Toast the bread in the oven until golden brown, about 5 minutes. While it is still warm, gently rub the bread with 1 clove garlic.

2. Coarsely chop the mushrooms and remaining 3 cloves of garlic. In a skillet, heat 2 tablespoons of the oil over medium heat. Cook the mushrooms and the peppers in the oil until softened. Add the shallots and remaining chopped garlic and cook, stirring, for 4–5 minutes longer. Season with the salt and black pepper. Remove the skillet from the heat.

3. In a small bowl, combine the basil or oregano, vinegar, and remaining 2 tablespoons of oil. Combine with the mushroom and pepper mixture, and season with additional salt and black pepper, if desired. Spoon onto the toasted bread. Garnish with basil or oregano leaves and serve immediately. **Serves 8.**

Lemon Artichoke Cream Potato Salad

YOU'LL LOVE *this unusual but satisfying variation on the classic potato salad. As an added enhancement, the potatoes are diced and then roasted before they're added to the lemon artichoke cream. The lemon artichoke cream also makes for a great salad dressing or a dip for crudités.*

note: For the fish recipe that accompanies this dish in the photo, see page 186.

ROASTED POTATOES

5 potatoes, peeled and diced

3 Tbsp. oil

• Kosher salt

• Fresh black pepper

LEMON ARTICHOKE CREAM

5 artichoke hearts, canned, freshly steamed, or roasted

½ cup oil

1 clove garlic, minced

2 Tbsp. fresh lemon juice

1 tsp. kosher salt

1. To roast the potatoes: Preheat the oven to 375° F. In a baking pan, drizzle the diced potatoes with the oil and season with the salt and black pepper. Roast, uncovered, until the potatoes are crispy and cooked through, about 1 hour and 10 minutes.

2. To prepare the lemon artichoke cream: In the bowl of a food processor, puree the artichokes, oil, garlic, lemon juice, and salt until smooth. Toss the roasted potatoes with the lemon artichoke cream. **Serves 4–6.**

Pesto Chicken or Sweetbreads with Tomato Basil Polenta Stacks

2 LB. sweetbreads or boneless skinless chicken thighs

• Oil

1 TUBE store-bought polenta, cut into eight ½-inch slices

8 beefsteak tomatoes

• Fresh basil leaves

PESTO SAUCE

1½ CUPS basil leaves

⅓ CUP pine nuts or walnuts (or a combination of both)

3 CLOVES garlic

¾ CUP oil, plus extra for coating the sweetbreads

1 lemon, juiced

• Kosher salt

• Fresh black pepper

1. To prepare the pesto sauce: In a food processor, puree the basil leaves, nuts, and garlic. Gradually add the oil and lemon juice, continuing to puree until blended. Add the salt and black pepper to taste.

2. To prepare the sweetbreads: Rinse the sweetbreads well and place in a saucepan. Add water to cover, bring to a boil, and simmer for 15 minutes. Drain immediately and pat dry with paper towels.

3. Trim the sweetbreads, removing any visible gristle or membranes with your fingers. Separate into 1½-inch pieces (by hand or with a knife) and toss with oil. Grill on an oiled grill rack on an indoor or outdoor grill over medium–high heat until golden brown, about 7–9 minutes per side. Transfer the sweetbreads to a platter and cover loosely with foil. Let stand for 5 minutes, then coat lightly with the pesto sauce, seasoning with additional salt and black pepper if necessary.

4. Broil the polenta slices, 2–3 minutes per side. Cut the tomatoes into slices the same size as the polenta rounds. Seed the tomatoes and drain the juices.

5. To serve, place a polenta slice on each plate. Top with basil leaves, then a tomato slice. Spread the tomato round with pesto sauce. Add another layer of polenta slice, basil leaf, tomato, and pesto sauce. Top with the sweetbreads or serve the sweetbreads on the side. **Serves 4.**

WHAT'S IN *a name?*
Making certain foods not only taste delicious but also sound delicious to my children has become a diligent work in progress. Sometimes sophisticated foods also need clever and inventive names to appeal to adults. Sweetbreads are neither sweet nor are they a bread, but I don't think "thymus glands" would survive on any menu.

Contrary to popular belief, sweetbreads are not the brains, but either the thymus gland (located in the throat or neck) or the pancreas of a young calf. Thawed or fresh sweetbreads are very perishable and should be cooked within twenty-four hours of purchase. If they were previously frozen and defrosted that day, do not refreeze them. Sweetbreads can be poached, braised, or sautéed, but my personal preference is to grill them. Grilling sweetbreads gives them a crispy crust that contrasts perfectly with their tender interior.

chicken option: *Use boneless skinless chicken thighs instead of sweetbreads. Cut chicken thighs into 1½-inch pieces and skip the boiling step.*

Minced Garlic and Rosemary Garlic Pita Crisps

4 pita breads

1 egg white, beaten

• Sea salt

• Fresh black pepper

• Dried minced garlic

• Fresh or dried rosemary, chopped

SOME SUPERMARKETS sell single-layer pitas so you don't have to divide the pita bread in half. You can also make these crisps using three different colored tortillas—white, green, and orange. Alternatively, in order to yield a thicker wedge, don't slit the pita in half

Before baking the pita chips (or tortilla chips), you can season them according to your personal preference: try cumin, oregano, basil, chives, sesame seeds, or parmesan cheese.

1. Preheat the oven to 350° F. Carefully slit open each pita bread and cut it in half to make two circles. Slice each circle into 8 wedges, as though you were slicing a pie. Lay the triangles flat on large, rimmed baking sheets.

2. Brush the tops of each pita wedge with the egg white. Sprinkle the wedges with the salt, black pepper, and minced garlic. Add the chopped rosemary, if desired. (You can use rosemary on just some of the triangles.)

3. Bake the pita wedges until crisp and lightly browned, about 20 minutes. Allow to cool. Store in an airtight container at room temperature for up to one day. Serve with Black and Green Olive Tapenade (page 50) and Roasted Eggplant and Red Pepper Dip (page 60). **Yields 64 crisps.**

Butcher's Cut with Broccoli Mashed Potatoes

1 LB. hanger steak

5 TBSP. oil

2 CLOVES garlic, minced

• Fresh black pepper

BROCCOLI MASHED POTATOES

4 Idaho or red potatoes, peeled and diced

12 oz. broccoli florets

3 CLOVES garlic, minced

4 TBSP. oil

1½ TSP. sea salt or kosher salt

• Fresh black pepper

• Chicken stock

• Tofutti sour cream (optional)

THE **BEST-KEPT** *secret in your butcher shop is the butcher's cut, also known as hanger steak or onglet. Somewhat similar to skirt steak in cut and taste, it's a lean, well-marbled meat with a unique and bold flavor profile, making it one of the beefiest and most robust cuts. It earned the title "butcher's cut" because butchers liked to keep this sought-after cut for themselves.*

Because this cut is so flavorful, a simple seasoning of minced garlic and fresh black pepper allows for the flavors to emerge. To preserve its natural tenderness, be sure not to cook the meat past medium. The best way to check the temperature is with a meat thermometer. When the thermometer reaches 140°–145° F while it is being seared (and the center of the meat is pink), you know it's done.

Baking the potatoes and broccoli in the oven rather than cooking them in water yields a huge flavor difference. Water drains the flavor, while steaming them au naturel in the oven maintains the crispiness of the potatoes and the flavor and vitamins of the broccoli.

note: If the steak has a membrane running down its center, cut the steak into two pieces and discard the membrane.

1. To prepare the butcher's cut: Rub the hanger steak with 2 tablespoons of the oil, the garlic, and the black pepper. In a large, heavy skillet, heat the remaining 3 tablespoons of oil over medium–high heat. Sear the hanger steak in the oil, 4 minutes per side for medium rare or 6 minutes per side for medium. Transfer to a plate and let sit for 8 minutes. Slice against the grain.

2. To prepare the broccoli mashed potatoes: Preheat the oven to 350° F. In a baking pan, combine the diced potatoes, broccoli, garlic, oil, salt, and black pepper. Bake, covered, until the potatoes and broccoli are very tender, at least 1 hour. Mash the potatoes and broccoli.

3. Add the chicken stock, a little at a time, until the mash is creamy and smooth. Season with additional salt and black pepper, if needed. For added creaminess, add the Tofutti sour cream, 1 tablespoon at a time, until the desired consistency is achieved. Serve warm alongside the sliced meat. You can serve this dish as an appetizer in small individual portions or plate as a main dish. Serve with steak knives for ease of slicing. **Serves 4–6.**

Black & Green Olive Tapenade

1 CUP black olives, pitted

1 CUP green olives, pitted

1 TBSP. capers, rinsed and drained

¼ CUP oil

2 CLOVES garlic, chopped

1 TBSP. fresh basil, chopped

1 TBSP. fresh thyme leaves

1 TBSP. fresh parsley, chopped

1 TSP. fresh lemon juice

• Fresh black pepper

OLIVE TAPENADE *is a rich, piquant condiment that originated in Provence, France. Traditionally, olive tapenade recipes call for kalamata olives, but you can use any green or black olives or a combination of both.*

In a food processor, blend all the ingredients until coarsely pureed. Serve with the Minced Garlic and Rosemary Garlic Pita Crisps (page 46). **Serves 6.**

Tomato Basil Salad with a Duo of Vinegars

EVER WONDER *why the food in restaurants tastes so good? After all, the dishes on the menu are not all that different from the ones we experiment with at home. A lot of that great flavor is due to the sufficient seasoning of salt—the most basic (and vital!) ingredient in most recipes. Sometimes several more pinches of salt yields a world of difference. Whenever a recipe calls for salt and pepper to taste, keep tasting and pinching, and invariably you will create flavor perfection.*

In addition to good seasoning, this salad can be enhanced with your favorite additions, such as feta cheese, cubed mozzarella, or flavored croutons. For a pretty presentation and a filling side dish, serve this salad on the Asian Portobello Mushroom caps (see page 14).

note: For the method for cutting the basil leaves chiffonade style, see page 292.

2 CUPS grape tomatoes, halved

1 small red onion, finely diced

3 TBSP. finely diced scallions

¼ CUP basil leaves, cut chiffonade

4 TBSP. oil

1 TBSP. balsamic vinegar

1 TSP. red wine vinegar

3 CLOVES garlic, minced

• Kosher salt

• Fresh black pepper

In a bowl, combine the tomatoes, onion, scallions, basil, oil, vinegars, and garlic. Season with the salt and black pepper. Serve as a side dish or arrange the salad on top of the Asian Portobello Mushrooms. **Serves 4**.

Teriyaki Sesame Pasta

SUPER QUICK, *this pasta side dish goes well with a teriyaki salmon or chicken dish. If this dish is on your Shabbos lunch menu, bring it to room temperature before serving.*

note: For the Striped Sesame Teriyaki Salmon recipe pictured here, see page 194.

3 Tbsp. toasted sesame oil

4 Tbsp. teriyaki sauce

1 Tbsp. seasoned rice vinegar

1 Tbsp. honey

1 lb. spaghetti or angel hair pasta,
prepared according to package directions

• Sliced scallions, to garnish

In a bowl, combine the sesame oil, teriyaki sauce, rice vinegar, and honey. Toss the pasta with the teriyaki sauce. Garnish with the sliced scallions and let sit, allowing the flavors to mingle for several minutes, before serving. **Serves 4-6.**

Tarragon Egg Salad and Guacamole on Wonton Crisps

A RECIPE FOR *egg salad? You bet. Egg salad can go from ordinary to extraordinary by paying attention to the details. Even simply preparing egg salad with spicy mayo renews its appeal (see page 97 for the spicy mayo recipe).*

The recipe for this award-winning tarragon egg salad (Kosherfest 2009) was given to me by chef Pini Ben-Ami, owner of U Café on the Upper East Side. If you don't care for tarragon, basil or parsley is a comparable substitute.

Capers, which feature in this recipe, are herb buds that lend a piquant, intense, and salty flavor. Because the flavors are so sharp, most recipes require only a few for enhancement. When it comes to capers, smaller in size is better.

TARRAGON EGG SALAD

10 eggs, hard-boiled

2 Tbsp. mayonnaise

2 Tbsp. tarragon leaves, minced

1 medium red onion, finely diced

3 Tbsp. capers, drained

• Sea salt

• Fresh black pepper

WONTON CRISPS

• Oil, for frying

12 wonton wrappers (3-4 inches)

GUACAMOLE

3 Hass avocados

1 lime, juiced

½ tsp. sea salt

½ tsp. ground cumin

½ tsp. cayenne pepper

1 garlic clove (fresh or frozen), minced

1 Tbsp. mayonnaise

1 Roma tomato, diced (optional)

OPTIONAL GARNISH

• Black caviar or scallions

1. To prepare the tarragon egg salad: In a large bowl, mash the eggs with a fork. Stir in the mayonnaise, tarragon, onion, and capers. Season with the kosher salt and black pepper. Refrigerate, covered, until ready to serve.

2. To prepare the guacamole: Halve the avocados and remove the pits. In a large bowl, mash the avocado with the lime juice. Combine with the salt, cumin, cayenne pepper, garlic, and mayonnaise. Top with the tomatoes, if desired. Place the avocado pits in the center of the guacamole to prevent it from oxidizing.

3. To prepare the wonton crisps: In a skillet, heat the oil over medium heat until very hot. Fry the wonton wrappers in the oil for 10-12 seconds per side. Remove the wrappers and drain until cooled. Keep covered until ready to serve.

4. To serve, place a wonton crisp on a plate. With an ice cream scoop, place a scoop of guacamole on the wonton crisp and top with a second wonton crisp. Place a scoop of egg salad on top of the second crisp. Garnish with the black caviar or scallions. For best results, keep at room temperature for 1 hour prior to serving. **Serves 6.**

Pulled Meat Wontons with Honey Mustard Sauce

WHAT CAN *you do with your leftover brisket or flanken? Create these pulled meat wontons. Alternatively, you can prepare these with store-bought sliced deli pastrami, corned beef, or brisket—the wontons are a blank canvas for your imagination and will work with just about any poultry or meat. Here you have a choice of either brisket or deli sauerkraut for your wonton filling.*

note: If you prefer a thinner consistency for the honey mustard sauce, add a little bit of orange juice: start with one tablespoon and use more if needed. If you're making the deli sauerkraut wontons, set aside three tablespoons of the honey mustard sauce for the wonton filling before thinning the sauce with the orange juice.

1 PKG. 3½-inch precut frozen wonton wrappers

• Oil, for frying

HONEY MUSTARD SAUCE

1½ CUPS mayonnaise

4 TBSP. honey

½ CUP spicy brown mustard

2 CLOVES garlic, minced

1 TBSP. lemon juice

1–2 TBSP. orange juice

BRISKET WONTONS

½ LB. cooked brisket or flanken

2 TBSP. oil

1 small onion, diced

2 CLOVES garlic, minced

3 TBSP. honey barbecue sauce

DELI SAUERKRAUT WONTONS

2 TBSP. oil

1 small onion, diced

1 CLOVE garlic, minced

¼ LB. deli pastrami, shredded or diced

¼ LB. smoked turkey roll, shredded or diced

1 CUP sauerkraut, well drained

3 TBSP. honey mustard sauce (see recipe above)

1. To prepare the honey mustard sauce: In a bowl, combine all the ingredients for the sauce. Reserve 3 tablespoons of the sauce if you are making the deli sauerkraut wontons. Thin the sauce with the orange juice, if desired.

2. To prepare the brisket wontons: Pull the brisket or flanken by shredding it with 2 forks. In a skillet, heat the oil over medium heat. Sauté the onion and garlic in the oil until cooked through. Remove from the heat. In a bowl, combine the shredded flanken or brisket with the honey barbecue sauce. Add the meat mixture to the onion and garlic and stir until mixed.

3. To prepare the deli sauerkraut wontons: In a skillet, heat the oil over medium heat. Sauté the onion and garlic in the oil until cooked through. Remove from the heat. In a bowl, combine the pastrami, turkey, sauerkraut, and honey mustard sauce. Add the mixture to the onion and garlic and stir until mixed.

4. Place 1 full teaspoon of the brisket or deli sauerkraut filling in the center of each wonton wrapper. Brush the edges of the wrapper with water. Fold the wonton wrapper over the meat mixture by bringing each of the corners to the center so that they overlap slightly. In a skillet, heat the oil over medium heat. Fry the wontons until golden, 2 minutes per side. Serve immediately with the honey mustard sauce on the side for dipping. **Yields 35–38 wontons.**

Coconut Couscous with Scallion Lime Syrup and Mango

> **T**HERE ARE *two reasons this recipe will endure: it's super simple to prepare, and even if you're not a great fan of coconut, you'll still enjoy the tropical mélange of flavors it produces here. This dish does have a hint of sweetness, but that stems from the natural flavors of the mango and coconut; they impart a mellow flavor that's perfectly suited to couscous.*

COCONUT COUSCOUS

- 2 PKG. (8.8 oz.) Israeli couscous
- 1 CUP coconut milk
- 2 CUPS water
- 1 TBSP. kosher salt or sea salt
- • Fresh black pepper
- 1 CUP coconut flakes
- 2 mangos, diced
- ½ CUP slivered almonds, toasted

LIME SYRUP

- 2 limes, juiced
- 2 TBSP. oil
- ½ CUP scallions, thinly sliced
- ½ CUP red onion, minced

1. In a medium saucepan, toast the couscous over medium heat until golden. Add the coconut milk, water, salt, and black pepper and bring to a boil. Immediately reduce the heat and simmer, covered, until the couscous is cooked, 6–8 minutes. Remove from the heat and keep the pot covered for several minutes to allow the couscous to continue to steam. This will keep it extra moist.

2. Meanwhile, in a skillet, toast the coconut flakes over medium heat until golden, stirring continuously.

3. To prepare the scallion lime syrup: Combine the lime juice, oil, scallions, and red onion until mixed.

4. Combine the couscous with the toasted coconut flakes, scallion lime syrup, mango, and almonds. Serve warm. **Serves 8.**

Roasted Eggplant and Red Pepper Dip

2 medium eggplants, peeled and diced

1 red bell pepper, seeded and diced

1 red onion, diced

2 garlic cloves, minced

3 Tbsp. oil

½ tsp. red pepper flakes

1½ tsp. kosher salt

¼ tsp. fresh black pepper

2 Tbsp. lemon juice

I OWN ALL of *Ina Garten's Barefoot Contessa cookbooks and adore her recipes. They're simple to prepare and rely on quality, fresh ingredients. This dip is adapted from one of her cookbooks. Serve it with Minced Garlic and Rosemary Garlic Pita Crisps (page 46).*

1. Preheat the oven to 400° F. Spread the diced eggplant, red pepper, and onion on a baking sheet with the garlic, oil, red pepper flakes, salt, and black pepper. Roast for 55 minutes. Toss and allow to cool slightly.

2. Place the roasted vegetables in a food processor with the lemon juice and pulse several times to blend. Add additional salt and black pepper if needed. Serve with pita crisps. **Serves 4–6.**

Cauliflower Mash

NOTICE THE *creamy cloud of what looks like mashed potatoes peeking out from behind the Delmonico Roast? That's cauliflower mash—a wonderful low-carb alternative to mashed potatoes. For enhanced flavor and presentation, season with chopped chives or chopped parsley.*

note: For the Delmonico Roast recipe, see page 164.

1 HEAD (8 cups) cauliflower, chopped

5 CLOVES garlic, chopped

1½ TSP. kosher salt

• Fresh black pepper

4 OZ. chicken stock

2 TBSP. trans-fat-free margarine

1. Preheat the oven to 375° F. Place the cauliflower, garlic, salt, black pepper, and chicken stock in a baking pan and bake, covered, until the cauliflower is soft, about 1½ hours.

2. Add the margarine and mash with a fork until creamy and smooth. Season with additional salt and black pepper if needed. Serve warm. **Serves 6.**

Roasted Asparagus and String Bean Bundles

1 LB. fresh asparagus spears, root ends discarded and trimmed to even lengths

1 LB. string beans, trimmed to even lengths

1 TBSP. oil

2 cloves garlic, minced

- Sea salt

- Fresh black pepper

- Deli pastrami or corned beef slices

DIPPING SAUCE

- Teriyaki sauce

- Sesame seeds

- Scallions, sliced

1. Preheat the oven to 400° F. On a baking sheet, coat the asparagus and string beans with the oil and garlic. Sprinkle with the salt and black pepper. Roast, uncov-ered, until tender, 20–25 minutes.

2. To prepare the dipping sauce: Pour the teriyaki sauce into a small bowl. Add the sesame seeds and sliced scallions.

3. When ready to serve, wrap small bundles of asparagus and string beans with a slice of deli pastrami or corned beef and serve with the dipping sauce. (Keep the bundles covered until ready to serve to prevent them from drying out.) **Serves 6.**

Trio of Spiced Olive Tapas

WHEN OTHER *babies were munching on Cheerios, mine were savoring sliced olives. Because of my family's fondness for olives, I throw them onto pasta, pizza, chicken, fish, eggs, and salads...practically anything. And, of course, every Shabbos meal includes olives in more than one shape or form.*

Adding spices to olives enhances their explosive flavor and makes them perfect for a tapas, the Spanish word for "appetizer." These olives can be whipped up in almost no time and will last awhile if stored tightly covered in the refrigerator. In fact, the flavor deepens as the spices meld.

You can serve these olives at room temperature, or warm them to bring out their heady aroma and bold taste.

CITRUS DILL OLIVES

2 CANS (12 oz.) pitted green or black olives, drained

1 lemon, juiced and zested

1 orange, zested

½ orange, juiced

1 TSP. honey

1 TBSP. fresh dill, chopped

4 TBSP. oil

1 CLOVE garlic, minced

½ TSP. fennel seeds

MEDITERRANEAN OLIVES

2 CANS (12 oz.) pitted green or black olives, drained

3 CLOVES garlic, minced

2 CUBES frozen basil, minced

1 JAR (3½ oz.) capers, drained

2 TBSP. sun-dried tomatoes, thinly sliced

1 TSP. oregano

• Fresh black pepper

4 TBSP. oil

SAVORY GARLIC OLIVES

2 CANS (12 oz.) pitted green or black olives, drained

5 CLOVES garlic, sliced

2 CLOVES garlic, minced

1 TBSP. fresh rosemary, minced

½ TSP. dried thyme

1 TSP. red pepper flakes

¼ TSP. fresh black pepper

4 TBSP. oil

In a large bowl, toss the olives with the other ingredients for the spiced olives of your choice. Store tightly in an airtight container and refrigerate for at least 24 hours to allow the flavors to marinate and mingle. Shake well before serving. **Serves 8–10.**

Mini Mushroom Beef Sliders

> **MY FAMILY** *prefers hamburgers without any fillers, but they do enjoy these super-tasty sliders—much of which is inspired by Debbie R.'s incredible sliders recipe that she shared with me.*
>
> *Slider is a cryptonym for mini burgers. They're small, dainty, and irresistible—the perfect healthy alternative to the American obsession with supersizing. Served with mini fries, it doesn't get much cuter than this!*
>
> *For this recipe, purchase the larger variety of white mushrooms since the mushroom caps are used in place of a standard bun.*

MUSHROOM BUNS

20 large white mushrooms

1 TBSP. Worcestershire sauce

- Kosher salt
- Fresh black pepper

ADDITIONS

- Barbecue sauce

10 fresh basil leaves

2 plum tomatoes, thinly sliced (10 slices total)

- Fresh rosemary sprigs, to garnish

SLIDERS

1 LB. chuck ground beef

1 TSP. dried rosemary

1 TSP. dried thyme

1 TSP. basil, minced

4 CLOVES garlic, minced

2 TSP. kosher salt

¼ TSP. fresh black pepper

1 egg, beaten

½ CUP bread crumbs

16 mushroom stems, minced

1. Preheat the oven to 350° F. Remove the mushroom stems from the caps. Mince the stems and set aside for making the sliders. On a baking sheet, spray the mushroom caps with nonstick cooking spray and drizzle with the Worcestershire sauce. Sprinkle the caps with the salt and black pepper. Bake, uncovered, for 25 minutes. Remove from the oven.

2. In a bowl, combine the ground beef, herbs, garlic, salt, black pepper, egg, bread crumbs, and minced mushroom stems. Form into small patties the same size as the mushroom caps. Grill the patties on an indoor or outdoor grill or sear in a nonstick skillet in hot oil for 4–5 minutes per side.

3. To assemble the sliders, spread the barbecue sauce on the insides of two mushroom caps. Place a patty on one mushroom cap, add a basil leaf and a slice of tomato, and top with the other mushroom cap. Garnish with a sprig of rosemary: stick the sprig through the top of the mushroom cap and pierce all the way through. (This will also help keep the slider intact.) **Yields 8–10 burgers.**

simmered to perfection

SOUPS

Cream of Roasted Butternut Squash Soup with Herbes de Provence Tuiles

1 HEAD garlic, halved

3 LB. fresh butternut squash, peeled and cubed

4 TBSP. oil

1 large red onion, chopped

1 large sweet potato, peeled and diced

1 large potato, peeled and diced

6 CUPS chicken stock

2 TSP. kosher salt or sea salt

⅛ TSP. fresh black pepper

¼ TSP. red pepper flakes

2 CUPS coconut milk, plus extra to garnish

• Greens, to garnish

TUILES

• Wonton dough

• Dried herbes de Provence

• Dried minced garlic

• Sea salt

ONE OF *the perks of having Dina S. proofread my column is that she loves to try new recipes and she gives honest feedback. After she made this soup, she reported that even her son, a super-picky eater, ate it—and he usually eats only chicken soup. Her husband loved the complexity of this dish, which is coconutty and garlicky at the same time.*

The soup gets an extra dose of creaminess from the coconut milk, and you can use the leftover coconut milk to drizzle on the soup as a garnish. And roasting the garlic transforms its flavor from robust and potent to mellow and sweet.

The accompaniment for this soup, herbes de Provence tuiles, adds an elegant touch. Herbes de Provence is an herb blend made of Tuscan-inspired dried herbs. It's also great on chicken, fish, and roast potatoes.

Tuile, French for "tile," is a slightly curved wafer-thin cookie that can be savory or sweet. Use store-bought wonton dough for the tuiles, and they're a snap to prepare.

1. Preheat the oven to 400° F. In a large roasting pan, roast both garlic halves and the butternut squash, uncovered, until the garlic is very soft, 35–40 minutes.

2. In a large pot, heat the oil. Add the red onion and sauté in the oil until translucent, about 7–8 minutes. Add the roasted butternut squash and garlic, and sauté for 2 minutes. Add the sweet potato, potato, chicken stock, salt, black pepper, and red pepper flakes. Cook, covered, over medium heat until the vegetables are soft and cooked through, about 1 hour.

3. Puree the soup with an immersion blender. Stir in the coconut milk and cook over low–medium heat for 25 minutes longer.

4. To prepare the tuiles: Preheat the oven to 350° F. Cut the wonton dough into equal-size strips according to desired preference and arrange the strips on a baking tray. Spray the strips with nonstick cooking spray and sprinkle them immediately with the herbes de Provence, dried minced garlic, and sea salt. Gently press the seasonings into the dough to make sure they stick. Bake until crispy and lightly golden, about 6–8 minutes.

5. Serve the soup warm, drizzled with coconut milk, garnished with the greens, and accompanied by the tuiles. **Serves 10–12.**

Vegetable Dumpling Soup

1 HEAD garlic, halved

4 TBSP. oil

1 large onion, chopped

3 leeks (white and light green parts only)

2 large zucchini, peeled and sliced

2 CUPS fresh pumpkin or butternut squash, peeled and diced

5 large carrots, peeled and sliced

1 sweet potato, peeled and diced

1 tomato, diced

2 potatoes, peeled and diced

9–10 CUPS chicken stock

1–2 TBSP. kosher or sea salt

¼ TSP. fresh black pepper

DUMPLINGS

2 CUPS all-purpose flour

1 TBSP. salt

1 TSP. garlic powder

1 TSP. onion powder

½ TSP. fresh black pepper

¼ TSP. baking powder

2 eggs, beaten

½ CUP chicken stock

2 TBSP. oil

THE MYTH *about gourmet food is that it requires obscure ingredients and elaborate preparation. But gourmet food is simply food prepared well, using only fresh ingredients. When I serve pure, all-natural food to my family, I can't help but feel a tiny bit virtuous. Providing them nourishment that doesn't include any processed or artificial ingredients sometimes does require more time and effort, but it is well worth it.*

This family favorite reflects my grandmother's domestic prowess. She could transform common ingredients into culinary delights, ingeniously creating recipes with an abundance of natural produce, preparing food as we were meant to eat it: healthy and all natural. And gourmet, nonetheless.

healthy alternative: For the dumplings, use white whole wheat flour instead of all-purpose flour.

1. Preheat the oven to 400° F. In a roasting pan, roast both garlic halves, uncovered, until the garlic is very soft, 35–40 minutes.

2. In a large pot, heat the oil over medium heat. Sauté the onion and leeks in the oil until translucent, about 10 minutes. Add the remaining vegetables and stir-fry for 5 minutes. Add just enough chicken stock to cover the vegetables by 1 inch. Add the salt and black pepper. Cook, covered, until all the vegetables are soft and cooked through, at least 1½ hours

3. Meanwhile, prepare the dumpling mixture: In a bowl, with a hand mixer, combine the flour, salt, garlic powder, onion powder, black pepper, and baking powder. In another bowl, whisk the eggs, chicken stock, and oil until well combined. Add the liquid ingredients to the dry ingredients and mix for 1–2 minutes. Do not overmix.

4. Once the soup is cooked, add the roasted garlic and puree the soup with an immersion blender until smooth. Raise the heat and bring the soup to a boil. Drop the dumpling mixture 1 tablespoon at a time into the soup. When all the dumpling mixture has been added, cook for 7–8 minutes, stirring the soup to prevent the dumplings from sticking together. Reduce the heat and simmer for 30 minutes longer. Serve immediately. **Serves 8–10.**

Roasted Chestnut Pumpkin Soup

4 PKG. (3½ oz.) peeled chestnuts (14 oz. in total)

4 TBSP. oil

1 large onion, diced

5 CLOVES garlic, minced

3½ LB. pumpkin, peeled and diced

2 sweet potatoes, peeled and diced

2 potatoes, peeled

10 CUPS vegetable or chicken stock

1 TBSP. kosher salt or sea salt

• Fresh black pepper, to taste

½ TSP. crushed red pepper flakes

• Toasted pumpkin seeds and chopped chestnuts, to garnish

THE KEY to this great-tasting soup (as with most soups) is to let it simmer for a while. Although this recipe calls for more than two hours of cooking, I sometimes let it simmer over the lowest heat for at least three more hours.

I use packaged peeled chestnuts, since fresh chestnuts take a while to prepare and they're fragile and can break easily if you try to peel them yourself.

1. Preheat the oven to 350° F. On a baking sheet, roast the chestnuts, uncovered, for 10 minutes.

2. In a sauté pan, heat the oil over medium heat. Add the onion and garlic and cook until the onion begins to soften.

3. Add the chestnuts, pumpkin, sweet potatoes, potatoes, stock, salt, black pepper, and red pepper flakes. Simmer, covered, over low-medium heat for 1½ hours.

4. With an immersion blender, puree the soup. Simmer, covered, over low heat for 1 hour longer. Garnish with the toasted pumpkin seeds and chopped chestnuts and serve immediately. **Serves 8–10.**

Best Chicken Soup

A **CLASSIC JEWISH** *standby has been repackaged and fully loaded. This recipe has a long list of ingredients, but the results are truly worth it! As with most chicken soups, there is a nuance of difference every time you prepare this soup, but it's always sublime.*

This recipe has been years in the making. For the past decade, I've collected recipes of chicken soups that I have enjoyed. I borrowed the idea of adding a fresh tomato from my mother, a green bell pepper from my mother-in-law, and fresh corn on the cob (yes! corn on the cob) and jalapeno peppers from my grandmothers. Michelle suggested I replace chicken quarters with chicken bones, and the amount of fresh garlic cloves has gradually increased to culminate in at least a dozen. And then...I let it gently simmer for at least six hours—the longer chicken soup simmers, the better.

When it's done, I wait for the soup to cool before it goes into the refrigerator. Soups that contain animal proteins turn sour if refrigerated when hot. You can freeze the leftover stock or use it in the other soups featured in this cookbook. Or, use leftover chicken soup instead of water when you prepare your side dishes for the week (such as rice, couscous, quinoa).

Fresh or as a flavoring, this rich, full bodied broth will exceed your expectations.

1 PKG. (2½ lb.) chicken bones

1 LB. flanken and/or turkey necks

1 green bell pepper, halved and seeded

1 LB. carrots, peeled and halved

1 large sweet potato, peeled

4 celery stalks, trimmed

1 large potato, peeled

1–2 large onions, peeled and halved

3 leeks, trimmed

12 CLOVES garlic

2 ears fresh corn

1 parsnip, peeled

1 turnip, peeled and quartered

1 tomato

½ small jalapeno pepper, seeded

2 large zucchini, peeled and halved

1 bouquet garni of fresh dill and parsley

1–2 TBSP. kosher salt, or more to taste

• Fresh black pepper

• Fine egg noodles, cooked

GARNISH

• Julienned carrots and zucchini

• Fresh parsley and dill springs

1. Rinse the chicken bones and flanken or turkey necks and pat dry. Place the chicken bones on the bottom of a very large pot and add the vegetables, placing the flanken and turkey necks and the dill and parsley on top. Cover with water. Add the salt and black pepper and bring to a boil. Reduce the heat and simmer, covered, for at least 6–8 hours.

2. When ready to serve, remove the bones, dill, and parsley and discard. Add the egg noodles and garnish with shredded carrots and zucchini. If you prefer a super-clear broth, put the soup through a strainer before serving. If desired, you can refrigerate the soup, letting it cool first, and skim off the fat before reheating it. **Serves 12–14.**

Roasted Portobello Mushroom Soup

MEATY PORTOBELLO *mushrooms can be transformed into a lovely full-bodied soup. For a cream soup version, stir in some heavy cream and heat through, about ten minutes. When roasting the ingredients, your kitchen will permeate with a delightful earthy aroma.*

3 TBSP. oil

3 large onions, chopped

6 CLOVES garlic

8 fresh portobello mushroom caps, cut into ½-inch strips

1 TBSP. sea salt, or more to taste

• Fresh black pepper

1 TSP. fresh thyme, chopped, or ½ tsp. dried thyme

1 TSP. fresh oregano, chopped, or ½ tsp. dried oregano

2 TBSP. brandy

5 CUPS homemade chicken or vegetable stock

¼ CUP coconut milk (optional)

¼ CUP fresh parsley, chopped, to garnish

OPTIONAL GARNISHES
• Enoki mushrooms
• Fresh oregano
• Fresh thyme

1. Preheat the oven to 400° F. Grease the bottom of a medium-size roasting pan or ovenproof skillet with 1 tablespoon of the oil. Add the onions and garlic and top with the mushrooms. Drizzle the remaining 2 tablespoons of oil over the mushrooms, and season with the salt, black pepper, thyme, and oregano. Roast, uncovered, for 30 minutes, stirring once or twice.

2. Remove the roasting pan from the oven and pour the brandy over the mushrooms. Remove 7–8 mushroom strips from the pan and set aside (these will not be pureed).

3. Add the remaining contents of the roasting pan to a large pot, scraping any brown bits stuck to the roasting pan and adding them to the pot. Add the stock and bring to a boil. Simmer, covered, over low–medium heat, for 30 minutes.

4. Remove the soup from the heat and puree with an immersion blender until smooth. Add the reserved mushroom strips and additional seasonings to taste. Stir in the coconut milk, if desired, and simmer over low heat until heated through, about 10 minutes. Garnish with the fresh parsley and any other optional garnishes of your choice and serve immediately. **Serves 4.**

Beef Bourguignon

BEEF BOURGUIGNON (pronounced *boor-gee-NYON*) is a rich, luxurious French stew that was first made popular in America by Julia Child. It is a braised beef simmered in red wine and chicken stock with a host of fresh vegetables. This stew may seem like a lot of extra effort, but it's really quite simple to prepare. So much more than a soup, it's a meal in itself when served with garlic knots (see page 40) or a good crusty bread.

Goldy S. introduced Martha Stewart's beef bourguignon to the Ohr Naava auction committee. She set a gorgeous table with fruits and sweets, but one of the committee members had just come in from a long day and was hungry for REAL food. Goldy, in hostess mode, quickly served her some soup and fresh bread. Of course, as soon as everyone saw the expression on the lucky recipient's face when she took her first bite, they all wanted the soup, too; it was a hit!

note: *Peeling pearl onions is much easier than it looks—with the following trick, the onions practically peel themselves. Place the onions with the skins intact in a colander and rinse them under running water. Drop them into a pot of boiling water for 3 minutes. Drain and place in cold water for 3–4 minutes. One by one, cut off the root ends and squeeze the onions right out of their skins.*

2 LB. short ribs or short-cut flanken

1 TBSP. kosher salt

• Fresh black pepper

1½ TBSP. cornstarch

3 TBSP. oil

1 large onion, diced

6 CLOVES garlic, minced

10 OZ. white button mushrooms, quartered

3 fresh carrots, peeled and sliced

2 celery stalks, sliced

3 SLICES skinless deli pastrami, chopped

1 TBSP. tomato paste

1 CUP good-quality dry red wine

10 CUPS chicken stock

2 potatoes, peeled and diced

½ TSP. dried thyme or 1 Tbsp. fresh thyme

1 bay leaf

15–20 pearl onions, peeled

1. Season the ribs or flanken with the kosher salt and black pepper, and coat with the cornstarch. In a large pot, heat the oil over medium-high heat and brown the meat on all sides for 6–7 minutes. Transfer the meat to a plate.

2. Add the onion to the pot and sauté until translucent, about 7–8 minutes. Add the garlic, mushrooms, carrots, celery, and pastrami and sauté for 5 minutes longer. Stir in the tomato paste and return the meat with the plate juices to the pot.

3. Raise the heat to high for 1–2 minutes. Deglaze the pot by adding the wine and scraping off any bits stuck to the bottom with a spoon, then allow the wine to reduce for 1 minute. Add the chicken stock, potatoes, thyme, and the bay leaf and bring to a boil. Simmer, partially covered, for 2½–3 hours. Remove from the heat and season with additional kosher salt and black pepper if necessary.

4. Remove the ribs or flanken from the pot and remove the bones from the meat. Discard the bones and cut the meat into bite-size pieces. Return the meat to the pot and add the pearl onions. Cover the pot and simmer over low heat for 30–40 minutes. Serve hot with garlic knots. **Serves 8–10.**

Roasted Corn and Sausage Soup

IT'S ALWAYS *nice to get e-mails from my readers. I'm especially touched when a reader takes time out of her busy day to give me feedback on a particular recipe. One reader e-mailed me raving that this soup was "the crown jewel of her family's holiday meal." I'm not surprised. Other than chicken soup, this is the soup I prepare most often.*

Some butchers offer authentic freshly prepared sausages in a variety of flavors ranging from mild to spicy, but if you can't find them, you can use kielbasa.

This soup is best when simmered for several hours over the lowest heat. If you don't have chicken stock on hand, you can use an MSG-free consommé, preparing the appropriate amount for thirteen cups of water.

3 CUPS (4 ears) fresh corn

2 large onions, finely diced

4 TBSP. oil

6 CLOVES garlic, minced (fresh or frozen)

16 OZ. (1 bag) carrots, peeled and sliced

3 STALKS celery, sliced

13 CUPS chicken stock or chicken consommé

½ TSP. red pepper flakes

• Kosher salt

• Fresh black pepper

16 OZ. (1 bag) yellow split peas

1 LB. sausages, sliced

• Chives, to garnish

1. Preheat the oven to 350° F. Roast the corn until soft, about 30 minutes. Slice the corn off the cob.

2. Sauté the onions in the oil until soft. Add the garlic, carrots, and celery, and sauté for several more minutes. Add the chicken stock or consommé. Season with the red pepper flakes, salt, and black pepper.

3. Add the split peas and bring the soup to a rolling boil. Add the corn and cook, covered, over medium heat for 2 hours.

4. Add the sausages and cook over low–medium heat for 2 hours longer, stirring occasionally. Reduce the heat and simmer over the lowest heat until ready to serve. Serve hot. **Serves 12.**

Minestrone Soup

MINESTRONE IS *derived from the Italian word minestra, meaning "big soup." This soup certainly fits that description—it's thick, comforting, and absolutely rejuvenating. The amazing combination of flavors belies the fact that this soup is so incredibly simple to put together.*

When developing this recipe, I definitely had an opinion on what I wanted out of a minestrone soup: it had to include more than one bean type, as well as cabbage and fresh spinach to give it texture and heartiness.

For optimal results, use real chicken stock. If you don't have chicken stock on hand, you can use pareve chicken soup mix and water and add a package of chicken bones to the soup. Just remove the bones before serving.

2 onions, chopped

5 TBSP. oil

2 STALKS celery, sliced

3 carrots, peeled and sliced

6 CLOVES garlic, minced

8 CUPS chicken stock

1 CAN (28 oz.) diced tomatoes, undrained

1 CAN (15 oz.) cannellini beans, undrained

1 CAN (15 oz.) garbanzo beans, drained

1 TBSP. tomato paste

1 CUP cabbage, shredded

1 potato, cubed

2 TBSP. fresh basil, chopped

¼ TSP. sage powder

½ TSP. dried oregano or 1 Tbsp. fresh oregano, chopped

1 TBSP. salt, or more to taste

• Fresh black pepper

2 CUPS fresh spinach or Swiss chard

1 CUP uncooked shell pasta

1. In a large pot, heat the oil over medium heat. Sauté the onions in the oil until translucent. Add the celery, carrots, and garlic and sauté for 2–3 minutes longer. Add the chicken stock, tomatoes, cannellini beans, garbanzo beans, tomato paste, cabbage, potato, basil, sage powder, oregano, salt, and black pepper. Simmer, covered, until the vegetables are tender-crisp, about 1 hour.

2. Add the spinach or Swiss chard and pasta and cook, covered, for 30 minutes longer, adjusting the seasoning if necessary. Beans can sometimes soak up too much water so if the soup is too thick, just add another cup of chicken stock and heat through. **Serves 8–10.**

Creamy Broccoli Asparagus Soup

1 medium onion, chopped

4 TBSP. oil

6 CLOVES garlic, chopped

1 LB. asparagus, chopped

24 OZ. broccoli florets

1 avocado, peeled, pitted, and diced

7 CUPS chicken stock

1 TSP. kosher salt

• Fresh black pepper

AVOCADO IS *the secret ingredient in this soup. It adds an extra dose of creaminess, yet its mild flavor is barely detectable.*

All of you fellow avocado lovers, take the liberty of adding more than just one avocado. If you're entertaining, or just want to have some fun, serve a few soups in mini bowls on a rectangular plate as an individual serving (see photo opposite).

note: The other soups shown in this photograph are Cream of Roasted Butternut Squash Soup on page 70 and Roasted Tomato Vodka Soup on page 238. For a pareve version of the Roasted Tomato Vodka Soup, substitute the heavy cream with coconut milk.

1. In a large pot, heat the oil over medium heat. Sauté the onion in the oil until translucent. Add the garlic and asparagus and sauté for 3-4 minutes longer. Add the broccoli, avocado, chicken stock, salt, and black pepper and cook, covered, until the vegetables are very tender, at least 1 hour.

2. Puree the soup with an immersion blender and season with additional salt and pepper if needed. Simmer, covered, over low heat for 30 minutes. Serve warm. **Serves 8–10.**

sweet and savory

SALADS

Clementine Glazed Chicken and Baby Arugula Salad with Balsamic-Soy Vinaigrette

CHICKEN & MARINADE

½ CUP soy sauce

⅓ CUP oil

1 TBSP. toasted sesame oil

⅓ CUP honey

5 CLOVES garlic, minced

1 clementine, juiced (about ⅛ cup)

⅛ TSP. red pepper flakes

• Salt and fresh black pepper

2 LB. skinless boneless chicken thighs, cut into 1½–inch cubes

VINAIGRETTE

½ CUP oil

1 TBSP. toasted sesame oil

2 clementines, juiced (about ¼ cup)

2–3 TBSP. honey, to taste

1 TBSP. balsamic vinegar

2 TBSP. lite soy sauce

1 CLOVE garlic, minced

PINCH kosher salt and fresh black pepper

SALAD

6 OZ. baby arugula

1 small red onion, very thinly sliced

1 endive, very thinly sliced

1 CUP pomegranate seeds, plus extra to sprinkle on the clementines

⅓ CUP sunflower seeds

⅓ CUP slivered almonds, toasted

4 clementines, peeled and sliced into rounds

• Black sesame seeds, to sprinkle on the clementines

THE INSPIRATION *for this recipe came from a simple desire to sprinkle black sesame seeds and pomegranate seeds on freshly sliced clementines (well...just to see how gorgeous it would look). From there (and to make it print worthy) it evolved into an unforgettable salad that includes a vinaigrette with both soy sauce and balsamic vinegar—unusual, but the results are fantastic.*

This salad is so delicious and beautiful, it's generated overwhelming feedback. The consensus is that even men who won't brave "interesting salads" love this one, and the chicken itself has become such a favorite, it's prepared time and time again.

If you prefer, you can substitute the endive for fennel. Fennel is super crunchy and has a mild licorice flavor. I don't particularly care for fennel, but when I slice it superthin with a mandoline slicer, the flavor is subtle and it adds a mega-crunch factor to this salad.

---

1. First, prepare the marinade: In a bowl, whisk together the soy sauce, oil, sesame oil, honey, garlic, clementine juice, red pepper flakes, salt, and black pepper. Place the chicken in a Ziploc bag with the marinade and shake to mix. Seal and leave overnight in the refrigerator, or for at least 6 hours.

2. To prepare the vinaigrette: In a jar or cruet, combine all the dressing ingredients and shake until well combined.

3. Remove the chicken from the marinade and grill or broil for 6–8 minutes per side.

4. In a large bowl, combine the baby arugula, red onion, endive, pomegranate seeds, sunflower seeds, and slivered almonds. Toss with the vinaigrette. Arrange the clementine slices either on top of the salad or on the side, and sprinkle them with pomegranate seeds and black sesame seeds. Serve with the chicken. **Serves 6.**

Asian Slaw with Chow Mein Noodles and Sesame Dressing

DRESSING

4 TBSP. oil

3 TBSP. sugar

3 TBSP. lite soy sauce

1 TBSP. rice vinegar

1 CLOVE garlic, minced

1 TSP. toasted sesame oil

½ TSP. fresh ginger, minced

2 TBSP. toasted black or white sesame seeds

SLAW

1 PKG. (16 oz.) coleslaw mix

3 scallions, thinly sliced

½ small red onion, thinly sliced

1½ CUPS Chinese chow mein noodles

THE CHOW MEIN *noodles add a great crunch factor to this slaw. Though the salad maintains its crunch longer than others, I prefer to serve this salad immediately after adding the dressing.*

If you wish, you can double or triple the dressing and keep it refrigerated in an airtight container for later. Then just toss with the slaw ingredients and it's ready to serve.

1. To prepare the dressing: In a small saucepan, combine the oil, sugar, soy sauce, vinegar, garlic, sesame oil, and ginger. Cook for several minutes over medium heat, stirring continuously, until the sugar has dissolved, about 1–2 minutes. Allow to cool, then add the sesame seeds and mix well.

2. In a large salad bowl, combine all the slaw ingredients. Toss with the dressing and serve immediately. **Serves 8-10.**

Spring Mix with Candied Hazelnuts and Pecans and Balsamic-Strawberry Vinaigrette

CANDIED HAZELNUTS AND PECANS

¾ CUP pecans

¾ CUP hazelnuts

1 orange, juiced and zested

⅓ CUP pure maple syrup

2 TBSP. honey

1 TBSP. balsamic vinegar

DRESSING

½ CUP oil

⅓ CUP PLUS 2 TBSP. sugar

¼ CUP balsamic vinegar

6–7 large strawberries

PINCH salt

SALAD

8 CUPS spring mix

¾ CUP dried apricots, diced

1 CUP strawberries, quartered

6 oz. blueberries

½ small red onion, chopped (optional)

"I'M DREAMING *about it"* was Yali's text about this salad. Every now and then, a sweet salad comes along and becomes a part of your life—literally. It's on your table at almost every meal, it's in your fridge for when the mood strikes...and it even satisfies your sweet cravings so you forget about dessert for a while.

This recipe calls for spring mix, also known as mesculin salad, an assortment of crucifers and baby greens with gorgeous contrasts of intense burgundy and green. Tossed with berries and apricots, this dish is bursting with color and truly irresistible. Once you've tried it, I bet you'll be as enamored with this salad—vibrant and sweet but not cloying—as my family is.

note: Because the dressing requires a food processor, the recipe yields enough for two salads.

even simpler: Use honey-glazed pecans and hazelnuts instead of preparing the candied nuts yourself.

---

1. To prepare the candied hazelnuts and pecans: Preheat the oven to 350° F. Line a baking sheet with parchment paper. In a bowl, combine the pecans, hazelnuts, orange juice and zest, maple syrup, honey, and balsamic vinegar. Spread the mixture onto the prepared baking sheet and roast, uncovered, until the nuts appear glazed, 5 minutes, stirring occasionally to ensure that the nuts remain separated. Allow to cool completely.

2. To prepare the dressing: In a food processor, puree the oil, sugar, balsamic vinegar, strawberries, and salt until smooth.

3. In a large salad bowl, combine the salad ingredients, half the dressing, and half the candied hazelnuts and pecans. Sprinkle the remaining nuts over the salad and serve immediately, reserving the rest of the dressing for later use. If desired, you can chop the nuts into smaller pieces before adding to the salad. **Serves 8.**

Blackened Tuna with Tropical Salad and Honey-Lime Dressing

TUNA STEAKS *have a firm texture and a delicate flavor and create an aesthetically pleasing presentation. Well-prepared blackened tuna is charred on both sides, but the center remains moist and pink. Purchase good-quality tuna, since freshness is the key to achieving the best results.*

These well-seasoned tuna steaks are lightly seared, Cajun-style. The spice rub that gives this dish its wonderful flavor is also great on chicken and salmon.

This salad is filling enough to serve as a main dish and elegant enough to be an appetizer. Serve half a tuna steak for an individual portion as an appetizer or a whole tuna steak as a main dish.

2 TBSP. oil

4 TBSP. lime juice

2 CLOVES garlic, minced

4 tuna steaks (6 oz. each)

SPICE RUB

2 TBSP. paprika

1 TSP. cayenne pepper

1 TBSP. onion powder

2 TSP. kosher salt

½ TSP. fresh black pepper

1 TSP. dried thyme

1 TSP. dried basil

1 TSP. dried oregano

1 TBSP. garlic powder

4 TBSP. oil

DRESSING

4 TBSP. lime juice

2 TBSP. orange juice

1 TBSP. honey

¼ CUP oil

1 TBSP. sesame seeds

SALAD

1 fresh mango, diced

1 red bell pepper, finely diced

1 small red onion, finely diced

3 scallions, thinly sliced

½ CUP golden raisins

2 TBSP. fresh cilantro, chopped

1 jalapeno pepper, seeded and minced

1½ hearts of romaine, sliced

1. In a small bowl, whisk together the oil, lime juice, and garlic. Rub the tuna steaks with the mixture and marinate in the refrigerator for at least 3 hours in a sealed Ziploc bag.

2. To prepare the dressing: In a small bowl, combine the lime juice, orange juice, honey, oil, and sesame seeds.

3. To prepare the salad: In a large bowl, combine the mango, red pepper, red onion, scallions, raisins, cilantro, and jalapeno pepper. Add half the dressing and toss to combine.

4. To prepare the spice rub: On a plate, combine the paprika, cayenne pepper, onion powder, salt, black pepper, thyme, basil, oregano, and garlic powder. Remove the tuna steaks from the marinade and coat each side with the spice mixture. In a large nonstick skillet, heat the 4 tablespoons of oil over medium heat. Add the tuna steaks and cook for 2 minutes on each side. Transfer the steaks to a clean plate and allow to cool.

5. Set aside a third of the mango-and-pepper salad mixture to use as a garnish. Add the romaine hearts and the remaining dressing to the other two-thirds of the mixture. Slice the tuna lengthwise and arrange on a plate along with a generous serving of the salad. Sprinkle the reserved mango and pepper mixture over each portion of salad and serve immediately. **Serves 4.**

Baby Red Potato Salad with Caesar Dill Dressing

> **THIS POTATO** *salad gets its intense flavor from baking the potatoes in their skin while tightly covered rather than boiling them. This method is also so much easier than boiling. You can serve this salad at any temperature—warm or cold.*

2 LB. baby red potatoes, peels intact

1 TBSP. oil

4 TBSP. mayonnaise

1 TSP. Dijon mustard

1 CLOVE garlic (fresh or frozen), minced

1 TSP. lemon juice

½ TSP. Worcestershire sauce

3 gherkin dill pickles, finely diced

3 TBSP. fresh dill, chopped

• Kosher salt

• Fresh black pepper

1. Preheat the oven to 350° F. Wash and dry the potatoes. Leaving on the peel, cut each potato in half and place in a baking pan. Sprinkle the potatoes with the oil and bake, covered, until cooked through, about 1 hour.

2. In a large bowl, combine the baked potatoes with the mayonnaise, mustard, garlic, lemon juice, Worcestershire sauce, gherkins, and dill. Season with the salt and black pepper. Serve warm, at room temperature, or cold. **Serves 4–6.**

Crispy Kani Slaw with Spicy Mayo

IF **THERE** *is kani slaw on a menu, I'll order it. But whenever I used to prepare this salad in my own kitchen, I was disappointed with the watery dressing.*

The cucumbers were the culprits. They expel a lot of water after they're sliced, which dilutes the dressing and renders it thin and watery instead of creamy. The solution was to drain the cucumbers of their excess water content, resulting in a much crispier slaw. Also, I started using English cucumbers—they're crispier because of their lower seed content.

The toasted sesame seeds are not a garnish here—they have a huge flavor impact on this salad. There are some good-quality toasted black and white sesame seed combinations that have recently become available—look for them in your local supermarket. For added texture, top the salad with tempura flakes purchased from your favorite sushi takeout.

note: *Kani are imitation crab sticks often found in sushi rolls. They can be found in the freezer section of the supermarket. You can shred the kani easily by hand.*

2 (12 inches long) English cucumbers, peeled

16 oz. kani (imitation crab sticks), shredded

• Black and white sesame seeds, toasted

OPTIONAL GARNISH

• Store-bought tempura flakes

DRESSING

1 CUP mayonnaise

1 TSP. seasoned rice vinegar

1 TSP. sesame oil

2 TBSP. sriracha sauce

1 TSP. honey

1. Slice each cucumber in half lengthwise and scrape the seeds out with a spoon. Shred the cucumber in a food processor or julienne by hand. Place the shredded cucumber in a colander and allow to drain for at least 30–45 minutes. Pat completely dry with paper towels.

2. Mix all the dressing ingredients until well combined. In a bowl, combine the cucumbers, shredded kani, and sesame seeds. Add the dressing and toss to combine. Top with additional sesame seeds and the tempura flakes, if desired, and serve immediately. **Serves 6.**

BBQ Tortilla Chip Salad

CARROT CHIPS

3 large carrots, peeled

- Oil, for frying

DRESSING

½ CUP oil

½ CUP mayonnaise

1 TBSP. red wine vinegar

1 TBSP. Dijon mustard

1 TBSP. chili sauce

1 CLOVE garlic, minced

1–3 TBSP. sugar (optional)

SALAD

2 hearts of romaine lettuce, sliced

1 box grape or cherry tomatoes, halved

1 yellow bell pepper, thinly sliced

1 CUP Craisins

½ small red onion, thinly sliced (optional)

4 OZ. (1 box) alfalfa sprouts

8 OZ. (1 large bag) BBQ taco chips, crushed

TO GET *an idea of what a recipe entails, the first thing I always do is scan the ingredients list. You may pause at the alfalfa sprouts listed in this recipe and consider leaving them out. Don't. Sometimes the most unlikely ingredient is the one that yields a winning recipe.*

The crispy carrots are simple to prepare and you can add them to any salad for a dazzling garnish. Though carrots lend a more vibrant color than sweet potatoes, you may prefer the taste of crispy sweet potatoes—so pick your choice.

If you find that the dressing is a bit too thick, dilute it with one or two tablespoons of warm water.

1. To prepare the carrot chips: Slice the carrots lengthwise into long, thin strips. In a medium saucepan, pour enough oil into the skillet to reach a depth of 2 inches and heat over high heat. When the oil is very hot, add the carrots and fry until crispy and curled, about 1 minute. Remove from the oil and drain on a paper towel.

2. To prepare the dressing: Place all the dressing ingredients in a jar or cruet and shake well until smooth.

3. In a large salad bowl, combine the hearts of romaine, tomatoes, yellow pepper, Craisins, and red onion and toss with the dressing. Add the alfalfa sprouts and taco chips and gently toss until evenly combined. Top the salad with the carrot chips and serve. **Serves 4–6.**

Smoked Turkey and Chicken Salad with Creamy Avocado Dressing

DRESSING

1 ripe Hass avocado

2 Tbsp. lemon juice

¼ cup oil

2 Tbsp. mayonnaise

5 Tbsp. warm water

¾ tsp. kosher salt

⅛ tsp. fresh black pepper

1 tsp. Worcestershire sauce

2 cloves garlic, minced

1 tsp. sugar

SALAD

2 ears fresh corn

1½ hearts of romaine lettuce, sliced

1½ cups grape or cherry tomatoes, halved

1 cup baked bits, divided (I use Baker's Choice)

1–2 large chicken breasts (approximately ⅓ lb.), grilled and diced

1 thick slice smoked turkey (approximately ⅓ lb.) , diced

WHEN SEVERAL *of my daughter's friends were over on Shabbos, I served them this avocado dressing as a dip with crackers and some vegetables. They loved it. And so we discovered that avocado dressing can also double as a dip for fresh vegetables.*

The avocado dressing will remain fresh for several days if stored in the refrigerator in an airtight container. It stays creamy and even maintains its gorgeous green color. If this salad is on the menu for Shabbos lunch, bring the avocado dressing to room temperature before serving. Dilute the dressing with several tablespoons of warm water if it's too thick.

If you're serving this salad as a starter, double or triple the avocado dressing and spoon some into mini dishes for individual servings. Everyone will love having their own dipping bowl for bread, challah, or vegetable sticks.

For a pretty presentation, serve the individual portions of salad spilling out of radicchio cups (see the photo opposite).

1. Preheat the oven to 350° F. Remove the husks and silks from the corn. Roast the corn on oven racks until softened, about 35 minutes. Allow to cool.

2. Cut the kernels off the cob: Hold the corn upright on a large cutting board . With a large, sharp knife, slice down the length of the ear between the kernels and the cob. Rotate the cob and repeat until all the kernels are cut.

3. To prepare the avocado dressing: Mash the avocado with the lemon juice. In a food processor, puree the mashed avocado with the rest of the dressing ingredients until smooth.

4. In a large salad bowl, combine the corn, lettuce, tomatoes, ½ cup of the baked bits, the chicken, and the turkey. Add the avocado dressing and toss. Sprinkle the remaining baked bits over the salad. Serve immediately. **Serves 6.**

Terra Stix, Mushroom, and Bell Pepper Salad

I HAVE YET *to serve this salad without someone (even kids) commenting on how special and delicious it is. The delightful crunch will make kids forget they're eating vegetables.*

You can double or triple the dressing to make more salad later. The dressing will stay fresh in the fridge for up to two weeks if stored in an airtight container. For a beautiful presentation, serve this salad in martini glasses and garnish with endives and radish sprouts.

DRESSING

- ¼ CUP oil
- ¼ CUP ketchup
- 2 TBSP. sugar
- 1 CLOVE garlic, minced
- 3 TBSP. red or white wine vinegar
- 2 TBSP. water
- ½ TBSP. Dijon mustard
- ¼ TSP. kosher salt
- PINCH fresh black pepper

SALAD

- 2 hearts of romaine lettuce, thinly sliced
- 8 OZ. (1 box) white button mushrooms, stems removed and sliced
- 1 red bell pepper, finely diced
- 1 yellow or orange bell pepper, finely diced
- 3 GENEROUS HANDFULS Terra Stix, plus extra to garnish
- ¾ CUP honey-glazed peanuts or pecans

1. To prepare the dressing: Place all the dressing ingredients in a jar or cruet and shake well to combine.

2. In a large salad bowl, toss together the lettuce, mushrooms, and peppers.

3. When ready to serve, add the dressing to the salad and toss to combine. Add the Terra Stix and nuts and toss gently. Garnish the salad with additional Terra Stix and serve immediately. **Serves 8–10.**

Romaine with Avocado, Cucumber, Mango, and Red Onion Dressing

THE MELDING *of mango, avocado, and cucumber is reminiscent of a soothing spa treatment. Enriched with essential vitamins, it tastes just as revitalizing and refreshing.*

For a slight variation on taste and color, add some thinly sliced red onions to complement the red onion dressing. This dressing is fabulous with just about any salad. The recipe yields a large batch, so you can save half of it to use later in other salads.

Once the salad is ready to serve, store-bought blue potato chips make for a dazzling, versatile garnish. You can also use the blue potato chips as individual servers for mini scoops of guacamole, egg salad, or tuna salad.

SALAD

1 CUP slivered almonds

6 CUPS romaine lettuce, chopped

1 mango, peeled and diced

1 avocado, peeled and diced

1 Kirby cucumber, peeled and diced

1 CUP Craisins or dried cherries (optional)

DRESSING

½ red onion

2 CLOVES garlic

1 TSP. mustard

¾ CUP oil

¼ CUP sugar

⅓ CUP lemon juice

2 TBSP. orange juice

1. Preheat the oven to 350° F. Spread the almonds on a baking sheet and toast until fragrant, about 10 minutes.

2. In a large salad bowl, toss together the romaine lettuce, mango, avocado, cucumber, Craisins or dried cherries, and toasted almonds.

3. To prepare the dressing: In a food processor, puree all the dressing ingredients until smooth. Pour over the salad and toss to combine. Serve immediately. **Serves 6.**

Pesto Caesar Salad with Crispy Onions (in Tortilla Bowls)

THE **CLASSIC** *goodness of Caesar salad is perfectly embellished with pesto paste, minced chili, and crispy onions. The tortilla bowls are super simple to prepare and can be used to present almost any salad. You can find nonstick tortilla bowl makers in most specialty bakeware shops.*

To further enhance your Caesar salad experience, choose your favorites from this list of possible additions:

- *Baked salmon, cubed*
- *Grilled chicken, sliced into strips*
- *Smoked turkey breast, cubed*
- *Mushrooms, sautéed or roasted*
- *Edamame*
- *Roasted peppers*
- *Artichoke hearts*
- *Grape tomatoes, halved*
- *Roasted sweet potatoes, diced*
- *Capers*
- *Avocado, diced*
- *Freshly grated parmesan*
- *Crumbled goat cheese*
- *Feta cheese, cubed*

note: *If you find the dressing too thick, dilute it with some warm water.*

dairy version: *Add ⅓ cup parmesan cheese to the dressing.*

4 CLOVES garlic, minced

¾ CUP mayonnaise

1 TBSP. lemon juice

1 TSP. Worcestershire sauce

1 TSP. Dijon mustard

1–2 frozen chili cubes

2 TBSP. prepared pesto sauce

- Salt
- Fresh black pepper

2 HEADS romaine lettuce, sliced

8 OZ. canned French-fried onions (I use French's)

- Tortilla wraps (any color)

1. Place the garlic, mayonnaise, lemon juice, Worcestershire sauce, mustard, chili, pesto sauce, salt, and black pepper in a jar or cruet and shake until well combined.

2. Toss the lettuce with the dressing. Add three-quarters of the French-fried onions and blend gently, reserving the rest of the fried onions to garnish.

3. To prepare the tortilla bowls: Preheat the oven to 350° F. Press the tortilla wraps gently into nonstick tortilla bowl makers, making sure to press down on all sides so the tortillas mold to them. Bake, uncovered, for 10 minutes. Remove from the oven and allow to cool. Keep uncovered at room temperature until ready to serve. Before serving, spoon the salad into the tortilla bowls. Sprinkle the remaining fried onions on top of the salad. **Serves 6-8.**

Purple Cabbage and Yellow Bell Pepper Slaw

LIKE MOST ever-evolving salads, slaws have been expanded way past the traditional coleslaw. This cabbage slaw boasts a pretty medley of crunchy and colorful tastes and textures.

You can slice the yellow pepper very thinly on a mandoline slicer, or chop it into small dice, depending on your preference. Prepare this salad several hours in advance to allow the flavors to mingle.

DRESSING

⅓ CUP oil

3 TBSP. white wine vinegar

3 TBSP. sugar

1 TSP. Dijon mustard

½ TSP. kosher salt

⅛ TSP. fresh black pepper

SLAW

1 BAG shredded red cabbage

1 large yellow bell pepper, thinly sliced or finely diced

1 CUP Craisins

¾ CUP slivered almonds, toasted

4 scallions, thinly sliced

2 TBSP. fresh parsley, finely chopped

• Black sesame seeds

1. To prepare the dressing: Place all the dressing ingredients in a jar or cruet and shake very well until combined.

2. In a large salad bowl, combine the cabbage, yellow pepper, Craisins, almonds, scallions, and parsley. Toss with the dressing. Refrigerate the salad until ready to serve. Just before serving, sprinkle with the black sesame seeds. **Serves 6-8.**

Arugula Waldorf Salad with Maple Walnuts

IN THIS *wonderfully light version of Waldorf salad, mayonnaise-drenched apples are a thing of the past. This American classic gets a makeover with just a tinge of mayo. The combination of crisp apples, arugula, endives, and walnuts gives this recipe a clean, fresh flavor, not to mention its delicious crunch.*

alternative: *Substitute the dried cherries with Craisins.*

1 CUP walnuts

½ CUP pure maple syrup

DRESSING

¼ CUP oil

¼ CUP pure maple syrup

2 TBSP. mayonnaise

2 TBSP. apple cider vinegar

1 TBSP. Dijon mustard

½ TSP. kosher salt

¼ TSP. fresh black pepper

SALAD

8 oz. arugula

1 endive, sliced

2 Granny Smith apples, peeled and diced

2 STALKS celery, sliced

¾ CUP dried cherries

¼ CUP golden raisins

1. Preheat the oven to 350° F. In a small bowl, coat the walnuts with the maple syrup and spread in single layer on a baking sheet. Bake for 10 minutes, or until fragrant. Allow to cool.

2. To prepare the dressing: Place all the dressing ingredients in a small jar or cruet and shake well to combine.

3. To prepare the salad: In a large salad bowl, combine the walnuts with the salad ingredients. Add the dressing and toss to combine. Serve immediately. **Serves 6-8.**

Crispy Beef Salad with Warm Peppers and Thai Sweet-Chili Vinaigrette

DRESSING

¼ CUP Thai sweet chili sauce

2 TBSP. lite soy sauce

2 TBSP. lime juice

2 TBSP. mayonnaise

½ CUP oil

2 CLOVES garlic, minced

2 TBSP. seasoned rice vinegar

SALAD

1 red bell pepper, thinly sliced

8 CUPS baby arugula

1 CUP pine nuts or slivered almonds

1 LB. ready-made crispy beef strips, warm or at room temperature

1. To prepare the dressing: Place all the dressing ingredients in a jar or cruet and shake well until combined.

2. To prepare the warm peppers: In a skillet, combine half of the dressing and the sliced red pepper. Stir-fry over medium heat until tender-crisp, 7–9 minutes, stirring occasionally.

3. To prepare the salad: In a large bowl, toss the remaining half of the dressing with the arugula and nuts. Add the warm red peppers together with the juices from the pan. To serve, place a mound of salad on a plate and top with strips of crispy beef. Serve immediately (so the salad doesn't get soggy). **Serves 6–8.**

THE CONTRASTING textures and flavors of the warm pepper, crispy beef, and sweet-sour-spicy dressing makes this salad a true knockout. No need to prepare the crispy beef from scratch; this salad is topped with ready-made crispy beef from your favorite Thai, Chinese, or Japanese takeout restaurant.

The dressing calls for seasoned rice vinegar, a wonderful flavor-packed condiment that has become easily available. I keep several bottles in my pantry since I know I'll be using it—often. The basic version is a combination of sake, sugar, and rice vinegar, but there are several variations to choose from. My personal favorites are the basic and roasted garlic versions.

note: Half of the salad dressing is used to stir-fry the peppers, while the other half is saved for dressing the arugula.

Caramelized Pear Spinach Salad with Pomegranate and Pecans

2 large Anjou pears, peeled, cored, and cut lengthwise into eighths

¼ CUP lemon juice

¼ CUP brown sugar

DRESSING

⅓ CUP oil

1 TBSP. red wine vinegar

1 TBSP. honey

2 TSP. Dijon mustard

1 CLOVE garlic, minced

½ TSP. kosher salt

⅛ TSP. fresh black pepper

• Juice from the caramelized pears

SALAD

10 oz. baby spinach

1 CUP honey-glazed pecans

¾–1 CUP Craisins

1 CUP pomegranate seeds

IF I WERE officially developing a pear salad, I'd naturally combine the sweetness of pears with peppery arugula. But this salad was an unexpected, delicious accident—I randomly teamed up pears with baby spinach after rummaging through my fridge for ingredients. The results were surprising—and amazing. I did know that fragrant ripe pears are lovely when caramelized, and I added some of the juice from the caramelized pears to the vinaigrette to lend the dressing a pear-infused taste.

I love testing my recipes on large crowds, and when we attended a fabulous dinner party hosted by Yali, I was presented with the perfect opportunity to test this recipe. Yali is the designer of ziccibea.com linens and her highly creative approach, whether with food or linens, is always fresh, clean, and never boring. So when Yali suggested that we should plate the salad individually as an appetizer instead of serving it in the center of the table, it was the perfect idea—and all the plates were wiped clean.

dairy version: Sprinkle the salad with grated goat or feta cheese before serving.

1. Preheat the oven to 425° F. Dip the flat sides of the sliced pears in the lemon juice and then in the brown sugar. In a large baking pan, arrange the pears in a single layer and roast for 25 minutes. Remove from the oven and allow to cool to room temperature. Cut each pear wedge into 1-inch slices. (Make sure to reserve the pear juice that was released during the roasting for the dressing.)

2. To prepare the dressing: In a small bowl, vigorously whisk together the oil, vinegar, honey, mustard, garlic, salt, black pepper, and the reserved pear juice until well combined.

3. In a large salad bowl, combine the baby spinach, pears, glazed pecans, and Craisins. Toss with the dressing and sprinkle evenly with the pomegranate seeds. Serve immediately. **Serves 6–8.**

Fusion Chef Salad with Triple Crunch (in Tortilla Wraps)

TRIPLE CRUNCH

2 Tbsp. oil

1 pkg. ramen noodles, crushed

¼ cup sesame seeds

½ cup slivered almonds

DRESSING

3 Tbsp. red wine vinegar

3 Tbsp. sugar

3 Tbsp. lite soy sauce

6 Tbsp. oil

SALAD

1½ heads romaine lettuce, thinly sliced

1 cup grape tomatoes, quartered, or 1 small red bell pepper, finely diced

1 thick slice (¼ lb.) smoked turkey, finely diced

1 thick slice (¼ lb.) turkey pastrami, finely diced

1 small Hass avocado, diced

1 small red onion, finely diced

8–10 tortillas (optional)

WE **ENJOYED** *this fabulous salad at Esther C.'s house at a Shabbos lunch. I loved how she wrapped the salad in tortillas before serving. Ingenious.*

Even if you don't want to bother with an extra step and would rather serve this salad in a serving bowl— "unwrapped"—you'll still love this salad. The best part? Because the ramen noodles are sautéed, they don't get soggy, leaving you with a triple dose of crunch from the ramen noodles, slivered almonds, and sesame seeds.

1. To prepare the triple crunch: In a skillet, heat the oil over medium heat. Sauté the crushed ramen noodles, sesame seeds, and slivered almonds, stirring, until deeply golden and very crunchy. Allow to cool completely. Keep tightly covered until ready to serve.

2. To prepare the dressing: Place all the dressing ingredients in a jar or cruet and shake until combined.

3. In a large salad bowl, combine the lettuce, tomatoes or red pepper, turkey, pastrami, avocado, and red onion. Toss the salad with the dressing and triple crunch. Serve immediately.

4. To prepare the optional tortilla wraps: Spoon the desired amount of salad down the center of each tortilla, stopping short of the edges. Roll the tortilla tightly and serve immediately. **Serves 6-8.**

Avocado, Tomato, and Hearts of Palm Salad

I LOVE THE *simplicity and versatility of this salad. I usually serve this salad as is, but you can add spring mix or serve it on bruschetta or mini tortilla crisps.*

Canned hearts of palm, one of the featured ingredients in this salad, are packed in brine, giving them a nice, gentle flavor—a little sweet and a little bit salty.

SALAD

1 CAN (14-15 oz.) sliced hearts of palm

1 PINT grape tomatoes, halved

2 avocados, peeled and diced

1 very small red onion, diced

DRESSING

2 TBSP. mayonnaise

1 TBSP. lemon or lime juice

1 TSP. warm water

1 frozen or fresh garlic clove, minced

¾ TSP. kosher salt

⅛ TSP. fresh black pepper

1. To prepare the salad: In a large salad bowl, combine the hearts of palm, tomatoes, avocados, and red onion.

2. To prepare the dressing: In a small jar, combine all the dressing ingredients. Add the dressing to the salad and toss well. Refrigerate until ready to serve. **Serves 6.**

Roasted Portobello Chicken Salad

THIS VIBRANT *salad is a combination of perfect pairings. Marinated chicken and a light salad mingle with meaty, robust mushrooms that are gussied up with thyme and a teriyaki-honey marinade and then roasted or grilled.*

When selecting portobello mushrooms, make sure they are plump, solid, and firm. A slippery mushroom indicates decomposition.

I found the bamboo skewers decorating the salad in the photo at Crate & Barrel. For a quicker method of presentation, cut the chicken into strips and place on top of the salad with the portobello mushroom strips. If you're serving this salad for Shabbos lunch, bring the mushroom caps and chicken to room temperature before serving.

6 large chicken cutlets (dark or white)

6 large portobello mushroom caps

¾ CUP oil

½ CUP teriyaki sauce

¼ CUP honey

1 TSP. fresh thyme leaves or ½ tsp. dried thyme

5 CLOVES garlic (frozen or fresh), minced

1 TSP. fresh black pepper

SALAD

10 oz. mesculin salad

2 different colored peppers, cut into strips, or 2 cups cherry tomatoes, halved

1 CUP pine nuts, toasted

DRESSING

⅓ CUP oil

2 TBSP. soy sauce

3 TBSP. sugar

2 TBSP. seasoned rice vinegar

¼ TSP. fresh black pepper

1 CLOVE garlic, minced

1. With a sharp knife, shape the chicken cutlets into rectangles by trimming the edges. Wash and clean the mushroom caps. Place the oil, teriyaki sauce, honey, thyme, garlic, and black pepper in a jar and mix until well combined. In one bowl, pour half the marinade over the chicken. In another bowl, pour the remaining marinade over the mushrooms. Marinate the chicken and mushrooms in the refrigerator for at least 6 hours.

2. Preheat the oven or grill to 450° F. With a slotted spoon, remove the chicken and mushrooms from the marinade. Roast or grill the mushrooms, gill side down, for 20 minutes. Grill the chicken on an indoor or outdoor grill on high heat, about 6–8 minutes per side.

3. In a large salad bowl, combine the mesculin mix, peppers or tomatoes, and the pine nuts, reserving some of the pine nuts to garnish.

4. To prepare the dressing: Place all the dressing ingredients in a jar or cruet and shake well until well combined. Toss the salad with the dressing.

5. To serve, place a piece of grilled chicken on a plate. Insert a bamboo skewer into each corner of the chicken. Fill the center with salad, being careful not to overfill, and top with the sliced mushrooms. Sprinkle some of the reserved pine nuts on top. **Serves 6.**

Tropical Kani Salad with Sriracha Lime Dressing

DRESSING

3 TBSP. mayonnaise

½ TBSP. sriracha sauce

1 TSP. lime juice

1 CLOVE garlic, minced

½ TSP. kosher salt

• Fresh black pepper

SALAD

7 kani (imitation crab sticks), finely diced

1 medium English cucumber, finely diced

1 mango, finely diced

THE SLIGHTLY *spicy dressing in this salad is nicely balanced with the cool cucumbers and sweet mango. If you prefer the salad even spicier, you can add more sriracha sauce.*

This salad contains long and slender English cucumbers, commonly referred to as "hothouse cucumbers." This variety is crispier and sweeter than standard cucumbers due to the low seed content.

The salad can be served in one of two ways. To prepare it as a slaw, shred the imitation crab sticks (kani) by hand and julienne the mango and cucumber in a food processor. Serve each portion with an avocado wedge as a garnish. Or serve this salad in avocado halves: cut an avocado in half, remove the pit, and fill each hollowed avocado half with the kani salad.

1. To prepare the dressing: In a small jar or bowl, combine the mayonnaise, sriracha sauce, lime juice, garlic, salt, and black pepper.

2. In a large bowl, combine the kani, cucumber, and mango and toss with the dressing. Serve immediately. **Serves 6.**

banish chicken boredom

POULTRY

Apricot Balsamic Cornish Hens

2 Cornish hens (4 chicken quarters or 1 whole chicken)

4 CLOVES garlic

4 SPRIGS thyme

1 CUP apricot jam

¼ CUP balsamic vinegar

• Kosher salt

• Fresh black pepper

5 fresh or dried figs

4 fresh apricots, halved and pitted, or 8 dried apricots, plus extra to garnish (optional)

1. Preheat the oven to 375° F. Rinse the Cornish hens and pat dry. In a roasting pan, sprinkle the cavities and outsides of the Cornish hens with the kosher salt and black pepper. Place 2 cloves of garlic and 2 sprigs of thyme in each cavity (if you are using chicken quarters, place the garlic cloves and thyme sprigs on top of the chicken).

2. In a small bowl, combine the apricot jam and balsamic vinegar. Pour the mixture over the chicken in the roasting pan. Add the figs and apricots to the pan and bake, uncovered, for 1½ hours. Before serving, drizzle plenty of sauce over the chicken, and each Cornish hen can be halved. **Serves 4.**

GROWING UP, *I rarely ate figs. When I started to develop my own recipes, I began to appreciate the grace of a beautiful, plump fig with its lingering sweet flavor.*

Figs and balsamic vinegar are a match made in heaven, and chicken is my top contender to partner this fruit. The figs make a rich crimson syrup, and their fruity notes of acidity lend a sweeter-than-honey sweetness to the dish. I've also created this dish using dried figs with equally spectacular results.

Good-quality balsamic vinegar is essential for infusing the sauce with an incredible flavor. Baking the chicken uncovered allows for a rich reduction to thicken the sauce and intensifies and concentrates the flavor. It also caramelizes the chicken, allowing you to reap the benefits of a flavorful, moist, and tender dish.

For a pleasing presentation, serve the chicken with fresh halved figs and fresh or dried apricots and drizzle with the sauce.

even simpler: *Substitute the Cornish hens with a standard whole or quartered chicken.*

note: *The recipe for the rice pilaf pictured with this recipe can be found on page 21.*

Savory Chicken with Papaya Salsa

BIG, **BOLD** *flavors define this chicken recipe. It's sufficiently savory to appeal to adults, but delicately spiced to accommodate children. For palates that prefer more heat, double the quantities of black pepper and cayenne pepper.*

Preparing a large batch of the spice rub will make this dish effortless to prepare in the future. Coriander, one of the featured seasonings in the spice rub, is the dried seed of cilantro. Its flavor is reminiscent of citrus peel. Toasting the coriander seeds and then coarsely grinding them gives the chicken an appealingly rustic look and an intense, fragrant flavor, but you can also use conventional ground coriander.

Boneless chicken thighs make for a more elegant presentation, but you may also use standard chicken quarters for this recipe. Credit for the papaya salsa goes to chef Aviv Mosovich.

4 boneless chicken thighs, skin intact, or 4 chicken quarters

• Thai sweet chili sauce (optional)

SPICE RUB

1 TSP. onion powder

½ TSP. chili powder

1 TSP. kosher salt

½ TSP. cumin

1 TSP. garlic powder

1 TSP. brown sugar

1 TSP. coriander

⅛ TSP. cayenne pepper

⅛ TSP. black pepper

PAPAYA SALSA

1 CUP tomatoes, finely diced

1 CUP papaya (1 papaya), finely diced

½ small red onion, finely diced

2 TBSP. fresh cilantro or parsley, chopped

1 lemon, juiced

1 TSP. oil

• Kosher salt

• Fresh black pepper

DASH cayenne pepper

1. Preheat the oven to 400° F. Rinse the chicken and pat dry. In a small bowl, combine all the ingredients for the spice rub and rub it on both sides of the chicken to coat. Bake, uncovered, skin-side up, 45 minutes for boneless chicken thighs and 1½ hours for chicken quarters.

2. To prepare the salsa: In a bowl, combine all the salsa ingredients. Serve the chicken warm, with the salsa and the sweet chili sauce on the side, if desired. **Serves 4.**

One-Pot Chicken Dinner

4 chicken bottoms, quartered

1 LB. baby potatoes, halved or quartered

10 CLOVES garlic

20 OZ. duck sauce

• Montreal steak seasoning (I like McCormick)

• Paprika

• Onion powder

• Fresh black pepper

2 TBSP. fresh chopped herbs of your choice (basil, rosemary, sage), plus extra to garnish

12 OZ. broccoli or cauliflower florets (fresh or frozen), or a combination of both

THIS RECIPE *is dedicated to busy moms everywhere. A balanced meal that takes less than ten minutes to prepare—what more could you ask for?*

You don't need lots of time or hard-to-find ingredients to put delicious wholesome food on the table quickly, and this recipe is the perfect example. And who knew that a one-pot dinner could go haute chic? This dinner is versatile enough that it can go from casual to elegant with some simple garnishing. And if you're lucky enough to find multicolored cauliflower or broccoli, you can use the combination of colors to up the elegance factor.

For a fabulous last-minute side dish, combine some of the broccoli with some of the chicken gravy and sprinkle with toasted sesame seeds. This side will make a broccoli lover out of even your most finicky eater.

1. Preheat the oven to 375° F. Rinse the chicken and pat dry. Place the chicken, baby potatoes, and garlic cloves in a large baking pan. Pour the duck sauce over the chicken and potatoes. Sprinkle with the Montreal steak seasoning, paprika, onion powder, black pepper, and chopped herbs. Bake, uncovered, for 1¾ hours. Remove from the oven and spoon the gravy from the pan over the potatoes and chicken.

2. Add the florets and continue to bake, uncovered, until the broccoli is cooked through yet still slightly crunchy, about 15 minutes. Pour the gravy generously over the broccoli, chicken, and potatoes and serve warm, garnished with fresh chopped herbs. **Serves 4.**

Sun-Dried Tomato and Basil Capons

10 boneless capons, skin intact

STUFFING

4 TBSP. oil

1 large onion, finely diced

3 CLOVES garlic, minced

1 STALK celery, thinly sliced

½ CUP sun-dried tomatoes, finely diced

1 BAG (5.25 oz.) Mediterranean-style onion and garlic croutons

½ TSP. kosher salt

⅛ TSP. fresh black pepper

¼ TSP. red pepper flakes

2 TBSP. chicken stock

¼ CUP fresh basil, chopped

2 TBSP. fresh chives, chopped

½ TSP. dried oregano

2 TBSP. fresh parsley, chopped

SEASONING SPICES

• Montreal steak seasoning

• Paprika

• Garlic powder

• Onion powder

THE KEY to getting your stuffed capons to have a nice, round, plump presentation is to stuff them generously and then mold them into shape. The stuffing in this recipe works well in veal pockets, too.

I prefer to use sun-dried tomatoes that are not packed in oil, so that the tangy burst of flavor you get from the tomatoes is subtle, not strong.

For a slight variation, pour French dressing on top of the capons before sprinkling them with the spices.

---

1. To prepare the stuffing: In a large skillet, heat the oil. Add the onion and sauté in the oil until soft. Add the garlic, celery, sun-dried tomatoes, croutons, salt, black pepper, and red pepper flakes. Stir in the chicken stock, basil, chives, oregano, and parsley and cook for several more minutes, until all the ingredients are evenly incorporated and the croutons are softened. The mixture should not be mushy, only slightly soft, and should still resemble a crumbly mix with the croutons mostly intact. (The croutons will soften completely while the capons are baking.) Remove from the heat.

2. Preheat the oven to 350° F. Rinse the capons and pat dry. Stuff the capons generously with 2 heaping tablespoons of stuffing per capon and mold each capon into a round shape. Place the capons in a baking pan and sprinkle with the steak seasoning, paprika, garlic powder, and onion powder. Bake in a tightly covered pan for 1½ hours. **Serves 8–10.**

Chicken Fire Poppers

2 EGGS

½ TSP. garlic powder

½ TSP. onion powder

1 LB. chicken cutlets, cut into bite-size (1½-inch) pieces

• Cornflake crumbs

• Oil, for frying

SAUCE

½ CUP sugar

½ CUP brown sugar

¼ CUP honey

⅓ CUP hot sauce (I use Frank's)

• Sliced chives, to garnish (optional)

WHEN I *prepared this dish at home, I asked my then two-year-old daughter if she wanted fire poppers. "No," she replied seriously, "it's dangerous." We all shared a laugh and then got on to the serious business of eating. By the end of the meal, I realized that these chicken poppers are indeed dangerous—once you start, it's hard to stop.*

note: *When preparing these poppers, use chicken cutlets that are not thinned so there's a substantial bite.*

1. Preheat the oven to 350° F. In a small bowl, beat the eggs with the garlic powder and onion powder. Dip the chicken pieces in the egg mixture, then coat with cornflake crumbs.

2. In a large skillet, heat the oil over medium heat. Fry the coated chicken pieces in the oil on both sides until golden and crispy. Let drain on paper towels for a few minutes, then transfer the chicken to a baking pan.

3. In a bowl, combine all the sauce ingredients. Pour the sauce over the fried chicken. Bake the chicken, covered, for 20 minutes (do not overbake). Spoon the sauce from the bottom of the pan over the chicken, garnish with the chives, if desired, and serve warm. **Serves 4-6.**

Pomegranate Honey Glazed Duck Breast with Sesame Roasted Sweet Potatoes

2 duck breasts (7 oz. each), skin intact

• Kosher salt

• Fresh black pepper

POMEGRANATE HONEY GLAZE

¼ cup Dijon mustard

2 Tbsp. whole-grain mustard

2 Tbsp. pomegranate molasses

3 Tbsp. honey

Dash cayenne pepper

• Fresh black pepper

ROASTED SWEET POTATOES

5 sweet potatoes, peeled and diced

2 Tbsp. sesame oil

1 Tbsp. oil

3 cloves garlic, minced

• Kosher salt

• Fresh black pepper

• Paprika

BECAUSE DUCKS *are well in-sulated with fat, there's no need to sear the duck breast in oil; the skin is fatty enough. Scoring the skin of the duck breast with a knife before searing will slowly render most of the fat as it cooks to produce a nice, crispy skin.*

This dish pairs well with a simple side dish like mashed or roasted sweet potatoes, wild rice, or quinoa.

note: What to do with the rest of the duck if your butcher only sells whole duck? Check out the recipe for Duck a l'Orange on page 148.

---

1. Preheat the oven to 350° F. Rinse the duck breasts and pat dry. With a sharp knife, score the skin of the duck breasts in a crosshatch *X* pattern. Season both sides of the breasts lightly with the kosher salt and black pepper to taste.

2. Heat a large nongreased nonstick skillet over medium–high heat. Sear the duck breasts skin-side down in the skillet until nicely browned, 7–8 minutes.

3. Prepare the pomegranate honey glaze: In a small bowl, whisk the Dijon mustard, whole-grain mustard, pomegranate molasses, honey, cayenne pepper, and black pepper.

4. Brush both sides of the duck breasts with half the glaze. Bake the glazed duck breasts skin-side up in the oven until medium-rare, about 12 minutes. Remove the duck from the oven and brush generously on both sides with the remaining glaze.

5. To prepare the roasted sweet potatoes: Preheat the oven to 450° F. Toss the sweet potatoes with the sesame oil, oil, garlic, salt, black pepper, and paprika. On a baking sheet, spread the diced sweet potatoes in a single layer and roast, uncovered, until lightly browned and slightly crispy on the outside, about 45 minutes.

6. To serve, cut the duck breast against the grain into slices. Fan the slices on plates and serve warm with the roasted sweet potatoes. **Serves 2-4.**

Grilled Chicken Satay with Peanut Butter Barbecue Sauce

I**T WAS** *Malky who suggested I create a peanut butter barbecue sauce. When I developed this recipe, the flavors worked out perfectly after the very first try, which is unusual—no extra tweaking was necessary. It was meant to be.*

PEANUT BUTTER BARBECUE SAUCE

¼ CUP peanut butter

1½ CUPS ketchup

3 TBSP. light brown sugar

3 TBSP. lite soy sauce

2 TBSP. brown rice vinegar

4 CLOVES garlic, minced

½ TSP. crushed red pepper flakes

⅛ TSP. fresh black pepper, or to taste

½ TSP. kosher salt

CHICKEN

3 LB. boneless skinless chicken thighs, cut into 1½-inch cubes

2 TBSP. oil

• Kosher salt

• Fresh black pepper

2 CLOVES garlic, minced

1. To prepare the sauce: In a small pot, combine all the sauce ingredients over medium heat. Heat, stirring constantly, until well combined. Set aside.

2. To prepare the chicken: Preheat the grill. Rinse the chicken and pat dry. Season with the oil, salt, black pepper, and garlic and toss to coat. Grill the chicken until cooked through, 6–8 minutes per side. Serve on skewers with the peanut butter barbecue sauce. **Serves 8.**

Crispy Sesame Chicken Cutlets with Avocado Hummus

2 LB. chicken cutlets

• Oil, for frying

MARINADE

2 eggs, beaten

4 TBSP. soy sauce

1 TSP. garlic powder

1 TSP. onion powder

½ TSP. paprika

MAYO COATING

6 TBSP. light mayonnaise

6 TBSP. hot and spicy duck sauce

2 TBSP. warm water

SESAME CRUMB COATING

2 CUPS cornflake crumbs or panko bread crumbs

4 TBSP. sesame seeds

AVOCADO HUMMUS

2 avocados

1½ TBSP. fresh lime juice

1 CLOVE garlic (fresh or frozen), minced

½ TSP. sea salt

½ TSP. minced chili pepper (½ fresh chili pepper or ½ frozen chili cube)

1 TBSP. prepared hummus

• Fresh black pepper

1. Rinse the chicken cutlets and pat dry. With a sharp knife, slice the cutlets into strips 3–4 inches wide. (The cutlets should not be too thin, to give more of a bite.)

2. To prepare the marinade: In a Ziploc bag, combine the eggs, soy sauce, garlic powder, onion powder, and paprika. Add the chicken to the marinade and shake to coat. Refrigerate and marinate for at least 5 hours.

3. To prepare the coatings: In a medium bowl, combine the mayonnaise, duck sauce, and water for the mayo coating. In another medium bowl, combine the cornflake or panko crumbs and sesame seeds for the sesame crumb coating.

4. Remove the chicken from the marinade and coat each piece with the mayo coating, then coat well with the crumb coating. In a skillet, heat the oil over medium heat until very hot. (If the oil is not hot enough, the chicken will stick to the skillet.) Fry the chicken pieces in the hot oil until crispy, 5 minutes per side. Transfer them to a plate lined with a paper towel to absorb the excess oil.

5. To prepare the avocado hummus: In a bowl, mash the avocados with a fork. Add the remaining ingredients and mix until creamy and smooth. Serve the chicken cutlets with the avocado hummus or another dipping sauce of your choice. **Serves 4-6.**

INTRODUCING A *marriage between hummus and guacamole—a surprisingly winning combination.*

I prefer the taste of fresh lime juice to the usual lemon juice used in guacamole; the limes add a nuance of sweetness, while lemons infuse a sour taste. Using sea salt to season the guacamole imparts a huge flavor difference as well.

For other dipping sauce alternatives, combine 1 cup of light mayonnaise with 2-3 tablespoons of either honey, sweet chili sauce, or duck sauce.

low-fat option: Arrange the chicken cutlets on a wire rack lightly sprayed with nonstick cooking spray and place in the oven. Place a cookie or baking sheet lined with parchment paper just under the wire rack. Bake the chicken at 375° F until the cutlets are cooked through and crispy, about 18 minutes. This eliminates the need to turn the cutlets during the baking and keeps the coating from coming off.

note: After handling the chili peppers, wash your hands thoroughly with warm soap and water. Avoid touching the eye area for several hours afterward.

Tuscan Chicken with Spaghetti

THIS IS *a nice alternative to meat-balls and spaghetti, and it takes less time to prepare. The olives give this dish a nice zing, and the cannellini beans are a nutritional powerhouse. You can substitute or add your favorite legumes and vegetables of your choice to the chicken before baking. Mushrooms, bell peppers, sun-dried tomatoes, and garbanzo beans are all choices that work well.*

If you are using olives, there is no need to add salt. If you're substituting another vegetable or legume for the olives, be sure to add kosher salt to taste.

CHICKEN

- 4–6 chicken quarters
- 1 JAR (26 oz.) marinara sauce
- 5 CLOVES garlic, minced
- 1 CUP pitted olives, drained
- 1 CAN (15 oz.) white cannellini beans or great northern beans, drained
- ¼ CUP fresh basil, chopped
- • Onion powder
- • Fresh black pepper

SPAGHETTI

- 1 LB. spaghetti, prepared according to package directions
- 2 firm Roma tomatoes, diced
- 1 CLOVE garlic, minced
- 3 TBSP. fresh basil, chopped
- • Kosher salt
- • Fresh black pepper

OPTIONAL GARNISH

- • Fresh parsley or basil

1. To prepare the chicken: Preheat the oven to 375° F. Rinse the chicken and pat dry. In a roasting pan, combine the chicken, marinara sauce, garlic, olives, beans, and fresh basil. Sprinkle with the onion powder and black pepper.

2. Bake, covered, for 1 hour, then uncover and bake for 30 minutes longer. Pour some of the sauce from the roasting pan over the chicken and remove the chicken from the pan, reserving the rest of the sauce to toss with the spaghetti.

3. Mix the reserved sauce in the pan to evenly incorporate all the flavors. Toss the spaghetti with the sauce. Add the diced tomatoes, garlic, basil, salt, and black pepper. Serve with the chicken, garnished with fresh parsley or basil, if desired. **Serves 4–6.**

Cashew Chicken Stir-Fry with Sweet Chili Glaze

ON AN *impulse I once bought a bottle of Thai sweet chili sauce. We started eating sweet chili sauce with practically everything: fish, chicken, eggs, egg rolls, pizza. It even replaced ketchup as a dipping sauce. Since then my family has developed quite an obsession with it, and I stock up on several bottles at a time. This recipe is just one of the many ways we thoroughly enjoy using sweet chili sauce.*

The sweet chili sauce is added at the end of the cooking process. Otherwise the vegetables will be quite watery. Practically any of your favorite vegetables will work with this recipe—I especially love adding bean sprouts for a crunchy texture. If you have a can of baby corn or sliced water chestnuts on hand, you can add that as well. Serve this chicken stir-fry over a bed of rice, pasta, or orzo.

1½ LB. boneless skinless chicken breasts, cut into strips

• Kosher salt

• Fresh black pepper

3 TBSP. oil

1 TBSP. toasted sesame oil

1 onion, chopped

4 CLOVES garlic, minced

12 oz. broccoli florets

8 oz. mushrooms, quartered

1 red bell pepper, sliced

½ CUP carrots, thinly sliced

½ CUP salted roasted cashews

SWEET CHILI GLAZE

2 TBSP. lite soy sauce

4 oz. Thai sweet chili sauce

½ CUP chicken stock

1½ TSP. cornstarch

1. Season the chicken with the salt and black pepper. In a large skillet, heat the oil and sesame oil over medium-high heat until very hot. Add the seasoned chicken and onion and cook until lightly browned, 4–5 minutes.

2. Add the garlic, broccoli, mushrooms, red pepper, and carrots and cook for an additional 5–6 minutes, stirring frequently.

3. Prepare the sweet chili glaze: In a medium bowl, combine the soy sauce, sweet chili sauce, chicken stock, and cornstarch. Add the sauce to the chicken and vegetable mixture. Reduce the heat to low-medium heat, and simmer until the sauce thickens, 2–3 minutes, stirring occasionally. Season with additional salt and black pepper, if needed. Sprinkle with the roasted cashews and serve warm with hot cooked rice, orzo, or pasta. **Serves 4.**

Pickled Dark Turkey Roast with Brown Sugar Horseradish Sauce

1 large onion, sliced

3–4 LB. pickled dark turkey roast

• Water, to cover

SAUCE

⅔ CUP ketchup

4 TBSP. oil

3 TBSP. red horseradish, drained

3 TBSP. Dijon mustard

¾ CUP brown sugar

3 TBSP. red wine vinegar

> **T**URKEY CAN *easily get tough and dry, but with this recipe you will enjoy super-flavorful and moist turkey. The recipe also works well with pickled corned beef. To vary it, you can cook the pickled turkey or corned beef in Coca-Cola instead of the water.*

1. Arrange the sliced onion on the bottom of a medium saucepan. Add the turkey roast and enough water to cover the turkey. Bring to a boil over high heat. Reduce the heat and cook, covered, over low–medium heat for 2½–3 hours. Remove the roast from the water and discard the onion. Allow the roast to cool, then refrigerate for at least 6 hours.

2. Preheat the oven to 350° F. In a small saucepan, combine the sauce ingredients over medium heat until the brown sugar has dissolved. Slice the turkey roast and place in a roasting pan. Pour the sauce over the sliced turkey and bake, covered, until the turkey is tender, 45–60 minutes. To serve, spoon the sauce over the turkey slices. Serve warm. **Serves 6–8.**

Cranberry Blueberry Orange Chicken

4 chicken bottoms, quartered or cut into eighths

½ CAN (7 oz.) cranberry sauce

½ CAN (10 oz.) blueberry pie filling

2 TBSP. lite soy sauce

¼ CUP honey

1 orange, juiced and zested

6–7 CLOVES garlic

• Steak seasoning

• Fresh basil, sage, rosemary, or parsley, chopped (optional)

IF YOU *share my penchant for purple, try finding purple basil or edible purple flowers. As a garnish, this will make any dish pop. No need to overwork the plate with excessive decoration—sometimes it's a simple garnish that makes a dish dazzle. If nothing else, even just chopped parsley sprinkled on the chicken adds aesthetic appeal.*

note: Use the rest of the cranberry sauce and blueberry pie filling to prepare the crispiest of crisps. See page 358 for the recipe.

1. Preheat the oven to 375° F. Rinse the chicken and pat dry. Place the chicken in a baking pan.

2. In a medium bowl, combine the cranberry sauce, blueberry pie filling, soy sauce, honey, orange juice, and zest and pour the mixture over the chicken. Sprinkle the garlic cloves and steak seasoning over the sauce.

3. Bake the chicken, uncovered, for 1½ hours. Before serving, spoon sauce from the bottom of the pan over the chicken and garnish with the chopped herbs, if desired. Serve warm. **Serves 4.**

Balsamic Duck a l'Orange

1 whole duck or chicken (3-4 lb.)

• Fresh black pepper

10 CLOVES garlic

2 CUPS duck sauce

1 TBSP. balsamic vinegar

1 JAR (8-10 oz.) orange marmalade

1 orange, peel intact, sliced

1. Preheat the oven to 350° F. Rinse the duck and pat dry. In a baking pan, season the duck with the black pepper. Stuff the cavity of the duck with half the garlic cloves and sprinkle the remainder of the cloves on top. Bake, covered, for 1 hour. Drain the fat from the pan.

2. In a bowl, combine the duck sauce, balsamic vinegar, and orange marmalade. Pour half the mixture over the duck. In the pan, arrange the orange slices around the duck.

3. Cover tightly and cook the duck for an additional 3 hours. Add the remaining sauce and continue to cook, uncovered, for 30 minutes longer. **Serves 6.**

Caramelized Baked Sticky Sesame Chicken

THE **CHICKEN** *is smothered with the familiar taste of the classic Chinese takeout dish—but without the extra fat that you get from frying. This sauce is also fabulous with grilled chicken nuggets made from boneless skinless chicken thighs. Nuggets is the key word here—somehow I get my children's attention better if I offer them "nuggets" rather than "chicken."*

¼ CUP sugar

⅓ CUP honey

¼ CUP ketchup

3 TBSP. rice vinegar

3 TBSP. soy sauce

½ TBSP. sesame oil

6 CLOVES garlic, minced

1 TSP. chili (fresh or frozen), minced

1 TSP. kosher salt

⅛ TSP. fresh black pepper

¼ CUP cornstarch

½ CUP cold water

½ CUP toasted sesame seeds, plus extra to garnish

12–16 chicken drumsticks, skin removed

1. To prepare the sesame sauce: In a medium saucepan, combine the sugar, honey, ketchup, rice vinegar, soy sauce, sesame oil, garlic, chili, salt, and black pepper. Heat the mixture over medium heat, stirring constantly, for several minutes.

2. In a small bowl, dissolve the cornstarch in the cold water. Add the cornstarch mixture to the sauce in the saucepan and cook until thickened, 3-4 minutes. Stir in ¼ cup of the toasted sesame seeds. Remove the sauce from the heat and set aside.

3. Preheat the oven to 350° F. Rinse the chicken and pat dry. Place in a pan and spray with nonstick cooking spray. Bake, uncovered, for 1 hour. Drain the chicken juices from the pan. Pour the sesame sauce over the chicken to cover completely, sprinkle with the remaining toasted sesame seeds, and bake, uncovered, for 20 minutes longer. Remove the chicken from the oven and toss with the sauce. Sprinkle with additional sesame seeds, if desired. Serve warm**. Serves 6-8.**

a cut above

MEAT

....

Savory Club Steak with Caramelized Onions

6 club steaks (6-8 oz. each)

3 CLOVES garlic, minced

• Kosher salt

• Fresh black pepper

1 TBSP. MSG-free onion soup mix

2 TBSP. oil

1 large onion, thinly sliced

10 OZ. (1 box) white mushrooms, sliced

¼ CUP A-1 steak sauce

¼ CUP dry white wine

ONE OF the most tender cuts of meat, club steak is taken from the short loin and lies next to the rib. This cut of meat is a favorite of my family's, partly because baking the meat for several hours renders it buttery soft, and they love its melt-in-the-mouth texture. It's easy even for my youngest child to chew.

If you don't have A-1 steak sauce on hand, you can substitute it with Worcestershire sauce. And if you prefer a creamy sauce, add ¼ cup of coconut milk to the steak sauce and white wine mixture. Either way, this dish is a guaranteed winner.

1. Preheat the oven to 350° F. Rinse the steaks and pat them dry. Place the steaks in a roasting pan and rub them with the minced garlic. Season with the salt and black pepper and sprinkle with the onion soup mix. Bake, tightly covered, for 2 hours.

2. In a skillet, heat the oil over medium heat. Sauté the onion and mushrooms in the oil until soft.

3. In a bowl, combine the steak sauce and white wine. Remove the steaks from the oven and top with the sautéed onion and mushrooms. Pour the steak sauce and wine mixture over the top. Reduce the oven temperature to 250° F. Cover tightly and bake for 50 minutes longer. **Serves 6.**

Orange-Scented Rack of Veal

6 garlic cloves, minced

4 TSP. basil, minced, or 4 frozen basil cubes

1 TSP. ground coriander

1 orange, zested

1 TSP. sea salt

¼ TSP. fresh black pepper

1½ CUPS hot and spicy duck sauce

1 CUP store-bought crispy fried onions (I use French's)

1 rack of veal (5 lb.)

RACK OF veal is a cut of meat you may want to prepare for special occasions, since it makes for a dramatic presentation. This is usually a special-order cut, so call your butcher in advance. When you do, request that he remove the backbone, also called the "chine bone"—this allows for easier carving between the ribs.

Roasting a whole rack of veal is likely to be the most succulent and softest way you'll enjoy this type of meat. Enhancing its natural flavor is fresh basil, coriander, and orange zest. The coriander is ample yet not excessive. The pairing of coriander and orange has always been a chef favorite, since the orange lends a citrusy vibe that blends marvelously well with the slightly lemony coriander.

1. Preheat the oven to 400° F. In a small bowl, combine the garlic, basil, coriander, orange zest, salt, black pepper, and duck sauce.

2. In a baking pan, brush the veal with the sauce mixture on all sides. Rub the crispy fried onions onto the meat to create a crispy coating. Roast, uncovered, for 3–3½ hours.

3. Remove the meat from the oven and allow to sit for 15–20 minutes. Transfer the whole rack to a platter or cutting board and carve at the table for a neater presentation. Serve warm. **Serves 6–8.**

Pasta Bolognese

MY CHILDREN *prefer this dish to meatballs and spaghetti. The key to pasta Bolognese is to use real chicken stock and allow the Bolognese sauce to simmer for a bit so that the combination of flavors resonates throughout the dish. And don't think Bolognese should be reserved just for everyday. The photo opposite shows how a commonplace recipe like this one can be served elegantly as an hors d'oeuvre.*

4 TBSP. oil

1 large onion, finely chopped

4 CLOVES garlic, minced

2 celery stalks, finely chopped

2 TBSP. tomato paste

1 LB. chuck beef, chopped

1 CUP chicken stock

½ TSP. chili, minced

1 TSP. liquid smoke

1 TSP. Worcestershire sauce

¾ TSP. kosher salt

¼ TSP. fresh black pepper

14 OZ. tomato sauce

1 CAN (14 oz.) finely diced tomatoes in sauce

1 LB. spaghetti pasta, cooked al dente

2 TBSP. basil, finely chopped

1. In a large saucepan, heat the oil. Sauté the onion in the oil over medium-high heat for 3–4 minutes. Add the garlic, celery, and tomato paste and sauté for another 2 minutes. Add the chopped beef and sauté until browned, gently breaking up the meat with a fork, about 5 minutes. Add the chicken stock, chili, liquid smoke, Worcestershire sauce, salt, and black pepper and cook until most of the stock has evaporated, 7 minutes.

2. Add the tomato sauce and the diced tomatoes and cook for 3 minutes longer. Reduce the heat to medium and simmer for 30 minutes, stirring frequently. Add the cooked pasta and basil to the sauce and toss over low heat. Serve warm. **Serves 4.**

Rack of Flanken with Cola Marinade and Coffee Barbecue Sauce

1 5–bone rack of flanken (6-8 lb.)

1 BOTTLE (1 liter) Coca-Cola

• Kosher salt

• Fresh black pepper

8 CLOVES garlic, sliced

COFFEE BARBECUE SAUCE

1 CUP chili sauce

½ CUP brown sugar

⅓ CUP honey

4 TBSP. Worcestershire sauce

2 TBSP. lite soy sauce

2 CLOVES garlic, minced

1 TBSP. liquid smoke

1 TBSP. Dijon mustard

1 TSP. coffee, dissolved in several drops of hot water

2 TBSP. lemon juice

½ TSP. kosher salt

½ TSP. fresh black pepper

WHEN I'M *entertaining guests for the first time, this is one of the dishes that makes its way onto the menu. It's foolproof and it always brings rave reviews.*

No matter what rib recipe you're experimenting with, the key to transforming a rack of ribs (or, in this case, flanken) into a juicy, "fall-off-the-bone" dish is to bake it "low and slow." This recipe entails baking the flanken for at least four hours to get the meat soft and succulent.

Rack of flanken is a specialty cut, so you'll have to ask your butcher to prepare it for you in advance. If you don't have flanken, this recipe works equally well with any other meaty rack of ribs.

The meat is marinated in cola overnight, so have in mind that you'll have to begin preparing this recipe in advance. Don't use diet cola for the marinade, since it's the sugar and phosphoric acid in regular cola that work wonders in tenderizing the meat.

1. Place the flanken and the cola in a large heavy-duty plastic bag and marinate in the refrigerator overnight.

2. Preheat the oven to 325° F. Remove the flanken from the marinade and transfer it to a large baking pan. Season with the salt and black pepper and sprinkle with the sliced garlic cloves.

3. Prepare the coffee barbecue sauce: In a bowl, whisk all the sauce ingredients until well combined. Pour half of the sauce over the ribs, reserving the rest.

4. Cover the ribs tightly and bake until the meat is fork tender, at least 4 hours. Pour the remaining sauce over the ribs and bake, uncovered, for 30 minutes longer. Serve warm. **Serves 6.**

Creole Veal Burgers with Remoulade Sauce

My **FAMILY** likes our burgers straight up—no fillers like eggs or bread crumbs, just light seasoning that won't mask the meat flavor. And we don't use packaged buns. Aside from all the preservatives they contain (even the whole wheat variety), the taste doesn't compare to fresh, warm buns. Try fresh multigrain, round sesame or ciabatta rolls to give your burgers a wholesome, delicious package.

These burgers get their flavor from Creole and Cajun cuisines, both fusion styles of cooking known for their savory, well-seasoned food. Remoulade, a staple of Cajun cuisine, is a flavorful and pungent sauce that traces its origins to France and has become a fixture on New Orleans menus. It's also kid-friendly thanks to all the pickles. This remoulade also makes a great dip for French fries and fish. If you prefer uber crunch, add celery or, for a piquant-tangy twist, capers.

To really get the most out of the burger experience, don't leave out the alfalfa sprouts and the sauce—they add essential texture and flavor. Since this recipe will likely become a staple at your dinner table, you can vary the sauces to maintain its appeal. For a super-simple barbecue sauce in place of the remoulade, mix equal parts of light mayo with your favorite barbecue sauce.

6 warm buns

REMOULADE SAUCE

1 CUP light mayonnaise

6 TBSP. (2 large) Israeli pickles, finely chopped

4 CLOVES garlic, minced

4 TSP. parsley, minced

2 TSP. lemon juice or Worcestershire sauce

1 TSP. mustard

3 TBSP. celery, chopped (optional)

2 TBSP. capers, finely chopped (optional)

CREOLE VEAL BURGERS

¾ LB. veal, chopped

¾ LB. chuck beef, chopped

1½ TSP. Cajun seasoning

3 CLOVES garlic, minced

1½ TBSP. teriyaki or Worcestershire sauce

• Kosher salt

• Fresh black pepper

GARNISHES

• Lettuce

• Tomatoes, sliced

• Alfalfa sprouts

• Red onions, thinly sliced

1. To prepare the remoulade sauce: In a small bowl, combine all the sauce ingredients.

2. To prepare the veal burgers: Preheat an indoor or outdoor grill. (An indoor grill pan works well for this, too.) Combine the veal, chuck beef, Cajun seasoning, garlic, and teriyaki or Worcestershire sauce. Form the meat into 6 round patties. Sprinkle the tops of the patties with the salt and black pepper. Grill the burgers for 6 minutes per side. To prepare in the oven, broil in the oven for 5–6 minutes per side. Remove from the grill or the oven and let sit for 5 minutes.

3. Place a leaf of lettuce and sliced tomatoes in each bun, and top with a burger. Spoon remoulade sauce generously over each burger. Top with alfalfa sprouts and sliced onions. Serve warm. **Yields 6 burgers.**

Lemon-Thyme Delmonico Roast

3 LB. Delmonico roast

4 TSP. kosher salt

2 TSP. dried thyme

1½ TSP. fresh black pepper

2 CLOVES garlic, minced

1 lemon or lime, zested

• Oil

THIS IS *my favorite and breeziest way to prepare a Delmonico roast. Contrary to popular belief, Delmonico is not a specific cut of meat; it simply means "the best cut available." It originated in the mid-1800s at the Delmonico Restaurant in Manhattan, where the house cut was dubbed "Delmonico." The exact cut of of Delmonico steak is unknown, but since Delmonico means the best, when you request a Delmonico roast from your butcher, you're likely to get a prime cut.*

A good cut of meat doesn't require frills. This recipe is proof of that—it preserves the intrinsic flavor of the roast, complementing it with a light, flavorful spice rub. When the meat is seared, it may appear that the roast is burning; it's not. Searing the roast gives it a crispy crust to lock in all the juices, while keeping it tender inside.

1. Preheat the oven to 350° F. Rinse the meat and pat dry. In a small bowl, combine the salt, thyme, black pepper, garlic, and lemon or lime zest.

2. Coat the roast with the oil. Spread the rub over the top, bottom, and sides. In a skillet, sear the meat over high heat for 10 minutes per side.

3. Transfer the roast to a baking pan. Scrape all the drippings from the skillet onto the top of the roast and bake, uncovered, 45–60 minutes for medium-rare. Let the meat stand for 10 minutes before slicing. Slice the meat against the grain and serve warm. **Serves 6.**

Marinated Cherry-Soy London Broil

2 LB. London broil beef

MARINADE

⅓ CUP oil

⅓ CUP lite soy sauce

⅓ CUP balsamic vinegar

4 TBSP. cherry preserves
(from a 12 oz. jar)

2 TBSP. honey

6 CLOVES garlic, minced

¼ TSP. fresh black pepper

OPTIONAL CHERRY SAUCE

5 TBSP. shallots, finely chopped

• Oil

8 OZ. cherry preserves
(the remainder of the jar)

2 TBSP. trans-fat-free
margarine

MARINATE THE *meat overnight to tenderize, turning it once or twice to allow both sides of the meat to fully absorb the marinade. Then you can either grill the meat on an indoor or outdoor grill or sear it in a skillet.*

The cherry reduction sauce is completely optional. If you're short on time, the London broil is special on its own as a main dish served with a salad.

note: London broil is a flavorful but mostly chewy cut of meat, so it's best enjoyed when it is served very thinly sliced. Always slice meat against the grain.

---

1. To prepare the marinade: In a small bowl, whisk the oil, soy sauce, balsamic vinegar, cherry preserves, honey, garlic, and black pepper. Place the meat in a bag. Pour the marinade over the meat. Seal the bag and turn to coat. Refrigerate overnight or at least 8 hours. Remove the meat from the marinade, reserving the marinade for the cherry reduction sauce.

2. To prepare the cherry sauce: In a small saucepan, sauté the shallots in the oil. Add the reserved marinade and remaining cherry preserves. Bring to a boil over medium-high heat. Boil for 5 minutes, stirring continuously, until the sauce thickens. Stir in the margarine. Remove from the heat.

3. Grease a grill pan or a heavy skillet with oil and heat over medium-high heat. Add the meat and cook 10–12 minutes per side for medium-rare, or until it reaches the desired level of doneness depending on the thickness of the meat. Transfer the meat to a cutting board and let sit for 5 minutes before slicing.

4. Slice the meat thinly against the grain. Serve with the cherry sauce. **Serves 6.**

Garlic Teriyaki Roast

WHOEVER COINED the phrase "No pain, no gain" hasn't checked out this recipe. It's simple and easy to prepare but you'd never guess it from the taste.

If this is your first time using steak seasoning, you'll be instantly hooked. There are many brands available, but I prefer McCormick and use it to season everything from salmon and chicken to potatoes. It enhances the great flavor of the meat without masking it. Another of my nearly effortless favorite uses for it is to sprinkle salmon with fresh lemon juice and Montreal steak seasoning and bake it at 350° F, uncovered, for half an hour. Fast, easy, delicious!

For this recipe, brick, top of the rib, standing rib roast, or New York strip steak all work well.

note: Use a meat thermometer to measure the temperature accurately: 135°–140° F for medium-rare, 140°–145° F for medium, and 155°–160° F for well done.

3–4 LB. roast

- Oil

7 CLOVES garlic, minced

- Montreal steak seasoning

- Teriyaki sauce

1. Preheat the oven to 375° F. Rinse the roast and pat dry. Brush with the oil and place in a baking pan. Rub the minced garlic and steak seasoning over the entire roast, then drizzle with teriyaki sauce. Bake, uncovered, until it reaches the desired doneness, 1½–3 hours.

2. Slice thinly against the grain and serve warm. **Serves 8–10.**

Smoked Sweet-and-Sour Ribs

I CAME ACROSS *an article that suggested the proper ladylike method for eating spare ribs "gracefully" in public. These were the rules: Gingerly hold a small rib between your forefinger and thumb in one hand and a heavy cloth dinner napkin in the other. Raise the rib to your mouth and nibble gently while keeping your mouth in a half smile so as to avoid getting your lips dirty with sauce. Try not to eat the fatty areas of the rib and dab at your mouth often. If it's socially acceptable, repeat often.*

Let's get real. If you really want to enjoy ribs, the only way to approach them is with reckless abandon. Otherwise, it's not worth the bother. So forget the pretenses and have plenty of napkins nearby!

3–4 LB. flanken ribs, spare ribs, or rack of ribs

• Kosher salt

• Fresh black pepper

1 JAR thick-style rib sauce (I use Mikey's)

2 TBSP. liquid smoke

8 CLOVES garlic

1. Preheat the oven to 325° F. Season the ribs with the salt and black pepper. In a baking pan, coat the seasoned ribs with three-quarters of the jar of rib sauce and the liquid smoke. Sprinkle with the garlic cloves.

2. Bake, tightly covered, until the ribs are buttery soft, about 3–4 hours. Pour the remaining rib sauce over the ribs 20 minutes before the end of the cooking time. Serve warm. **Serves 4.**

New York Strip Steak with Cabernet Merlot Reduction Sauce and Crispy Shallots

NEW YORK STRIP STEAK

- 2 LB. New York strip steak
- Kosher salt
- Fresh black pepper
- 4 CLOVES garlic, minced
- 2 TBSP. Worcestershire sauce
- Oil

CRISPY SHALLOTS

- 2 CUPS oil
- Shallots, sliced into thin rounds
- All-purpose flour
- Oil, for frying
- Kosher salt
- Fresh black pepper

MERLOT REDUCTION

- 3 TBSP. oil
- ½ CUP shallots, minced
- ½ CUP cabernet merlot
- 2 CUPS chicken or beef stock
- Kosher salt
- Fresh black pepper

NEW YORK *strip steak has a deeply satisfying beef taste, and the cabernet merlot reduction sauce adds a robust flavor to the meat.*

The most valuable meat preparation tip I can share with you is this: invest in a meat thermometer. A meat thermometer allows you to check the level of doneness and saves you from the guesswork. Medium-rare registers at 135°–140° F.

to prepare mini carrot boxes: To plate this dish with a side of mashed potatoes wrapped in mini carrot boxes as shown, slice thin strips of carrot lengthwise on a mandoline slicer. Boil the carrots and chives for several minutes until tender, then blanch immediately in cold water to retain their color. Wrap mashed potatoes with the carrot strips and tie with the chives.

1. Rub the strip steak with the salt, black pepper, garlic, and Worcestershire sauce. In a skillet, heat the oil over high heat until very hot. Add the meat and cook until browned, about 1–2 minutes per side. Reduce the heat to medium and continue to sear, about 3–4 minutes per side for medium-rare. Transfer the meat to a plate and tent loosely with foil.

2. To prepare the cabernet merlot reduction sauce: In the same skillet that the meat was seared in, heat the oil over medium–high heat. Add the shallots and sauté for 1 minute. Add the cabernet merlot and stock, raise the heat, and bring to a boil. Boil until the sauce is reduced by half and achieves a syrupy consistency, about 10 minutes. Remove from the heat and season with the salt and black pepper to taste.

3. To prepare the crispy shallots: In a medium saucepan, heat the oil until very hot. In a medium bowl, toss the shallot slices with the flour to coat. Test the oil heat by dropping in one shallot slice. The oil should bubble. If it doesn't, heat the oil for a little longer and retest. Fry the shallots in small batches until golden brown. Remove them from the oil with a slotted spoon and drain on a paper towel. Season with the salt and black pepper to taste.

4. Serve the meat topped with the crispy shallots and the cabernet merlot sauce on the side for dipping. **Serves 4.**

Grilled Steak with Herb and Garlic Tapenade

4 oz. (½ cup) trans-fat-free margarine, melted

1 TSP. fresh parsley, finely chopped

1 TSP. fresh thyme, finely chopped

2 TBSP. fresh chives, minced

1 TBSP. fresh basil, minced

1 TBSP. fresh rosemary, minced

2 TBSP. lemon juice

3 CLOVES garlic, minced

6 rib-eye or club steaks, each about 1 inch thick

• Oil

• Kosher salt or sea salt

• Fresh black pepper

IF YOU'RE *a barbecue purist and prefer your meat without added enhancements or marinades—simply grilled with just salt and pepper—this one's for you. This recipe maintains the meat's distinctive flavor, enhanced with the unique aroma produced by grilling.*

Immediately after the steaks are grilled or pan-seared, a savory paste is spread thinly and evenly on the steaks for melt-in-your-mouth flavor. You can keep any leftover tapenade in the refrigerator for future use. Spread it on corn on the cob, fresh bread, or grilled salmon.

1. To prepare the tapenade: In a small mixing bowl, combine the margarine, parsley, thyme, chives, basil, rosemary, lemon juice, and garlic. Place the mixture onto a sheet of wax paper or plastic wrap and form into a log shape, wrapping the log tightly with the wax paper or plastic wrap. Chill the tapenade for at least 1 hour to allow the flavors to combine.

2. Preheat the grill to high heat. Rub each steak with a small amount of the oil and season with the salt and black pepper. Reduce the heat to medium and grill the steaks until an instant-read thermometer inserted in the steak registers 145° F; for medium-rare, about 5 minutes per side. Remove from the heat and let sit for 5 minutes before serving. In the meantime, cut slices of tapenade from the log and spread evenly on each steak.

3. For the pan-seared option: In a skillet, heat oil over high heat until very hot. Sear the steaks, 5 minutes per side for medium-rare. Let sit for 5 minutes before spreading with the tapenade. **Serves 6.**

Rack of Lamb with Orange Mustard Rosemary Sauce

1 rack of lamb

• Kosher salt

• Fresh black pepper

½ CUP fresh orange juice

2 TBSP. orange zest

4 TBSP. honey

4 TBSP. lite soy sauce

2 TBSP. toasted sesame oil

3 CLOVES. garlic (fresh or frozen), minced

1 TBSP. Dijon mustard

1 TBSP. rosemary, minced, plus extra sprigs to garnish

IT'S USUALLY *a good idea to sear meats before roasting to lock in the juices, but this recipe is hassle-free—there is no need to sear the lamb before roasting; it's just as flavorful without. Marinating the lamb overnight infuses the meat with the fabulous flavors of orange, soy, honey, garlic, and rosemary.*

To thoroughly marinate the lamb, turn the bag several times throughout the marinating process. You can serve the rack of lamb whole or carve between the ribs and then serve.

1. Rinse the lamb and pat dry. Season with the salt and black pepper and place in a large Ziploc bag or plastic shopping bag.

2. In a jar or cruet, combine the orange juice, orange zest, honey, soy sauce, sesame oil, garlic, Dijon mustard, and rosemary. Shake well to mix. Pour the sauce over the lamb. Seal the bag and turn to coat. Refrigerate overnight to marinate, turning the bag several times.

3. Preheat the oven to 400° F. Remove the meat from the marinade and bake until an instant-read thermometer inserted in the lamb registers 150° F; for medium-rare, about 45 minutes. Remove from the oven and let sit for 10 minutes before serving. Garnish with fresh rosemary sprigs. **Serves 4.**

Filet Mignon au Poivre

THIS SAVORY dish may serve as a midweek dinner or you can save it for your Friday night menu. If you're serving this dish alongside other main-course dishes, the portion sizes can be cut in half. If preparing this in advance, you can reheat it, uncovered, in an oven set to 175° F for no more than two hours.

Filet mignon, also known as "chateaubriand," is a French term, meaning "dainty slice". It first appeared in American cuisine in 1899 and is sometimes also called tournedos or medallion.

Filet mignon, prized for its melt-in-the-mouth texture, is considered a kosher cut, even though it is located near the sciatic nerve. According to kosher dietary laws, it's forbidden to eat the sciatic nerve, so it requires a very experienced butcher to separate the sciatic nerve from the filet mignon. For this reason, filet mignon is hard to obtain.

If you can't get kosher filet mignon, club steak and rib eye resemble the flavor of the well-marbled filet mignon in taste. Both of these cuts of meat work in this recipe; your butcher might even be labeling them "filet mignon."

For this recipe, I use port as the wine of choice because of its rich color, but cognac and madeira both work well, too.

- 4 round-cut filet mignon steaks (6 oz. each)
- Kosher salt
- Fresh black pepper
- 2 Tbsp. Worcestershire sauce
- 3 Tbsp. oil

DEGLAZING SAUCE

- 6 Tbsp. shallots, finely chopped
- 2 cloves garlic, minced
- ¼ cup port, madeira, or cognac
- 2 cups chicken stock
- 1 Tbsp. Dijon mustard
- 2 sprigs thyme
- 2 sprigs tarragon
- 3 Tbsp. trans-fat-free margarine

OPTIONAL ROASTED PATTYPANS & SQUASH

- Green and yellow pattypan squash
- Oil
- Kosher salt
- Fresh black pepper
- Minced garlic
- Yellow squash
- Zucchini
- Red onions, thinly sliced

---

1. Season the steaks with the salt and black pepper to taste, then sprinkle with the Worcestershire sauce. In a sauté pan, heat the oil over high heat. Sear the steaks in the oil until medium-rare or they reach the desired level of doneness, about 4–5 minutes per side. Remove the steaks from the pan.

2. To prepare the sauce: Add the shallots and garlic to the pan in which the steaks were pan-seared and sauté briefly, about 5 minutes. Leaning away from the stove, add the port, madeira, or cognac and cook for a few seconds. Add the chicken stock, mustard, thyme, and tarragon and bring to a boil, stirring occasionally to scrape up all the drippings. Reduce the heat to medium–high and continue to cook until the liquid is thickened and reduced by half, about 10 minutes. Remove from the heat and remove the sprigs of thyme and tarragon. Add the margarine and stir until incorporated.

3. To prepare the pattypans: Preheat the oven to 350° F. Sprinkle the pattypans with the oil and season with the salt, black pepper, and minced garlic. Roast in the oven for 20 minutes.

4. To prepare the squash, zucchini, and red onion: In a lightly oiled skillet, combine the vegetables. Season with the salt, black pepper, and minced garlic and sauté over high heat for 2 minutes. Remove from the heat.

5. Pour the sauce over the steaks and serve with the pattypans and squash medley. **Serves 4.**

Twenty-Garlic-Clove Standing Rib Roast

1 standing rib roast (6 lb.)

GARLIC HORSERADISH RUB

20 frozen garlic cloves, minced

¼ CUP oil

½ CUP white horseradish, drained

1 TBSP. Dijon mustard

1½ TBSP. kosher salt

¼–½ TSP. fresh black pepper

THIS IS *a knock-your-socks-off dish that's worthy of holidays and special occasions. I serve this roast half-sliced and leave the other half whole on a large cutting board with reservoirs to trap the juices. I continue carving the meat as needed at the table. You can serve the separated rack of bones for nibbling and the juices in a gravy boat on the side for those who want extra juices to spoon over their meat. Want to complete the ultimate meat and potatoes dish? Serve mashed potatoes mixed with the meat juices—it's unforgettable.*

The term "standing" means that the bones are included in the roast, making it easy for the roast to stand on its own while baking rib-side down. You should only purchase a rib roast that has the bones intact, since the bones enhance the flavor. Many roast recipes such as this one call for searing the meat before cooking or roasting to lock in the juices and flavors and brown the proteins present in the meat. There are two methods for searing meat. Whether you're pan-searing or roast-searing, they are both equally effective. Since this cut of meat is large, it's cleaner and more practical to roast-sear it.

Once you serve this dish and experience the onslaught of compliments and requests for doubles, you'll designate this as one of your signature dishes. And the best part is that it's foolproof, with consistent results every time you prepare it.

1. Preheat the oven to 450° F. Rinse the meat and pat dry. In a small bowl, mix the garlic, oil, horseradish, Dijon mustard, salt, and black pepper. Rub the mixture evenly over the roast on all sides. Set the roast bone-side down in a large roasting pan. Roast, uncovered, for 20 minutes, until the skin is slightly crispy.

2. Reduce the heat to 350° F. Bake for 30 minutes per pound of meat, or until a thermometer inserted into the center of the narrow end reaches 145° F for medium. Transfer the roast to a platter and let it sit in a warm place for 10 minutes, reserving the juices in the pan.

3. To slice a standing rib roast, using a sharp knife, make one slice to cut off the large end bones so you can easily sever the meat from the bones in one piece. Set the meat cut-side down and slice across the grain to the desired thickness. Serve with the reserved juices. **Serves 8–10.**

Tamari French Roast or Brisket

4 LB. French roast or brisket

6 CLOVES garlic, minced

1 onion, sliced

5 TBSP. tamari sauce

½ CUP packed brown sugar

½ CUP Thai sweet chili sauce

¾ CUP Coca-Cola

2 TBSP. lime juice

8 OZ. barbecue sauce

COOKING THIS *roast in a slow cooker renders this cut superlatively tender and flavorful. The roast cooks all day while you get to do other things. But if you prefer an oven roast, it's just as flavorful prepared in an oven; it doesn't have to be cooked in a slow cooker.*

Leftovers make for a fabulous pulled-brisket sandwich. Use two forks to pull apart and shred the meat, then mix with some extra gravy and sandwich between fresh bread, warm tortillas, or tacos.

Tamari, a featured ingredient in this recipe, is very similar to soy sauce and they are essentially interchangeable. The only difference is that tamari sauce is gentler and less salty than soy sauce and is also wheat-free, making tamari sauce a good option for a gluten-free diet.

note: These ingredients are equally good with skirt steak. Just omit the tamari sauce, since skirt steak is naturally salty. To prepare the skirt steak: section three pounds of skirt steak into nine equal pieces and place in a baking pan. Combine all the sauce ingredients (including the barbecue sauce), except for the tamari. Pour the sauce over the skirt steak and bake, covered, at 375° F until fork tender, about 2–3 hours.

1. Place the roast in a Crock-Pot. In a small bowl, combine all the remaining ingredients except for the barbecue sauce and pour over the roast.

2. Cook on high for 1 hour. Reduce the heat to low and cook until fork tender, about 6–8 hours longer.

3. About 1½ hours before the end of the cooking time, pour the barbecue sauce over the roast. Raise the heat to high and cook for another hour.

4. To prepare the roast in the oven: Preheat the oven to 375° F. Place the roast in baking pan. In a small bowl, combine all the remaining ingredients, including the barbecue sauce, and pour the sauce over the roast. Bake, tightly covered, until the meat is fork tender, about 3–3½ hours.

5. Let the roast chill before slicing. Thinly slice the roast against the grain and reheat as needed. Serve warm. **Serves 8.**

FISH

for compliments

···

Sixty-Second Cajun Salmon with Dill

SHORT ON *time? Skip the skewers. Baking the salmon fillet in the six-ounce slices that the recipe calls for, or as a single large thirty-six-ounce fillet, will take no more than five minutes in a baking pan. And if you prepare a large batch of the spice mixture in advance, it will take only seconds, making it perfect for a quick, healthy dinner or a first course on Shabbos.*

This recipe is a keeper, not only because of its incredible flavors and versatility (this spice rub is also great on chicken), but also for its innovative style of presentation—if you choose to use the skewers.

6 salmon fillets (6 oz. each), 1½ inches wide

• Paprika

• Fresh dill, chopped

SPICE RUB

1 TBSP. kosher salt

1 TBSP. garlic powder

½ TSP. sage powder

1 TSP. dried oregano

1 TSP. dried thyme

1 TSP. dried basil

½ TSP. black pepper

⅛ TSP. cayenne pepper

1. Soak 6 wooden skewers in water for at least 1 hour. Preheat the oven to 350° F.

2. In a small bowl, combine the ingredients for the spice rub. Spread the mixture evenly over the salmon fillets. Sprinkle with the paprika and fresh dill.

3. Thread each fillet onto a soaked skewer in the shape of an *S*. Transfer to a baking pan and bake, uncovered, for 30–35 minutes (for one large fillet, 45–50 minutes). Serve warm or at room temperature. **Serves 6.**

Sake-Glazed Salmon with Shitake and Portobello Mushrooms

½ CUP sake

4 TBSP. brown sugar

6 TBSP. lite soy sauce

2 CLOVES garlic (fresh or frozen), minced

3 TSP. toasted sesame oil

3 TBSP. oil

¼ LB. shitake mushrooms, sliced

¾ LB. portobello mushrooms, sliced

2 salmon fillets (24 oz. total), skin removed

• Kosher salt

• Fresh black pepper

• Chives or scallions, to garnish

THIS RECIPE *was inspired by a chicken dish my family enjoys. I decided to try it with salmon, and the results were just as fabulous. You'll love this perfect pairing of salmon and mushrooms—two super-healthy foods.*

When purchasing the salmon, request that the fish seller cut the slices across the width rather than along the length. Cut the wide pieces of salmon in half to make short, wide pieces, as opposed to long, narrow slices. These will retain their shape better when searing.

Sake, the featured ingredient in this recipe, is a rice-based Japanese alcoholic beverage that can be found in most liquor stores.

note: *Use a nonstick skillet for this recipe.*

1. Preheat the broiler. In a small bowl, whisk together the sake, brown sugar, soy sauce, garlic, and sesame oil.

2. In a large nonstick skillet, heat 2 tablespoons of the oil. Add the mushrooms and sauté over medium heat until tender and browned, about 4 minutes, stirring occasionally. Add the sake mixture and cook until the mushrooms are glazed and the sauce has thickened slightly, 3-4 minutes. Transfer the mushrooms and sauce to a bowl. Cover and keep warm.

3. Cut the salmon fillets in half along the width and sprinkle with the salt and black pepper. Wipe the nonstick skillet with a paper towel and heat the remaining 1 tablespoon of oil over high heat. Add the salmon fillets and cook over high heat for 3 minutes per side, turning them only once.

4. Transfer the salmon to the broiler and broil until the top is golden and just cooked through, watching carefully to ensure it doesn't burn, about 2 minutes.

5. Stir the mushrooms and sauce, then scoop the mushrooms out of the sauce and place them on a plate. Baste the tops and bottoms of the salmon fillets generously with the remaining sauce. Serve the salmon warm or at room temperature on a bed of mushrooms, garnished with two or three mushrooms and the chives or scallions. **Serves 4.**

Chilean Sea Bass with Chive Chimichurri

6 sea bass fillets (6 oz. each)

- Fresh lemon juice
- Kosher salt
- Fresh black pepper

OPTIONAL SQUARE FRENCH FRIES

- Potatoes, peeled
- Oil, for deep-frying

CHIVE CHIMICHURRI

½ CUP chives, thinly sliced

⅓ CUP oil

1 TSP. kosher salt

1 garlic clove, minced

1 TBSP. fresh lemon juice

¼ CUP walnuts, toasted

THE **PUNGENT** *flavor of the chives in this recipe is tempered by the mild sea bass so that they complement each other perfectly. Chimichurri is the Argentinian code word for "pesto." It's a green herb sauce that is primarily served with meats but, like pesto sauce, can be served with just about anything.*

For a complete meal, serve this dish with Lemon Artichoke Cream Potato Salad (see page 43), which makes a nice accompaniment for the sea bass. The chive chimichurri and the lemon artichoke cream both have an enduring, versatile appeal. They're also delicious as a salad dressing, a savory side dish when tossed with roasted potatoes, or a dip. Culinary ingenuity is intensified with the square french fries as a garnish.

1. Preheat the oven to 350° F. Rinse the sea bass and pat dry. In a baking dish, season the fillets with the lemon juice, salt, and black pepper. Bake, uncovered, until the fish is cooked through, about 25 minutes.

2. While the fish is cooking, prepare the chimichurri sauce: In the bowl of a food processor, puree the chives, oil, salt, garlic, lemon juice, and toasted walnuts until smooth and creamy.

3. To prepare the square french fries: Trim all 6 rounded sides of each potato to square it up. Slice the potatoes into long, even strips, then dice to create squares. Deep-fry until golden and crispy.

4. To serve, place lemon artichoke cream potato salad in the center of a plate in a circle (optional) . Place a fillet of sea bass on the plate, and spread a layer of chive chimichurri on top. Garnish with the french fried potatoes. **Serves 6.**

Coconut Tilapia with Apricot Teriyaki Sauce

4 SLICES tilapia (1 lb. total)

• Peanut oil, for frying

DIPPING SAUCE

1 CUP apricot jam

2 TBSP. Dijon mustard

2 TBSP. white or red horseradish, drained

2 TBSP. teriyaki sauce

COATING 1

½ CUP cornstarch

• Kosher salt

• Fresh black pepper

COATING 2

2 eggs, beaten

1 TSP. garlic powder

1 TSP. onion powder

½ TSP. cayenne pepper

1 TSP. kosher salt

¼ TSP. fresh black pepper

COATING 3

1 CUP fine ground coconut

1 CUP coconut flakes

YOU **WOULD** *be hard-pressed to find a tilapia recipe that comes close to this one. It's the only tilapia recipe I've included in this cookbook because I've yet to taste another tilapia dish that compares.*

What makes this coconut crust different from others is that it combines fine and flaked coconut. Since tilapia is a mild-flavored and tender fish, the combination of the two coconut textures gives it an extra boost of crunch and coconut boldness.

I find that when I fry fish or chicken cutlets I get a more intense flavor when I season the egg wash instead of the crumbs, flour, or cornstarch. Besides seasoning the egg wash, I also add some kosher salt and black pepper to the cornstarch coating.

1. To prepare the dipping sauce: In a small bowl, combine all the sauce ingredients.

2. Cut the tilapia into ¾-inch-wide strips (about 4 strips per slice). Trim the top and bottom of each strip to form a neat rectangular shape.

3. Prepare three bowls for the coatings. In one bowl, combine the cornstarch, salt, and black pepper. In a second bowl, combine the eggs, garlic powder, onion powder, cayenne pepper, 1 teaspoon salt, and ¼ teaspoon black pepper. In the third bowl, combine the fine coconut and the coconut flakes.

4. Coat the tilapia strips on all sides with the cornstarch coating, then coat with the egg mixture. Finally, coat the tilapia with the coconut coating.

5. In a frying pan, heat the peanut oil over medium–high heat. (Make sure the oil is very hot before frying or the fish will stick to the pan.) Fry the tilapia on both sides until it is golden brown and the crust is crispy, about 4–5 minutes per side. Remove the tilapia and drain on a paper towel. Serve with the dipping sauce. **Serves 6.**

Sushi Gefilte Fish

1 ROLL (20 oz.) gefilte fish, thawed

5 SHEETS nori seaweed

1 red bell pepper, thinly sliced

½ CUP carrots, shredded

DIPPING SAUCES

- Horseradish
- Soy sauce
- Wasabi sauce
- Mayonnaise

DON'T BE *overwhelmed by the photo. You'll find that this recipe is simple but produces dazzling results. For extra panache, add smoked lox along with the gefilte fish to mimic the look of fresh ginger. Your guests will be fascinated by this dish, so expect to share the recipe.*

alternative: Use salmon gefilte fish.

1. Preheat the oven to 350° F. Defrost the fish until it will spread evenly and divide into 5 equal portions. Place a sheet of nori seaweed, shiny side down, on a flat surface. Gently spread 1 portion of gefilte fish on the seaweed. Arrange the sliced red peppers in a single row along one edge of the sheet. Follow with a row of shredded carrots alongside the peppers. Starting from the side with the peppers and carrots, tightly roll up the nori sheet jelly-roll style.

2. Repeat with the 4 remaining nori sheets. Transfer the rolls to a baking pan and bake, uncovered, for 25 minutes. Allow to cool, then refrigerate until firm.

3. When ready to serve, slice the rolls into 1-inch pieces. Serve cold, with your choice of horseradish, soy sauce, wasabi sauce, or mayo for dipping. **Serves 5.**

Lime Sea Bass with Sweet Chili Apricot Relish

2 **WIDE SLICES** sea bass (24-32 oz. total), sliced in half lengthwise

• Kosher salt

• Fresh black pepper

GARNISH

• Lime slices

• Radish sprouts

• Pomegranate seeds

SAUCE

½ **CUP** Thai sweet chili sauce

1 lime, juiced

6 **TBSP.** apricot preserves

4 **TBSP.** brown sugar

THIS DISH *is the perfect example of how looks can be deceiving. It looks complicated, but it really isn't. You can easily duplicate the beautiful presentation shown in the photo—in mere minutes.*

You'll also love the fact that every bite of this gorgeous dish delivers spicy, zesty, sweet, and tangy all at the same time. All you need is several ingredients, and couture cuisine is served.

note: When purchasing the sea bass, request slices that are double the width you would normally buy. Cut each wide piece of fish in half lengthwise to yield two slices. These look prettier than long narrow slices, and they retain their shape better during searing or baking.

alternative: This sauce also works well with baked salmon or chicken.

1. Preheat the oven to 375° F. To prepare the sauce: In a small saucepan, combine the sweet chili sauce, lime juice, apricot jam, and brown sugar. Cook over low-medium heat, stirring continuously, until the sugar has melted, about 1-2 minutes. Set aside.

2. Rinse the fish and pat completely dry. Sprinkle with the salt and black pepper. Place in a baking dish and bake, uncovered, until cooked through, 20 minutes.

3. To serve, place a lime slice on a plate, position the sea bass on top, and drizzle the sea bass with the sauce. Garnish with the radish sprouts and pomegranate seeds. Serve warm or at room temperature. **Serves 4.**

Striped Sesame Teriyaki Salmon

1 large (36 oz.) salmon fillet

2 Tbsp. teriyaki sauce

¼ cup soy sauce

½ cup Dijon mustard

½ cup honey

1 lemon, juiced

5 cloves garlic, minced

• Black and white sesame seeds

THE IDEA *of striping the salmon with black and white sesame seeds came from Batsheva, who has a knack for upgrading a recipe's wow factor. You can also achieve this look with individual salmon slices. As for the salmon, this is not just any teriyaki salmon. It's by far the best version of teriyaki salmon I've tasted.*

tip: Serve the teriyaki salmon with Sesame Teriyaki Pasta (pictured) from page 53.

1. Place the salmon in an oversized, sealable plastic bag. Combine the teriyaki sauce, soy sauce, mustard, honey, lemon juice, and garlic and pour over the salmon. Turn the salmon to coat. Refrigerate overnight or at least 6 hours.

2. Preheat the oven to 350° F. Spray a large baking sheet with nonstick cooking spray. Remove the salmon from the marinade and place on the baking sheet.

3. Sprinkle the salmon with the black and white sesame seeds in diagonal stripes, alternating with the black and white seeds. Use the dull side of a large knife to help keep the lines even.

4. Bake for 50 minutes for a large fillet or 35–40 minutes for individual slices. Transfer to a serving platter and serve warm or at room temperature. **Serves 6.**

Tuna Steaks with Dijon Garlic Sauce

DIJON GARLIC SAUCE

- ¼ CUP soy sauce
- 3 TBSP. brown sugar
- 2 TBSP. oil
- 1 TSP. toasted sesame oil
- 1 TSP. Dijon mustard
- 2 CLOVES garlic, minced
- ⅛ TSP. fresh black pepper

TUNA STEAKS

- Soy sauce
- 4 tuna steaks (4-6 oz. each)
- Black or white sesame seeds
- Oil, for frying
- Store-bought fried onions (I use French's), to garnish

1. In a jar or cruet, combine all the sauce ingredients. Shake well until mixed.

2. Rub the soy sauce on the tuna steaks on all sides and immediately coat with the sesame seeds. In a nonstick skillet, heat the oil over medium heat until very hot. Sear the tuna for 30–60 seconds on each side, according to the desired level of doneness.

3. Remove the tuna from the skillet to a platter and allow to cool for several minutes. Cut the tuna against the grain into slices at least ¼ inch thick.

4. To serve, top the tuna slices with a mound of crispy onions, and drizzle the Dijon garlic sauce on the side for dipping. **Serves 4-6.**

Panko-Crusted Tomato Basil Chilean Sea Bass

PANKO CRUMB TOPPING

1 CUP panko crumbs

⅓ CUP oil

1 large clove garlic, minced, or 1 frozen garlic cube

¾–1 TSP. kosher salt

• Fresh black pepper

SEA BASS

4 Chilean sea bass fillets (6 oz. each)

2 CLOVES garlic, minced

• Kosher salt

• Fresh black pepper

2 plum tomatoes, seeded and thinly sliced into 8 rounds

2 basil leaves per fillet, sliced into chiffonade ribbons

1. Preheat the oven to 375° F. In a small mixing bowl, combine the panko crumb topping ingredients and set aside.

2. Rub half a minced garlic clove onto the top and sides of each sea bass fillet and season with the salt and black pepper.

3. Arrange two tomato slices on top of each fillet. Top with a layer of the sliced basil, then cover with the panko crumb mixture to form a crust.

4. Bake, uncovered, for 30–35 minutes. Once cooked, broil for 1–2 minutes to give the panko topping extra crispiness. **Serves 4.**

AFTER SPENDING *a lovely Shavuos at Yali's home, we left with this delicious recipe for sea bass. It was given to her by an Italian client who insisted that this was the authentic way of preparing Chilean sea bass in Italy. This is one example of how great food, simply prepared, can turn into a masterpiece.*

For accompaniment, the Tomato Basil Salad on Asian Portobello Mushrooms (see page 52) is an appetizer I've been preparing for years. When served with this tomato basil sea bass, they make the perfect pair.

By now you've probably noticed that my recipes usually call for fresh herbs. Once you use fresh herbs in your recipes, you'll never go back to using dried. They are nature's little parcels packed with flavor.

note: *For the method of slicing herbs chiffonade style, see page 292.*

dairy option: *Add ½ cup parmesan cheese to the panko crumb topping.*

Sweet Gefilte Fish with Caramelized Tomatoes, Mushrooms, and Onions

1 large onion, chopped

2 CUPS grape tomatoes, halved

10 OZ. white button mushrooms, quartered

2 TBSP. oil

⅓–½ CUP sugar

PINCH salt

1 loaf (20 oz.) gefilte fish

1. Preheat the oven to 350° F. In a 9x13-inch baking pan, combine the onion, tomatoes, mushrooms, oil, sugar, and salt. Roast, uncovered, until caramelized, 30-40 minutes.

2. Remove the pan from the oven and stir the roasted vegetables to combine. Add the gefilte fish loaf to the pan and bake, covered, for 1 hour and 15 minutes longer. Serve the gefilte fish warm, topped with the vegetables. **Serves 6-8.**

IF THE concept of a gefilte fish craving sounds foreign to you, well, that's about to change. At Toby E.'s house we're always served a glorious amount of fabulous food (which leaves me with a glorious amount of inspiration). This is one of Toby's recipes, and it's the kind of recipe that travels fast. You'll see...

note: If the frozen gefilte fish loaf is wrapped in parchment paper, let the fish thaw slightly. It will be easier to remove the paper before baking.

Pistachio-Crusted Salmon with Eggplant Puree

THIS RECIPE *is from The Dairy Gourmet by Sarah Lasry. We first enjoyed this dish at Toby's house and were instantly enamored. I have a copy of that cookbook, and I prepare the vegetable lasagna all the time, so how did I manage to skip this gem? I now prepare this dish often, with either sea bass or salmon. I wanted to publish the recipe in this book because of all the pistachio-crusted fish recipes I've experimented with, this one deserves another dose of recognition. No doubt the addition of crispy onions and all that fresh basil is responsible for its success.*

The eggplant puree that I've added to the original recipe is an optional addition. I include a little tahini in the puree, which renders a more nuanced sauce. To serve, either spoon the eggplant puree on the side or place a mound of puree in the center of the plate and position the fish on top.

2 CUPS green pistachio nuts, shelled

2 CUPS fried onions (I use French's)

1 PACKED CUP fresh basil

6 TBSP. oil

1 TSP. sage powder

1 TSP. onion powder

1 TSP. garlic powder

4 salmon fillets (6 oz. each)

• Kosher salt

• Fresh black pepper

2 lemons, juiced

1 cup mayonnaise

EGGPLANT PUREE

4 TBSP. oil

1 medium eggplant, peeled and finely diced

1 CUP MSG-free pareve chicken stock

3 CLOVES garlic, minced

1 TBSP. tahini

1 TBSP. lemon juice

1½ TSP. kosher salt

¼ TSP. red pepper flakes

⅛ TSP. fresh black pepper

1. In a skillet, sauté the eggplant in the oil over medium heat until the eggplant is shrunken and softened, about 4–5 minutes. Add the pareve chicken stock, garlic, tahini, lemon juice, salt, red pepper flakes, and black pepper. Cover and reduce the heat to medium–low. Simmer for 20 minutes. Cool for several minutes, then puree with immersion blender until smooth.

2. Preheat the oven to 350° F. In a food processor, place the pistachios, fried onions, basil, oil, sage powder, onion powder, and garlic powder. Pulse 5–6 times until the mixture has a grainy consistency. Set aside.

3. Rinse the fish and pat dry. Sprinkle with the salt, black pepper, and lemon juice. In a large nonstick skillet sprayed with nonstick cooking spray, pan-sear the fish on both sides to seal in the juices, about 2 minutes per side. Transfer the salmon to a baking pan and allow to cool for several minutes.

4. Spread the mayonnaise on the salmon, then pat the pistachio mixture evenly on top. The layer of pistachio mixture should be thick. Bake in the oven for 20–25 minutes. Serve warm or at room temperature with the eggplant puree. **Serves 4.**

Aburi Sesame Tuna with Wasabi Garlic Cream

1 LB. sushi-grade tuna steaks

- Kosher salt
- Fresh black pepper
- Teriyaki sauce
- Black sesame seeds

GARNISH

- Edamame peas
- Variety of herbs

WASABI GARLIC CREAM

2 TBSP. wasabi powder

¾ CUP mayonnaise

2 TBSP. water

1 TBSP. lemon juice

2 CLOVES garlic, minced

1 TSP. sugar

IF YOU'RE *a tuna enthusiast, but you aren't keen on the raw variety, this Aburi tuna is the perfect compromise. Aburi is the Japanese word for "flamed". The tuna is torched with a butane blowtorch to create a crispy, delicate skin (the same kind of blowtorch used to caramelize crème brûlée). If you don't own a blowtorch, you can still enjoy this recipe by searing the tuna for no longer than thirty seconds per side. The intention is not to cook the fish, but to caramelize it slightly and change the texture.*

Serve the tuna with a generous drizzle of wasabi garlic cream or serve the wasabi garlic cream on the side in a small dipping dish. The wasabi garlic cream is also great with other types of fish or even french fries.

For added flavor, you may substitute fresh cracked black pepper for the black sesame seeds to coat the tuna.

1. Rinse the tuna and pat dry. Sprinkle the tuna steaks with the salt and black pepper. Coat all sides of the tuna with the teriyaki sauce and then immediately coat with the black sesame seeds.

2. Slice the tuna steaks into desired thickness, keeping the slices together in a row. Place the tuna slices in a baking pan. Very carefully light the blowtorch and, holding it close to the tuna, sear the top of the fish, running the flame along the tuna slices just until the color begins to change, about 10 seconds.

3. Prepare the wasabi garlic cream: In a small bowl, combine the wasabi powder, mayonnaise, water, lemon juice, garlic, and sugar.

4. Serve the sliced tuna with a generous amount of wasabi garlic cream. Garnish with the edamame peas and herbs and serve with a green salad on the side. **Serves 2–4.**

Poached Sweet and Tangy Salmon

6 salmon fillets (4-6 oz. each)

1 cup hot and spicy duck sauce

1 cup ketchup

¾ cup brown sugar

4 Tbsp. lemon juice

4 Tbsp. apple cider vinegar

1 small red onion, thinly sliced

1. Rinse the salmon and pat dry. Fill a large saucepan with enough water to cover the salmon and bring to a boil over high heat. Reduce the heat to low and add the salmon to the pan, ensuring that it is completely covered with the water. Cover and simmer for no more than 18 minutes. Remove the pan from the heat. Remove the salmon from the water and place in a nonreactive dish (do not use foil).

2. To prepare the sauce: Mix the duck sauce, ketchup, brown sugar, lemon juice, vinegar, and sliced onion. Pour over the salmon. Refrigerate overnight to marinate before serving.

3. To serve, scoop a generous amount of sauce over the salmon. **Serves 6.**

DINING AT *Esther C. W.'s table is always a culinary adventure, and I never leave without a superb new recipe. I've eaten in her home countless times, and she has never repeated a dish—ever (think: wide array of dishes per meal).*

This recipe, an update of the traditional sweet-and-sour salmon, is one of the gems I acquired from Esther, and it has been a staple in my Shabbos repertoire for years. The key is to poach the salmon for no longer than eighteen minutes to ensure it is moist and flavorful and maintains its pinkish hue.

Now, whenever I serve this dish to guests, they always request the recipe, and it's become my daughter's favorite salmon dish—she refers to is as "candy salmon." It tastes even better the next day—making it perfect for Shabbos lunch. If you want to get the people in your life to eat more salmon, this recipe will do the trick.

Two-Toned Gefilte Fish Gift Squares

1 LOAF (20 oz.) gefilte fish, thawed

1 LOAF (20 oz.) salmon gefilte fish, thawed

• Chives, to garnish

1. Preheat the oven to 350° F. In an 8-inch square Pyrex or foil pan, spread the gefilte fish in an even layer. Cover tightly and bake for 30 minutes.

2. Remove the pan from the oven and spread the salmon gefilte fish evenly over the gefilte fish layer. Cover tightly and bake for 1 hour longer. Allow to cool, then refrigerate.

3. To serve, cut into 12 squares and wrap with chives. Serve with your favorite gefilte fish condiment. **Serves 8.**

HERE IS *a charming update on a traditional dish. A familiar classic is repackaged with a unique, exciting presentation. In this case, packaging IS everything.*

If you prefer your gefilte fish sweeter, add several tablespoons of sugar to the mixture. To soften the chives for easier wrapping, soak them in boiling water for several seconds.

delightfully

DAIRY

···

Haloumi Salad with Warm Mushrooms and Teriyaki Dressing

DRESSING

- 1 CUP lite soy sauce
- 1 TBSP. cornstarch
- ½ CUP good-quality semi-dry white wine
- 4 TBSP. oil
- ½ CUP sugar
- 3 CLOVES garlic, minced
- 1 TSP. fresh ginger, minced

SALAD

- 1 large red onion, thinly sliced
- ¼ CUP oil, plus extra for frying
- 8 OZ. (1 box) white button mushrooms, sliced
- 2 CUPS grape tomatoes
- • Haloumi cheese, cut into 1-inch slices
- 2 HEADS romaine lettuce, sliced
- 1 cucumber, diced

I'VE RECEIVED *several wistful requests to recreate a certain famed haloumi salad that is served in a Brooklyn cafe. After much trial and error, this is the spectacular result. Haloumi is a traditional Greek cheese that has a higher melting point than other cheeses, so it can be grilled and fried and still maintain its shape. If you don't have any on hand, you may substitute the haloumi with breaded fried mozzarella.*

The recipe for the dressing will leave you with more than enough for multiple servings, and it stays fresh in an airtight container in the fridge for several weeks. When you're ready to use the extra dressing, heat it for several minutes before serving. To prepare the cucumber bowls shown in the photo, use English cucumbers since they are longer. Simply slice the cucumber lengthwise on a mandoline slicer and then mold it into a round shape. Attach the two ends with a toothpick.

meat option: Substitute the cheese with bite-size pieces of boneless, skinless dark chicken cutlets. Grill or broil the chicken pieces, then toss with the dressing. Add half of the chicken pieces to the salad and sprinkle the rest on top.

1. To prepare the dressing: In a saucepan, combine the soy sauce and cornstarch over medium heat until the cornstarch is dissolved. Add the wine, oil, sugar, garlic, and ginger. Cook for several minutes, stirring occasionally. Once the mixture starts to thicken considerably, remove from the heat. Set aside.

2. To prepare the salad: In a sauté pan, sauté the red onion slices in the oil until soft. Add the mushrooms and tomatoes. Cover and simmer until the mushrooms are soft and cooked through, 6–8 minutes.

3. Heat oil in a frying pan over high heat. Fry the slices of haloumi cheese until golden brown and crispy, about 2 minutes per side.

4. In a large bowl, toss the romaine lettuce and cucumber with the hot onions, mushrooms, and tomatoes. Add half the dressing and half the haloumi cheese and toss well to combine. Sprinkle the remaining half of the haloumi cheese on top of the salad (about 5–7 pieces of cheese per person). Reserve the extra dressing for later use. **Serves 6–8.**

Cheese Truffles

YOU CAN *further enhance the flavor of these savory cheese truffles by adding minced herbs, seeds, wasabi, or pesto paste to the cheese mixture, or trying other coatings, such as chopped toasted nuts. Choose your own creative options to see what you prefer.*

The easiest method for coating the cheese balls is to put the coating into a plastic cup, drop the cheese ball into the mixture, and shake until completely covered. Serve with your favorite crackers and bunches of grapes.

CHEESE BALLS

8 oz. farmer cheese or goat cheese

1 TSP. garlic powder

½ TSP. onion powder

1 TSP. Dijon mustard

1 TSP. Worcestershire sauce

1–2 DASHES hot sauce

COATING

- Toasted sesame seeds
- Smoked or regular paprika
- Chopped chives
- Chopped pecans

1. Bring the cheese to room temperature. In a large mixing bowl, combine all the ingredients for the cheese balls until mixed. Cover with plastic wrap and refrigerate for a half hour.

2. Remove the cheese mixture from the fridge and form into balls. Combine the ingredients for the desired coating and pour into a plastic cup. Drop the cheese balls one at a time into the cup and shake to coat. Refrigerate until ready to serve. **Serves 6.**

No-Bake Cheesecake Mousse

THIS RECIPE *ended my quest for a melt-in-the-mouth cheese mousse. It's irresistibly creamy, but not too sweet. I kept the topping for this cheese mousse simple, so you won't be overwhelmed by multiple flavors, and so as not to detract from the goodness of the delicate mousse.*

Since the cheese filling is not baked, it should be refrigerated for at least twelve hours prior to serving to allow it to firm up.

DOUGH CRUMBS

⅞ CUP (1¾ sticks) butter

4 TBSP. sugar

2 egg yolks

2 CUPS all-purpose flour

1 TSP. baking powder

1 TSP. vanilla sugar

CHEESE FILLING

2 CUPS heavy cream

4 TBSP. sugar

4 CONTAINERS 9% soft cheese
(I use Tnuva or Norman's)

1¼ CUPS confectioners' sugar

2 TSP. vanilla sugar

1. Preheat the oven to 350° F. In a bowl, combine all the ingredients for the dough crumbs until the mixture is crumbly. Press two-thirds of the mixture onto the bottom and sides of a 9½-inch springform pan to form an even crust. Bake until golden, about 25 minutes. Remove from the oven and allow to cool.

2. In a baking pan, bake the remaining one-third of the dough crumbs for 25 minutes. Transfer the baked crumbs from the pan to a sealable plastic bag and crush to form fine crumbs. Set aside.

3. To prepare the cheese filling: Whip the heavy cream with the sugar. Set aside.

4. Beat the soft cheese with the confectioners' sugar and vanilla sugar. Fold gently into the heavy cream. Pour the mixture over the baked crust and sprinkle with the fine crumbs. Refrigerate for at least 12 hours before serving. **Serves 10.**

Strawberry Spinach Salad with Yogurt Poppy Seed Dressing

DRESSING

1 CUP vanilla yogurt

2 TBSP. smooth strawberry jam

2 TBSP. honey

2 TBSP. lemon or lime juice

1 TBSP. poppy seeds

SALAD

10 OZ. baby spinach

1 LB. strawberries, quartered

1 mango, peeled and thinly sliced

1 CUP pistachio nuts

1 CUP Craisins

• Granola (optional)

THIS SALAD *resembles a deconstructed fruit and yogurt parfait. You can add your choice of either crumbled feta or goat cheese, granola, Craisins, or raisins.*

pareve option: *Substitute the yogurt with ½ cup oil and 2 tablespoons balsamic vinegar.*

1. In a large bowl, combine all the ingredients for the dressing.

2. Toss the salad ingredients with the dressing. Serve immediately. **Serves 6-8.**

Better-Than-Snickers™ Dessert Bars

WHENEVER I *get a recipe from Batsheva, I know it will be fabulous. But when she sends me a recipe that's also simple like this one, it's a double bonus.*

Batsheva tasted this memorable dessert in Israel—the pareve version at Keyara and the dairy version at The Spaghettis in Mamilla—and was relentless in pursuing the recipe. This decadent adult treat appeals to the kid inside. It's rich and dense, so one serving per person is usually sufficient.

Although the recipe has a casual feel to it, this is a dessert that can go either way. For an elegant presentation, serve each bar with mint leaves and berries on the side or heaped with chocolate curls.

note: Make sure to use peanuts that are salted. They make a good complement for the sweet flavors.

LAYER 1

1 CUP all-purpose flour

¼ CUP sugar

2 TBSP. confectioners' sugar

PINCH salt

½ CUP (1 stick) butter, cut into squares

1 large egg yolk

LAYER 2

2 CUPS store-bought caramel cream (I like Baker's Choice), at room temperature

1½ CUPS roasted salted peanuts, chopped

LAYER 3

2 BARS (7 oz.) bittersweet milk chocolate

¼ CUP (½ stick) butter

• Chopped roasted salted peanuts

1. In the bowl of an electric mixer, combine the ingredients for the first layer until a dough forms. Press the dough onto the bottom of a 9x13-inch pan until smooth and thin. Preheat the oven to 350° F. Chill the dough layer in the freezer for 20 minutes. Remove from the freezer and bake immediately for 15 minutes. Allow to cool.

2. To prepare the second layer: Combine the caramel cream and peanuts. Pour the mixture over the first layer and spread evenly. Freeze until firm.

3. To prepare the third layer: Microwave the chocolate and butter until melted, taking care not to let it burn. With a spatula, smooth the chocolate and butter mixture over the caramel layer. Sprinkle with the chopped salted peanuts. Freeze until ready to serve.

4. To serve, slice the dessert into squares while still slightly frozen. Bring to room temperature for at least 15 minutes before serving. **Yields 20 bars.**

Cream of Spinach Soup

1 large onion, diced

¼ CUP (½ stick) butter

10 oz. frozen spinach

3 CLOVES garlic, minced

¼ CUP all-purpose flour

5 CUPS pareve chicken stock

1 TSP. kosher salt

⅛ TSP. fresh black pepper

DASH nutmeg

1 CUP whole milk

1 CUP heavy cream

OPTIONAL GARNISHES
- Toasted pine nuts
- Baby spinach leaves
- Herbed goat cheese

IF YOU enjoy cream of spinach, you'll love this soup. Quick, satisfying, and nutritious, the soup is pureed to blend the onions and create a smoother texture (though it's okay if the spinach pieces stay partially intact).

For a healthier alternative, replace the pareve chicken stock made from soup mix with MSG-free chicken soup powder mixed with water.

1. In a skillet, sauté the onion in the butter until translucent, about 5–7 minutes. Add the spinach and garlic and sauté for 2 minutes longer. Stir in the flour. Gradually add the pareve chicken stock and season with the salt, black pepper, and nutmeg. Simmer, uncovered, for 25 minutes. Add the milk and cream and continue to simmer, uncovered, for 15 minutes longer.

2. With an immersion blender, puree the soup until the onions are blended and the consistency is smooth. Simmer for an additional 15 minutes. Add more seasoning, if needed. Serve warm, garnished with the toasted pine nuts, fresh baby spinach leaves, and/or herbed goat cheese, if desired. **Serves 6.**

Fettuccine with Pistachio Pesto Alfredo Cream

FETTUCCINE WITH PISTACHIO PESTO ALFREDO CREAM

- 1 CUP fresh basil leaves, plus extra to garnish
- ½ CUP pistachio nuts, toasted
- 3 CLOVES garlic
- ¼ CUP oil
- 1 TSP. fresh black pepper
- ½ CUP parmesan cheese, grated
- 1¼ CUPS heavy cream
- • Kosher salt
- 1 LB. fettuccine, cooked al dente
- • Pine nuts (optional)

FOUR-INGREDIENT FETTUCCINE ALFREDO

- 1 CUP heavy cream
- 2 CLOVES garlic, minced
- ¾ CUP parmesan cheese, grated
- • Kosher salt
- • Fresh black pepper
- 1 LB. fettuccine, cooked al dente

THIS RECIPE *was created with my daughter in mind. She loves both fettuccine alfredo and all things pesto, so I decided to combine them. This is one of those dishes that generates demands for the recipe from whoever tastes it, it's that good. But to get good results, this dish is best served fresh.*

I've also included a recipe for Four-Ingredient Fettuccine Alfredo here. It's my daughter's absolute favorite food, and if we're going to prepare it often, it might as well be fast and easy. This dish is so simple that I open the stove top for my nine-year-old daughter and she prepares the sauce all on her own (she insists!). This allows her to tap into her own creativity—sometimes she'll add frozen basil cubes, fresh herbs, or the juice of half a lemon, or she'll play around with various garnishes. She especially loves to add "pinches" of salt and pepper.

It took some trial and error to figure out the exact amount of salt we like in this dish. For us, it's three-quarters of a teaspoon. Because we prepare this dish so often, we also cut out the butter that you'll usually find in this dish, making it a healthier, lighter version.

Directions for Fettuccine with Pistachio Pesto Alfredo Cream:

1. To prepare the pesto sauce: In a food processor, puree the basil, pistachio nuts, garlic, oil, and black pepper until smooth. Stir in the grated parmesan until mixed.

2. In a large sauté pan, heat the heavy cream over medium–high heat until it starts to thicken considerably, for several minutes. Stir in the pesto sauce until well combined. Season with the kosher salt, if needed.

3. Reduce the heat to low. Add the pasta to the sauté pan and cook for 1-2 minutes, tossing it with the sauce until it is evenly coated. Serve hot, garnished with basil leaves and/or pine nuts. **Serves 4.**

Directions for Four-Ingredient Fettuccine Alfredo:

1. In a large skillet, heat the heavy cream over medium–high heat. Stir in the garlic and cook until thickened, about 5 minutes. Stir in the grated parmesan and season with the salt and black pepper.

2. Reduce the heat to low. Add the pasta to the sauté pan and cook for 1-2 minutes, tossing it with the sauce until it is evenly coated. Serve warm. **Serves 4.**

Sole in Lime Caper Chili Sauce

THE **SAVORY** *sauce in this recipe complements the dainty, buttery flavor of the sole. You can adjust the amount of minced chili according to your taste, and you can use either jalapeno peppers, cayenne peppers, or habanero peppers. Jalapeno peppers range from mild to medium zesty, cayenne peppers pack a fiery punch, and habanero peppers are the spiciest peppers you can buy at most stores.*

To reduce the heat of the peppers, remove the seeds and membranes. Wear gloves to do this, or wash your hands immediately afterward with hot water and soap.

½ CUP all-purpose flour

1 TSP. kosher salt

¼ TSP. fresh black pepper

½ CUP (1 stick) butter

6 lemon sole fillets (4–6 oz. each)

¼ CUP fresh lime juice (juice of 2 limes)

1 TSP. lime zest

2 TBSP. capers, drained

1 CLOVE garlic, minced

2–3 TSP. chili peppers, minced or chopped

1. Preheat the oven to 350° F. On a plate, combine the flour with the salt and black pepper. Dredge each fillet in the flour mixture.

2. In a nonstick skillet, melt half of the butter over high heat. Fry each fillet for 2–3 minutes per side. Remove the fillets from the skillet and transfer to a baking pan. Bake, uncovered, until completely cooked through, for 12 minutes.

3. Using the same skillet, melt the remaining butter over medium heat. Add the lime juice, zest, capers, and garlic. Stir to mix thoroughly and bring to a boil. Let it boil for several seconds. Remove from the heat and stir in the desired amount of chili.

4. To serve, pour the sauce over the sole fillets. Serve warm. **Serves 6.**

Stuffed French Bread with Spinach, Herbs, and Cheese

STORE-BOUGHT *French bread makes this recipe simple and quick to prepare and yields satisfying results.*

To serve, slice the filled loaves on the diagonal. Arrange the entire loaf of French bread after it's been sliced on a platter to place in the center of the table, or serve the slices as individual portions.

2 LOAVES French bread (for about 12 servings)

2 TBSP. fresh parsley, chopped

2 TBSP. fresh chives, chopped

2 TBSP. fresh basil, chopped

¼ CUP fresh spinach leaves, chopped

2 CLOVES garlic, minced

¼ CUP oil

1 TSP. kosher salt

8 OZ. shredded mozzarella cheese

1. Preheat the oven to 350° F. Slice the loaves in half horizontally and hollow out the bottom half of each loaf. (You can reserve the hollowed-out bread to make fresh bread crumbs.)

2. In a bowl, mix the parsley, chives, basil, spinach, garlic, oil, salt, and cheese. Spread half of the mixture into each of the hollowed out halves of bread, and top with the other halves. Wrap tightly with foil and bake for 20 minutes. Serve warm. **Serves 12.**

Sour Cream Apple Pie with Walnut Streusel

2 9-inch frozen deep-dish pastry shells

APPLE FILLING

1¼ CUPS sour cream

¾ CUP sugar

¼ CUP all-purpose flour

¼ TSP. salt

1 egg

2 TSP. vanilla extract

3 Granny Smith apples, thinly sliced (⅛ inch thick)

3 Cortland apples, thinly sliced (⅛ inch thick)

1 Gala or McIntosh apple, thinly sliced (⅛ inch thick)

WALNUT STREUSEL TOPPING

¾ CUP chopped walnuts

¾ CUP all-purpose flour

⅓ CUP sugar

⅓ CUP brown sugar

1 TSP. ground cinnamon

⅛ TSP. salt

½ CUP (1 stick) butter, softened

OPTIONAL GARNISH

• Store-bought caramel sauce

1. To prepare the filling: Preheat the oven to 350° F. In a large bowl, whisk the sour cream, sugar, flour, salt, egg, and vanilla. Stir in the sliced apples. Pour the filling into the two frozen pastry shells and bake for 55 minutes.

2. Prepare the walnut streusel topping: In a bowl, combine the walnuts, flour, sugar, brown sugar, cinnamon, and salt. Add the softened butter and mix until the mixture is crumbly. Sprinkle the topping over the two pies and bake until golden, 30 minutes longer. Allow to cool at room temperature for several hours before serving. If the pie has been refrigerated, bring to room temperature before serving. Plate the pie slices garnished with the caramel sauce on the side, if desired. **Serves 12.**

Panko Mozzarella Sticks with Red Wine Vinegar Marinara Sauce

MARINARA SAUCE

1½ CUPS marinara sauce

1 TBSP. red wine vinegar

MOZZARELLA STICKS

14 STICKS mozzarella string cheese

½ CUP all-purpose flour

2 eggs, beaten

2 TBSP. milk

2 CUPS panko bread crumbs

½ CUP cornflake crumbs

• Oil, for frying

ALTHOUGH YOU'VE *vowed never to eat deep-fried dishes, not many can resist fresh, hot mozzarella sticks. The panko crumbs make them even crispier, and the cornflake crumbs, which are of a finer consistency, ensure that the sticks are completely coated. For dipping, add a hint of red wine vinegar to your favorite marinara sauce and serve on the side.*

1. To prepare the marinara sauce: In a small saucepan, heat the marinara sauce with the red wine vinegar for several minutes, stirring to combine.

2. To prepare the mozzarella sticks: Prepare three bowls for coating the sticks. In one bowl, place the flour. In the second bowl, combine the eggs and milk to make an egg wash. In the third, combine the panko and cornflake crumbs.

3. Cut each stick of string cheese in half widthwise to make 28 pieces. Dip each piece of cheese in the flour, then the egg wash, and finally the crumb mixture, coating the cheese completely. Place the sticks on a tray and freeze for at least 1 hour until firm.

4. In a skillet or saucepan, heat at least 1½ inches of oil over medium heat. Make sure the oil is very hot before you add the sticks. Place the sticks in the oil, spacing them so they are not touching. Fry until golden and crispy, before the cheese starts to melt and leak, about 2 minutes. Serve warm with the marinara sauce. **Yields 28 sticks.**

Key Lime Pie with Pecan Crust

PECAN CRUST

1 CUP ground pecans

1 CUP graham cracker crumbs

⅓ CUP brown sugar

PINCH salt

⅓ TSP. cinnamon

¼ CUP (½ stick) butter, melted

LIME FILLING

21 OZ. (2 jars) condensed cream (I use Baker's Choice)

½ CUP sour cream

1 TSP. lime zest, grated, plus extra to garnish

¾ CUP key lime juice (bottled or fresh)

SOUR CREAM TOPPING

1 CUP sour cream

8 TBSP. confectioners' sugar

• Lime slices, to garnish

EVEN IF *you're not a key lime pie aficionado, you will instantly enjoy this vibrant all-American dessert. Traditionally it is prepared with a graham cracker crust, but the pecans in this crust make a perfect foil for the tangy-sweet taste of the bright citrus filling. Authentic key lime pie contains condensed cream, so attempting a pareve version with the exact taste and texture is futile.*

You may be pleasantly surprised at how this pie stays together so well without the addition of eggs. There are many versions that call for eggs, but those yield a heavier, custard-like filling. The filling in this recipe is creamy and light, and the flavors are not overwhelming in either direction—not too sweet and not too tart. The sweet sour cream topping is unusual for a classic key lime pie, but it elevates the impeccable sweet-tart combination.

Key limes are smaller and more tart than Persian limes, the more common variety. If you can't locate key limes, Persian limes are good, too. Bottled key lime juice is available, but fresh lime juice does make a world of difference. Many brands of bottled lime or lemon juice contain water and citric acid, which drastically reduces the flavor.

even simpler: This filling yields enough to fill one store-bought 9-inch graham cracker pie crust.

1. To prepare the crust: Preheat the oven to 350° F. Toast the nuts in the oven until fragrant, about 8 minutes. Allow to cool. In a bowl, combine the toasted nuts, graham cracker crumbs, brown sugar, salt, and cinnamon. Stir in the butter until evenly combined and the mixture is crumbly.

2. Press the crumbs onto the bottom and sides of a 9-inch pie plate or 9-inch springform pan. If you are using a springform pan, cut parchment paper to line the base of the pan and spray the sides of the pan generously with nonstick cooking spray before forming the crust. Bake the crust until golden, 10–12 minutes. Remove from the oven.

3. To prepare the lime filling: In a bowl, beat all the filling ingredients with a hand mixer until smooth, about 1 minute. Pour the lime filling into the crust and bake until just set, 10 minutes. Do not overbake. Allow to cool at room temperature for 1 hour.

4. To prepare the sour cream topping: In a small bowl, whisk together the sour cream and confectioners' sugar until smooth. Spread on top of the key lime filling and refrigerate overnight. Serve chilled, garnished with the lime slices and lime zest. **Serves 8.**

Mini Cheese Babkas

WHEN **E. LEINER** *sent me one of her cheese babkas, she warned me that it was "dangerous"— and highly addictive it is. The aroma of this cheese babka baking in the oven will permeate your home and give you a hint of what's to come. Every bite combines sweet cheese with a perfect buttery crust, resulting in a sinfully rich and delicious treat.*

If you choose, you can make traditional round babka cakes by placing the unbaked buns (the 1½-inch slices of rolled-up filled dough) in tube pans and baking for 40–45 minutes. For optimal taste, serve warm.

note: *Instead of the crumb topping, you can drizzle the top of the babkas with icing. See the recipe for icing on page 312.*

DOUGH

3 oz. fresh yeast

1 TSP. sugar

1½ CUPS warm water

1 CUP milk

4 egg yolks

2 eggs

10 CUPS all-purpose flour

2 CUPS (4 sticks) butter

2 TBSP. vanilla sugar

1 CUP sugar

1 TSP. salt

CHEESE FILLING

2 LB. cream cheese

½ LB. farmer cheese

1⅓ CUPS sugar

3 TSP. vanilla extract

2 egg yolks

CRUMB TOPPING

¼ CUP (½ stick) butter

1 CUP all-purpose flour

½ CUP sugar

1. To prepare the dough: In a small bowl, dissolve the yeast and sugar in the warm water. In the large bowl of an electric mixer, beat together the dissolved yeast with the rest of the dough ingredients until evenly combined. Transfer the dough from the mixer to a large, nonreactive bowl (glass or plastic) and cover with plastic wrap.

2. Allow the dough to rise for 1 hour. Punch down the dough and allow to rise for an additional 30 minutes.

3. Divide the dough into 6 portions. Roll out each portion of dough into a thin square.

4. Prepare the cheese filling: In the bowl of an electric mixer, beat all the cheese filling ingredients until mixed. Spread an even layer of cheese mixture onto each square of dough. Roll the dough jelly-roll style, using a large stainless steel spatula to help you lift the dough off the counter, if necessary.

5. Slice the rolled-up dough into 1½-inch slices. Spray muffin tins with nonstick cooking spray and place 1 slice into each muffin slot. For large round babkas, spray 4 tube pans with nonstick cooking spray and arrange the slices in the tube pans.

6. In a bowl, combine the crumb topping ingredients. Sprinkle each babka with the crumb topping. Allow to rise for 30 minutes.

7. Preheat the oven to 350° F. Bake the mini babkas for 35–40 minutes or the large babkas for 40–45 minutes. Allow to cool slightly and serve warm, or allow to cool fully and serve at room temperature. **Yields 48–52 mini babkas or 4 round babka Bundt cakes.**

Strawberries and Cream Smoothies

16 oz. frozen strawberries

1 JAR (10.5 oz.) condensed cream (I use Baker's Choice)

6 ice cubes

1 TBSP. lime juice

4–6 TBSP. honey

1 TSP. vanilla extract

½ CUP milk

½ CUP plain yogurt

In a blender, puree the strawberries, condensed cream, ice cubes, lime juice, honey, vanilla extract, milk, and yogurt until smooth. **Serves 4.**

SWEETENED CONDENSED cream adds an extra measure of creaminess to smoothies. Condensed cream (available from Baker's Choice) is milk that has had most of its water content removed and sugar added to maintain freshness. If you're a vanilla kinda gal, you'll love strawberries dipped in condensed cream instead of melted chocolate.

This smoothie allows a lot of room for self-expression. Feel free to add your favorite fresh fruit to the recipe— if I have blueberries on hand, they are usually my first addition to this smoothie.

pareve option: Use orange juice or pomegranate juice instead of condensed cream and milk.

Creamy Roasted Tomato Vodka Soup

¼ CUP (½ stick) butter, cut into squares

10 tomatoes, quartered

1 large onion, diced

5–6 CLOVES garlic, minced

4 CUPS vegetable or pareve chicken stock

¼ CUP vodka

1 TBSP. tomato paste

¼ TSP. red pepper flakes

¼ CUP fresh basil leaves

2 TSP. kosher salt

• Fresh black pepper

2 CUPS heavy cream

GARNISH

• Whipped heavy cream or mascarpone

• Fresh cracked black pepper

• Basil leaves

WHILE ON *an Alaskan cruise, my friend Rikki W. couldn't get enough of the cream of tomato soup. For the first several days, Rikki helped herself to heaping bowl after bowl of the delicious soup that was served at every lunch. One day she actually scraped the bottom of the pot clean and requested more. To her dismay, she was told that she'd been consuming the vodka sauce meant to be poured over the penne a la vodka pasta! This story inspired me to develop a vodka tomato cream soup that's reminiscent of that popular pasta dish. I wanted the same delicious taste, but lighter.*

Do you happen to have pine nuts in your pantry? Try adding a cup of toasted pine nuts with the rest of the ingredients before cooking. And, if you prefer, complete the idea with a garnish of mini penne pasta, or enjoy it as is with a dollop of mascarpone or heavy cream on top.

1. Preheat the oven to 400° F. On a large baking sheet, sprinkle the butter on the tomatoes, onion, and garlic. Roast, uncovered, for 55 minutes, stirring halfway through to combine.

2. In a large pot, combine the roasted vegetables with the stock, vodka, tomato paste, red pepper flakes, basil leaves, salt, and black pepper. Cook, covered, over medium heat for 1 hour.

3. Puree the soup with an immersion blender. Add the heavy cream and cook over low heat for 20 minutes longer. Season with additional salt and black pepper, as needed. Garnish with a dollop of whipped heavy cream or mascarpone, fresh cracked black pepper, and basil leaves. Serve warm. **Serves 8.**

Linguine with White Wine Cream Sauce and Mushrooms

1 LB. linguine pasta, cooked al dente

SAUCE

½ CUP (1 stick) butter

16 OZ. (2 boxes) white button mushrooms, quartered

3 CLOVES garlic, minced

½ CUP good-quality dry white wine

1 CUP heavy cream

¾ CUP parmesan cheese, plus extra for sprinkling

1 TSP. kosher salt, or to taste

• Fresh black pepper

OPTIONAL GARNISHES

• Fresh basil or parsley

• Dried mushrooms

IN MOST *pasta dishes, I like using fresh herbs as a flavor booster, but I completely did away with them in this dish. The white wine adds enough complexity and aromatic distinction on its own. Like many children, my kids are picky eaters, but they love pasta. I tested this recipe many times to get just the right amount of white wine so the flavor isn't too overpowering for kids to enjoy.*

The key to great pasta is to cook it al dente—that is, only until it is firm and chewy. To ensure you don't over-cook the pasta, "undercook" it by one minute. Once the sauce is prepared, toss the pasta and sauce together over low heat for a minute until you have the sauce clinging to every bit of pasta. Prepared like this, it's a unified, well-executed dish.

To make this pasta dish a complete meal, add bite-sized pieces of baked salmon. If you don't have mushrooms on hand, broccoli florets work really well here, too (although your pasta will look green and may slightly re-semble a pesto sauce).

1. To prepare the sauce: In a large skillet, melt the butter over medium heat. Add the mushrooms and sauté until they are lightly browned and soft, about 5 minutes. Add the garlic and sauté for another minute. Add the wine and simmer gently to allow the sauce to reduce, 4–5 minutes. Add the heavy cream, parmesan, salt, and black pepper. Cook for 2–3 minutes longer, stirring occasionally, just until the sauce starts to thicken.

2. Reduce the heat to low and fold the linguine into the sauce until all the pasta is well coated. Add additional salt and black pepper to taste and sprinkle with additional parmesan cheese. Garnish with fresh basil or parsley leaves and/or dried mushrooms. Serve warm. **Serves 4.**

Eggnog Crème Brûlée

1 vanilla bean

2 CUPS heavy cream

¼ TSP. nutmeg

5 large egg yolks

1 large egg

½ CUP sugar

¼ TSP. kosher salt

2 TBSP. rum

6 TBSP. turbinado or raw sugar

AS CRÈME *brûlée is the last dessert I will order from a restaurant menu (I always order dessert), I was determined to find a crème brûlée recipe that would tempt me. For several weeks, my kitchen was in full crème brûlée mode. I tested a host of crème brûlée recipes that included various flavors such as pumpkin, amaretto, and cheesecake.*

I discovered that vanilla beans provide a more pungent and complex flavor than vanilla extract, and that it's crucial to bake the ramekins in a water bath. I also concluded that I prefer crème brûlée chilled in the refrigerator rather than at room temperature. The cold custard is still soft and creamy, but stiff enough in structure to cut through cleanly. Finally, this Eggnog Crème Brûlée struck a harmonious chord of flavors.

Eggnog is a rich, sweetened custard beverage. The word eggnog literally means "eggs in a small cup," and the word nog is also Old English lingo for "rum" or a rum-based drink. The base of crème brûlée is nearly identical to eggnog: sugar, cream, and egg yolks. It's the addition of rum and a touch of nutmeg that adds the distinctive eggnog flavor.

note: *Don't substitute the rum with rum extract.*

pareve option: *Use non-dairy whip topping instead of heavy cream.*

1. Preheat the oven to 350° F. Scrape out the vanilla bean: Halve the bean lengthwise. With the cut side up, scrape out the seeds with a knife. In a medium saucepan, combine the vanilla bean and its pulp, the cream, and the nutmeg. Cook over medium heat until the mixture starts to bubble around the edges of the pan, about 7–8 minutes. Remove from the heat as soon as the cream starts to boil.

2. In a medium bowl, whisk the egg yolks and egg with the sugar and salt until the sugar is dissolved. To temper the eggs, add a ladle of the hot cream mixture to the egg mixture and whisk to combine. Whisk in the remaining cream, one ladle at a time. Strain the mixture through a medium sieve to remove any lumps or pieces of vanilla bean. Add the rum and whisk to combine.

3. Divide the mixture evenly among 6 six-ounce ramekins or 4 eight-ounce ramekins. Place the ramekins in a large roasting pan. Pour hot (not boiling) water into the pan so that the water level is halfway up the sides of the ramekins.

4. Place the pan in the oven and bake until the custard is set, about 35–40 minutes (they should be slightly jiggly in the center). Remove the ramekins from the oven and allow to cool at room temperature. Cover and refrigerate for at least 4 hours and up to 3 days.

5. To caramelize the top of the custard, remove the ramekins from the refrigerator and allow the custard to reach room temperature, about 30 minutes. Sprinkle the top of each custard with 1 tablespoon of turbinado sugar. Heat the sugar with a butane torch until the top is caramelized and a crispy crust has formed. Alternatively, you can broil the ramekins in the oven until you get a thick, crunchy sugar crust, about 4 minutes. Allow the custards to harden at room temperature for at least 15 minutes before serving, or refrigerate for several hours or overnight and serve chilled. **Serves 4–6.**

Chocolate Chunk Pudding Cookies

1 CUP (2 sticks) butter, softened

1 CUP packed dark brown sugar

¼ CUP sugar

1 PKG. (2.8 oz.) instant vanilla pudding

1¼ TSP. vanilla extract

2 eggs

2¼ CUPS white whole wheat flour or all-purpose flour

1 TSP. baking soda

⅛ TSP. salt

1½ CUPS chocolate, chopped, or chocolate chips

1. Preheat the oven to 375° F. In the bowl of an electric mixer, cream together the butter and sugars until smooth. Beat in the vanilla pudding, vanilla extract, and eggs.

2. In a small bowl, combine the flour, baking soda, and salt. Beat the dry ingredients into the creamed mixture. Fold in the chopped chocolate or chocolate chips.

3. Drop spoonfuls of the cookie mixture onto a baking sheet. Bake for 14–15 minutes until golden and the edges are lightly browned. **Yields 32-36 cookies.**

THIS IS *my son's favorite pudding cookies, and they never fail to put a huge grin on his face. We bake these cookies together regularly, usually on Friday after school. My son is a picky eater and goes through stages when he'll eat just pizza and cucumbers and nothing else for weeks and then abruptly tire of them, but he never needs to be asked twice to eat these cookies. (I was a notoriously picky eater myself as a child, and my mom teasingly refers to this as karmic retribution.) Because these cookies go fast, I use whole wheat flour—if my children are going to eat that many cookies, they may as well be healthy. Well...healthier, at least.*

The chocolate chunks give this cookie character and lend a touch of finesse to an otherwise modest chocolate chip cookie. But if you prefer to save the time needed for chopping the chocolate, go ahead and use chocolate chips instead.

note: I'm not one for unnecessary kitchen gadgets, but investing in a cookie scoop will yield perfect uniform round cookies and save you time.

pareve option: Use 1 cup of oil instead of butter.

just for you

Heirloom Caprese Salad on Rosemary Skewers

A **SIMPLE CAPRESE** *salad is threaded onto rosemary skewers for an innovative presentation. If you can't get fresh buffalo mozzarella cheese, you can substitute with mozzarella string cheese.*

- Rosemary sprigs
- Assorted colored heirloom tomatoes
- Mozzarella cheese or mozzarella string cheese, cut into 1-inch slices
- Oil
- Balsamic vinegar
- Sea salt
- Fresh black pepper
- Oregano, dried or fresh
- Basil, dried or fresh

1. To prepare the rosemary skewers: Working with one rosemary sprig at a time, hold the leafy end of the sprig in one hand. Strip the leaves off the sprig with the other hand, leaving 1–2 inches of leaves attached to the leafy end. Repeat with the remaining rosemary sprigs.

2. Thread the tomatoes and cheese slices onto the rosemary skewers. In a small bowl, mix equal quantities of oil and balsamic vinegar and pour over the skewers. Season with the salt, black pepper, oregano, and basil.

Halibut in Balsamic Honey Butter Sauce

ROASTED ASPARAGUS *pairs really well with the fish in this recipe. When serving, place some roasted or grilled asparagus in the center of the plate and drizzle it with the sauce, then place the halibut on the asparagus and drizzle the fish and plate with more sauce. Salmon and mahi mahi can be used in place of the halibut if you wish.*

note: *Always pat fish completely dry with a paper towel after rinsing or it will become mushy while cooking.*

⅓ CUP balsamic vinegar

2 CLOVES garlic, minced

2 TBSP. honey

½ CUP PLUS 2 TBSP. (1 stick plus 2 tbsp.) butter, cut into small pieces

4 halibut fillets (6 oz. each)

• Kosher salt

• Fresh black pepper

1. To prepare the sauce: In a small saucepan, combine the balsamic vinegar, garlic, and honey over medium heat. Cook until thickened, about 5 minutes. Add ½ cup of the butter to the balsamic sauce and whisk until smooth.

2. Rinse the fish and pat dry, then season with the salt and black pepper. In a large skillet, melt the 2 tablespoons of the butter over medium heat. Sear the fish in the butter for 3 minutes per side. To serve, drizzle the sauce over the halibut. Serve warm. **Serves 4.**

Green Tea Lychee Berry Tart

CRUST

1 CUP confectioners' sugar

1¾ CUPS all-purpose flour

PINCH salt

½ CUP (1 stick) butter, softened

1 large egg

TOPPING

8 oz. fresh lychees, pitted and halved

1 PINT berries or cherries, pitted and halved

• Fresh mint leaves

GREEN TEA FILLING

1 TSP. powdered gelatin

1½ CUPS heavy cream

2 OZ. cream cheese

5 TBSP. sugar

1–2 TBSP. green tea powder

1 CUP crème fraîche

HERE IS *a tart that is nothing short of dazzling. The lychees, berries, and mint imbue the green tea cream with vibrant color contrasts, yielding a simple yet sophisticated dish. The dough recipe yields enough for two pies, so half of it can be frozen for the next time you prepare this dessert. This lovely recipe was graciously shared by chef Stephane Lemagnen.*

note: *Crème fraîche is a creamier and more decadent version of sour cream with a little less tang. If you cannot locate creme fraîche, full-fat sour cream stands in well as a quick substitute. To prepare authentic crème fraîche from scratch, whisk equal parts heavy cream and sour cream in a jar. Leave at room temperature for 12–15 hours until it is thickened, stirring several times. It will keep in the refrigerator for up to seven days.*

alternative: *Instead of raspberries, you can use halved strawberries or pitted, halved cherries.*

1. To prepare the tart crust: Sift the confectioners' sugar, flour, and salt together into a bowl. In a food processor, process the butter until smooth. Sprinkle the flour mixture over the butter. Add the egg and process just long enough for the dough to form; do not overmix. Wrap the dough in plastic wrap and refrigerate for at least 1 hour.

2. Grease a 9-inch tart ring. Divide the dough in two. Roll out one half of the dough into a circle and place in the tart ring—it's important to keep the tart crust very thin. Chill for 30 minutes. The remaining half of the dough can be frozen for another time.

3. Preheat the oven to 375° F. Line the tart crust with aluminum foil and fill with pie weights, dry rice, or beans. Bake for 15 minutes, then remove the aluminum foil and weights. Return the tart to the oven and bake for 15 minutes longer. Remove the tart from the oven and allow to cool on a rack.

4. To prepare the green tea filling: In a small bowl, sprinkle the gelatin over ½ cup of the heavy cream to soften. In a small saucepan, bring another ½ cup of heavy cream, the cream cheese, sugar, and green tea powder to a simmer over low–medium heat. Whisk until smooth, then whisk together the warm green tea mixture with the heavy cream and gelatin mixture until smooth. Allow to cool.

5. In a medium bowl, whip the crème fraîche and remaining ½ cup of heavy cream until soft peaks form. Fold the whipped cream mixture into the cooled green tea cream. Pour the filling into the tart shell and refrigerate for at least 2 hours.

6. When ready to serve, arrange the lychees, berries or cherries, and mint on top of the tart. **Serves 8.**

Slow-Cooked French Onion Soup

6 onions, chopped

6 CLOVES garlic, minced

½ CUP (1 stick) butter

8 CUPS pareve chicken or beef stock

¼ CUP port wine or dry red wine

2 TBSP. Worcestershire sauce

2 TBSP. balsamic vinegar

1 bay leaf

½ TBSP. sea salt or kosher salt

• Fresh black pepper

1 SPRIG thyme

8 baguette slices

• Shredded cheese of choice

WITH SO *many renditions of French onion soup recipes around, you'll wonder how this one differs from the rest. All the recipes I've experimented with call for too short a cooking time, which result in the onions being crisp-tender (when I like them melt-in-your-mouth tender) or a broth that isn't rich enough and lacks flavor intensity. The other choice is to cook the soup for longer, but who wants to coddle a simmering pot of soup for hours?*

The answer is this recipe for slow-cooked French onion soup. The virtue of this soup is that it's cooked until the onions are deep brown and caramelized, allowing time to draw out all the flavor from the ingredients to yield an incomparable depth to the taste. Since it's made in a slow cooker, you can prepare this soup in the morning, leave it on its own to simmer all day, and enjoy it for dinner.

1. Preheat the oven to 400° F. In a roasting pan, roast the chopped onions and minced garlic with the butter, uncovered, for 1 hour, stirring the onions and garlic with the butter once.

2. Transfer the roasted onion mixture to a 5-quart slow cooker and add the pareve chicken or beef stock, wine, Worcestershire sauce, balsamic vinegar, bay leaf, salt, black pepper, and thyme. Cover and cook on low until the onions are very tender, at least 6 hours. The soup can be cooked for up to 10–12 hours.

3. Around 15 minutes before serving, prepare the baguette slices: Preheat the oven to 450° F. Arrange the baguette slices on a cookie sheet and bake until toasted, 5 minutes. Remove from the oven, top with the shredded cheese, and bake until the cheese is browned and bubbling, about 10 minutes.

4. To serve, place some shredded cheese in each bowl, fill with soup, and allow the cheese to melt. Top with the toasted baguettes. **Serves 8.**

Easy Cheesecake with Berry Cups

IT TOOK me a while to get this cheesecake just right, but after batch number six, this cheesecake was spectacular—the best I've ever had. The texture was exactly what I wanted: creamy, fluffy, and "doesn't-stick-to-your-mouth" smooth.

It doesn't take much to transform the easiest cheesecake into a sophisticated dessert—just add a berry cup. Add your choice of fresh berries to melted sorbet and serve in mini shot glasses with a mint leaf. For an added touch, you can also crust the top of the shot glass with colored sugar.

For this cheesecake, I prefer to use light whipped cream cheese—it yields a cheesecake that's rich and creamy but not too dense. I'm a cheesecake purist and prefer no frills, but if you want added decadence, melt seven ounces of white chocolate into the heavy cream over a double boiler before adding the cream to the filling.

The trick to this cheesecake is to leave it to cool in the oven for one hour after turning off the heat. This allows for uniform cooling and a moister cake. The recipe yields three 9-inch pies. No worries—regardless of the number of people you are serving, there won't be much left over.

CHEESECAKE

3 CONTAINERS (8 oz. each) light whipped cream cheese

1 PKG. (7.5 oz.) farmer cheese

1 CONTAINER (16 oz.) sour cream

1½ CUPS sugar

5 eggs

1 CUP heavy cream

1 TBSP. lemon juice

1 TBSP. vanilla sugar

3 store-bought 9-inch graham cracker pie crusts

TOPPING

1 CONTAINER (16 oz.) sour cream

2 TBSP. sugar

1 TSP. vanilla sugar

1. Preheat the oven to 350° F. In the bowl of an electric mixer, or with a hand mixer, cream together the cream cheese, farmer cheese, sour cream, and sugar. Beat in the eggs, one at a time. Add the heavy cream, lemon juice, and vanilla sugar and mix until well combined.

2. Divide the mixture evenly among the 3 graham cracker pie crusts and bake for 50 minutes. Turn off the heat and leave the pies in the oven to cool for 1 hour.

3. To prepare the topping: In a bowl, combine the sour cream, sugar, and vanilla sugar. Spread over the top of the 3 cooled cheesecakes. Refrigerate for at least 5 hours before serving. Serve with berry cups. **Serves 24.**

Mascarpone Cheese Danishes

MASCARPONE IS *a very rich cow's milk cheese with a creamy buttery taste commonly used in tiramisu. If you find it hard to locate mascarpone, whipped cream cheese is a suitable substitute.*

1 LB. (16 oz.) mascarpone cheese

1¼ CUPS sugar

1 egg

½ PKG. (1.4 oz.) instant vanilla pudding

1 TBSP. vanilla sugar

1 TBSP. lemon juice

PINCH salt

1 lemon, zested

25–30 store-bought 3-inch mini puff pastry squares

• Confectioners' sugar, for sprinkling

EGG WASH

1 egg, beaten with 1 tablespoon water

1. To prepare the cheese filling: In the bowl of an electric mixer, cream together the mascarpone cheese and sugar on low speed until smooth. Beat in the egg, vanilla pudding, vanilla sugar, lemon juice, salt, and lemon zest until just combined—do not overmix. Refrigerate for 30 minutes.

2. Preheat the oven to 350° F. Line a baking sheet with parchment paper. Place a small amount of filling (about 1 generous tablespoon) in the center of each pastry square. Brush the edges of each pastry square with the egg wash and fold the corners toward the center, overlapping the corners so they stick firmly together. Place the pastries on the prepared baking sheet and brush the tops with the egg wash. Refrigerate for 15 minutes.

3. Bake the pastries until puffed and golden brown, 30–35 minutes, rotating the pan halfway through the baking. Dust with confectioners' sugar before serving and serve warm or at room temperature. **Yields 25–30 danishes.**

Mini Chocolate Chip Cheesecakes

YOU CAN *have lots of fun with this recipe: the crust is made out of your favorite cookie. Simply place a cookie on the bottom of each cupcake holder and fill with the easy-to-prepare cheesecake filling.*

alternative: Instead of cookies, place peanut butter cups on the bottom of the cupcake holders.

2 CONTAINERS (8 oz. each) whipped cream cheese

½ CUP PLUS 2 TBSP. sugar

3 eggs

1 TSP. vanilla extract

1 CUP milk chocolate chips

18 cookies

1. Preheat the oven to 350° F. In the bowl of an electric mixer, beat the cream cheese and sugar until well combined. Beat in the eggs and vanilla extract. Stir in the chocolate chips.

2. Line a muffin tin with paper cupcake holders. Place a cookie in each cupcake holder. Top with the cheese mixture so that each cupcake holder is two-thirds full. Bake until the center of each cake is firm and a toothpick inserted into the center comes out clean, about 35 minutes. Allow to cool, then refrigerate. **Yields 18 cheesecakes.**

Penne Vodka

1 medium onion, chopped

¼ CUP (½ stick) butter

5 CLOVES garlic, minced

1 CAN (28 oz.) whole peeled tomatoes, with the juice

1 TSP. kosher salt

⅛ TSP. fresh black pepper

½ TSP. red pepper flakes

¼ CUP vodka

1½ CUPS heavy cream

½ CUP parmesan cheese

¼ CUP fresh basil, chopped (optional)

1 LB. penne pasta, prepared according to package directions

"TOO GENERIC" *was my initial thought when I contemplated including this recipe. But, although there are many recipes for penne vodka, finding a good one is tricky. The preparation process is as important as the ingredient list.*

Vodka is mostly odorless and flavorless, but the acids released during the cooking process provide the catalyst that brings out the flavor compounds and caramel-like taste of the tomatoes. The trick is to cook a modest amount of vodka for at least thirty minutes so you don't have an overwhelmingly bitter aftertaste, but rather a slight undertone that gives the cream sauce its character.

Some authentic Italian recipes call for the sauce to be simmered for hours, but I find that thirty minutes of cooking out the vodka is long enough to deem this recipe restaurant worthy.

note: If you prefer a smooth vodka sauce without small chunks, puree the peeled tomatoes and liquid together in a food processor or use a 28-ounce can of your favorite marinara sauce.

1. In a large skillet, sauté the onion in the butter over medium heat until cooked through, 7–8 minutes. Add the garlic and cook for another minute.

2. Add the tomatoes with the juice, salt, black pepper, red pepper flakes, and vodka and cook for 20 minutes, starting to break up the whole tomatoes into small pieces with a spoon after about 10 minutes.

3. Stir in the heavy cream and cook for 8 minutes longer. Add the parmesan and fresh basil and cook for another minute until combined. Add the penne pasta and toss with the sauce until well combined. Cook for another minute. Serve warm. **Serves 4.**

there's always room for

DESSERTS

Chocolate Toffee Torte

½ CUP PLUS 2 TBSP. (5 oz.) trans-fat-free margarine

1 BAR (3.5 oz.) bittersweet chocolate (I use Rosemarie)

1 CUP sugar

⅓ CUP honey

½ TSP. salt

¼ CUP all-purpose flour

1 TSP. vanilla extract

3 eggs

1 9-inch graham cracker pie crust

8 OZ. (1 cup) non-dairy whip topping

GARNISH

• Store-bought berry sauce

• Cocoa powder (optional)

THE **DESSERT** *chapter in this book is dedicated to Esty, who doesn't possess a single sweet tooth and prefers spicy foods. There are nearly fifty-five reasons (recipes) loaded with unabashed decadence in this chapter to convince her otherwise.*

After Esty tasted this sumptuous dessert at Batsheva's Friday night meal, she informed me that it was absolutely necessary to include the recipe in my book. Of course, I promptly tested the recipe and complied. Finally, a dessert that awakened Esty's sweet tooth!

There's a lot more than meets the eye in this torte. It isn't the most photogenic of desserts, but its taste more than makes up for its lack of aesthetics (though a garnish of store-bought berry sauce and whipped cream certainly enhances its appeal). Everyone who tasted this dessert finished it until the very last gooey chocolatey drop, including my yoga instructor, Jodi, who kept murmuring, "This is heaven!" in between each bite.

dairy option: *Substitute butter for the margarine.*

1. Preheat the oven to 350° F. Over a double boiler, melt the margarine with the chocolate, stirring constantly. Remove from the heat and allow to cool for several minutes.

2. Pour the chocolate-margarine mixture into a mixing bowl. Add the sugar, honey, salt, flour, vanilla, and eggs and beat with a hand mixer, beat until evenly combined, about 1 minute. Pour the batter into the graham cracker pie crust and bake for 30 minutes. Do not overbake. Allow to cool for 20 minutes. Freeze the pie for at least 8 hours.

3. In the bowl of an electric mixer, beat the whip topping until peaks form. Refrigerate until ready to serve.

4. To serve, remove the pie from the freezer and slice. Allow the slices to thaw for 5 minutes and serve immediately with a generous dollop of whip topping. If desired, dust the whip topping with cocoa powder and serve berry sauce on the side. **Serves 8.**

Warm Cinnamon Buns with Flambéed Rum Bananas

4 store-bought large cinnamon buns or 8 small cinnamon buns

• Store-bought vanilla ice cream

BANANA RUM SAUCE

6 Tbsp. trans-fat-free margarine

⅞ cup sugar

½ cup orange juice

4 Tbsp. rum (not rum extract)

2 firm, barely ripe bananas, sliced

• Pecans (optional)

SOMETHING MAGICAL *happens to bananas when they're combined with the right ingredients. Flambé means to heat rum or brandy with food. When that food is bananas, you'll agree that it can indeed be magical.*

I've tried many banana flambé recipes with less than thrilling results. Either the rum taste was overpowering or the sauce would harden. So...after much playing around, I finally hit the jackpot with orange juice. The orange juice adds balance to the rum and doesn't allow the sauce to harden.

In this recipe, a subtle amount of rum and orange juice are heated and added to sliced fresh bananas. This is the only preparation required here: the banana rum sauce is served over store-bought ice cream and your favorite store-bought cinnamon buns. You can use mini buns if you prefer to serve smaller portions or if you're serving more than one dessert. The sauce is also amazing spooned over French toast or crepes.

note: *If you are serving this dessert on Friday night, keep the sauce warm (not hot) and place the banana slices in the rum sauce 10 minutes before serving. If you are adding pecans to the recipe, stir them into sauce just before serving.*

1. Preheat the oven to 350° F. In a baking pan, warm the cinnamon buns, covered, in the oven for 15–20 minutes. Keep them tightly covered so they don't dry out or get crispy.

2. To prepare the banana rum sauce: In a saucepan, melt the margarine with the sugar over medium–high heat, stirring constantly, until the mixture starts to bubble, about 1 minute. Add the orange juice and rum. Cook, stirring constantly, until the mixture is bubbling and slightly thickened, about 1 minute. Remove from the heat and let sit until the bubbling subsides. Stir in the banana slices and, if desired, the pecans.

3. To serve, place a warm cinnamon bun on a plate. Top the bun with a scoop of ice cream. Spoon the banana rum sauce over the ice cream. Serve the sauce warm. **Serves 4–8.**

Chocolate French Macarons with Caramel Cream

1⅓ CUPS confectioners' sugar

1 CUP ground almonds (about 6 oz. sliced almonds, pulverized)

4 TBSP. unsweetened, Dutch-process cocoa powder

PINCH salt

3 large egg whites, at room temperature

PINCH cream of tartar

¼ CUP sugar

CARAMEL CREAM FILLING

4 OZ. (½ cup) non-dairy whip topping

2 TSP. light corn syrup

1 TBSP. trans-fat-free margarine

FRENCH MACARONS *have been sweeping the pastry scene in a variety of hues. These ethereal mini macarons don't contain any food coloring, so you can serve them to your children guilt-free. To save time, buy ready-made cream in a variety of flavors. For a playful twist, substitute the filling with sorbet and serve immediately.*

alternatives:
- *To make a chocolate filling, add 4 ounces of finely chopped semisweet chocolate to the caramel cream when heating.*
- *For vanilla macarons, replace the cocoa powder in the batter with 4 tablespoons of confectioners' sugar.*
- *For coffee macarons, add 1 tablespoon of instant coffee to the food processor before processing the dry ingredients for the cookie batter.*

1. Preheat the oven to 350° F. Line 2 baking sheets with parchment paper. In a food processor, combine the confectioners' sugar, ground almonds, cocoa, and salt and pulse for 30 seconds until smooth.

2. In the bowl of an electric mixer, beat the egg whites on medium speed until foamy. Add the cream of tartar and beat until stiff peaks form. Gradually add the sugar and beat on high speed until the mixture is very stiff, about 6–7 minutes.

3. With a spatula, gently fold the confectioners' sugar, almond, and cocoa mixture into the egg whites, adding the mixture in several batches. Do not overwork the batter. When the batter is smooth and shiny and no traces of egg whites remain, scrape the batter into a pastry bag with a plain ½-inch tip.

4. Pipe 1 tablespoon of the batter onto a prepared baking sheet, forming a 1- to 1½-inch diameter disk. Continue to pipe disks onto the baking sheets, leaving at least 1½ inches between them. Let stand at room temperature for 12 minutes to allow the batter to dry. Bake for 15–17 minutes, rotating the sheet once for even baking. Allow to cool for several minutes at room temperature, then remove the macarons from the baking sheet and allow to cool completely on a wire rack.

5. To prepare the caramel cream: In a saucepan, bring the whip topping to a boil over high heat. Stir in the corn syrup and margarine until smooth. Remove from the heat and refrigerate until the sauce has thickened to a spreadable consistency, 10–15 minutes.

6. To assemble the macarons, spread the caramel filling onto the flat side of a macaron and top with a second macaron, flat-side down, pressing slightly so that the filling spreads to the edges. Continue until all the macarons are filled. **Yields 16 macarons.**

Sorbet and Ice Cream Sandwich Trifle

1 **PINT** mango sorbet, melted

6 mini vanilla-flavored ice cream sandwiches
(I like Tofutti Cuties)

1 **PINT** berry or strawberry sorbet, melted

THIS DESSERT *is so easy to prepare. All the ingredients are store bought, and all you have to do is assemble the layers to create a stunning effect.*

It's a good idea to line the loaf pan with plastic wrap so that it will be easier to remove the entire trifle with one swift motion. Although the ice cream sandwiches are placed frozen in the pan, you still need to freeze the ice cream sandwich layer until it is solid—this will prevent the top sorbet layer from dripping into the crevices of the ice cream sandwich layer.

1. Line a 3-pound loaf pan with plastic wrap so that the plastic wrap hangs over the sides of the pan. Spread the mango sorbet onto the bottom of the loaf pan. Freeze until very firm.

2. Arrange the 6 ice cream sandwiches on the mango sorbet layer in three rows of two, with the narrower side of the ice cream sandwich facing the narrow side of the pan. Make sure there is no space at either end of the pan, so don't arrange the ice cream sandwiches too tightly packed. Freeze until very firm.

3. Spread the berry or strawberry sorbet over the ice cream sandwich layer. Freeze until firm. Holding the edges of the plastic wrap on both sides, pull out the entire trifle from the pan. Slice and serve immediately. **Serves 8.**

Pretzel-Crusted Lemon Lime Pie

PRETZEL CRUST

½ CUP sugar

4 CUPS salted mini pretzels

12 TBSP. trans-fat-free margarine, melted

TOPPING

16 OZ. (2 cups) non-dairy whip topping

1 CAN (21 oz.) lemon pie filling

8 OZ. (1 cup) marshmallow fluff

1 TBSP. lime juice

• Lemon or lime peel or zest, to garnish

• Pretzels, to garnish

COMPRISED OF *a slightly salty and crispy crust topped with a mass of lemony lusciousness, each bite of this dessert delivers a flawless combination of tart and sweet. The synergy of the saltiness of the pretzels and the sweetness of the citrus is simply spectacular.*

This dessert is not only for lemon lovers—it's a no-fail recipe with a shortcut option that's great when you're pressed for time. Served in a prepared pie crust, the lemon topping still maintains the same creamy loveliness. You may have some leftover lemon filling, but it's so good, you won't mind at all. The filling will stay fresh in the freezer for several weeks.

even simpler: Skip the pretzel crust preparation and fill 2 graham cracker pie crusts instead.

dairy option: Substitute the margarine for butter and the non-dairy whip topping for heavy cream.

1. To prepare the crust: In a food processor, combine the sugar and pretzels and process until the pretzels are finely crushed with some small pieces remaining. Add the melted margarine and process until crumbly. Press the crumbs evenly onto the bottom and sides of a 9-inch Pyrex pie plate. Set aside.

2. To prepare the filling: In the bowl of an electric mixer, whip the non-dairy whip topping until very firm peaks form. Add the lemon pie filling, marshmallow fluff, and lime juice. Beat for several minutes until the ingredients are evenly incorporated and the mixture becomes firm. Pour the filling into the pretzel crust. Cover and freeze overnight. Before serving, garnish with your choice of lemon or lime peel, zest, or pretzels. **Serves 8.**

Pomegranate Strawberry Mocktail with Sorbet

2 CUPS pure pomegranate juice

2 CUPS (1 16-oz. box) strawberries

5 TBSP. honey

30 large mint leaves, plus extra to garnish

½ CUP ice

• Store-bought coconut sorbet (I use Sharon's brand)

18–24 extra-large cinnamon sticks

A BEAUTIFULLY *crafted dessert that's perfect for serving to large crowds, this recipe requires very little preparation time but it is fabulously elegant. This drink is also popular with kids—and healthy!*

The thirty mint leaves in the recipe may seem like a lot, but that's what makes this drink so crisp and aromatic.

The inspiration for this presentation comes from chef Aviv Mosovich. The purpose of the cinnamon sticks is twofold: they're pretty, and they act as a support for the sorbet.

1. In a food processor, puree the juice, strawberries, honey, mint, and ice. Refrigerate until ready to serve.

2. To serve, pour the drink into wine glasses, filling them halfway. Place three large cinnamon sticks in each glass, spreading them out around the sides. Place a scoop of coconut sorbet in the center of each wine glass so that it is cradled by the cinnamon sticks. Garnish with a mint leaf. **Serves 6–8.**

Orange Mousse in Phyllo Baskets with Citrus Punchsietta

1 PKG. phyllo dough
(extra-fine sheets)

ORANGE MOUSSE

¾ CUP sugar

4 egg yolks

1 TBSP. orange zest

2 TBSP. cornstarch

8 OZ. (1 cup) non-dairy whip topping

½ CUP fresh orange juice

CITRUS PUNCHSIETTA

• Orange juice

SPLASH lime juice

SPLASH lemon juice

• Rum

OPTIONAL GARNISH

• Clementines, thinly sliced

• Sugar

MY **KITCHEN** *houses many of the books in my cookbook collection. On the second-to-lowest shelf is one of my many Martha Stewart Living cookbooks with a photo of Martha on the spine. When my daughter was a baby, she used to point to the photo and exclaim, "Look, that's Bubby!"*

The similarities don't end there. My mother is quite the domestic diva herself. This exquisite recipe and presentation is one of her signature desserts. It's elegant and refined, and the taste is deliciously delicate.

dairy option: *Substitute the non-dairy whip topping with heavy cream.*

1. To prepare the phyllo baskets: Preheat the oven to 400° F. Cut the sheets of phyllo dough into 4-inch squares (you may cut through a few sheets at a time).

2. On a flat surface, spray a square of phyllo dough with nonstick cooking spray. Place a second square of phyllo dough on top of the first to form a star shape (you should be able to see all 8 corners of the two squares). Spray the second square with the nonstick cooking spray. Add a third square at the same angle as the first. Spray. Add a fourth square at the same angle as the second. Spray. Each phyllo basket will be 4 sheets thick.

3. Spray a muffin tin or round ramekins with the nonstick cooking spray. Cup the phyllo star loosely in your hand to form a 4-inch round shape and gently press it onto the muffin tin or ramekin. Repeat with the remaining squares of phyllo dough. Bake until lightly browned, 7–8 minutes. Remove from the oven and allow to cool. Cover and let stand at room temperature until ready to serve.

4. To prepare the mousse: In the bowl of an electric mixer, beat the sugar and egg yolks. Beat in the orange zest and cornstarch. Remove the mixture from the bowl and set aside.

5. In the bowl of the mixer, whip the non-dairy whip topping until stiff peaks form. Add the orange juice and beat for 30 seconds. Beat in the egg yolk and sugar mixture for several minutes until evenly incorporated. Refrigerate the mousse in an airtight container until ready to serve.

6. To prepare the punchsietta: Combine all the punchsietta ingredients and pour into shot glasses or mini stemware.

7. To prepare the optional baked clementine slices: Coat both sides of the clementine slices with sugar. Bake, uncovered, at 350° F until golden, about 10–15 minutes. Allow to dry on parchment paper for 15 minutes before serving.

8. To serve, spoon the mousse into the phyllo baskets, garnish with a clementine slice, and serve the punchsietta on the side. **Serves 6.**

Plum Torte

THIS PLUM *torte recipe will re-place all your others. It's adapted from Marian Burros's famous plum torte recipe that was printed in the New York Times every year for nearly twenty years in response to readers' demands. The last time the New York Times printed this recipe, they advised their readers to laminate it. It's now the most requested recipe in the New York Times' archives, and there are countless blogs praising its merits.*

Because this torte boasts a delicate cake batter, I've reduced the amount of plums. I prefer to get more cake than plums per bite. Fresh apricots, blueberries, apples, and even cherries also work well in this recipe.

¾ CUP sugar

4 OZ. (½ cup) trans-fat-free margarine or butter

1 CUP all-purpose flour

1 TSP. baking powder

2 eggs

6–8 dinosaur plums, cut into eighths

1 TSP. cinnamon

1 TSP. sugar

1. Preheat the oven to 350° F. Generously spray an 8- or 9-inch springform torte pan with nonstick flour-and-oil combination baking spray.

2. In the bowl of an electric mixer, or with a hand mixer, cream the sugar and margarine. Beat in the flour, baking powder, and eggs.

3. Arrange the dinosaur plums on the bottom of the torte pan in a single layer. Pour the batter over the plums, and sprinkle with the cinnamon and sugar. Bake for 1 hour. Allow to cool before serving. **Serves 8.**

Bavarian Strawberries 'n' Cream Napoleon

THE EXTRAORDINARY *thing about this dessert is that it looks impressive, but it's so easy to prepare. You'll notice that the dough squares puff up considerably, but they'll be cut in half before the dessert is assembled.*

There are many varieties of store-bought cream fillings available. My personal favorites are the Bavarian cream sold at the Peppermill and the custard from Baker's Choice.

15 frozen puff pastry squares

2 CUPS store-bought Bavarian cream or custard

3 PINTS (3 16-oz. boxes) fresh strawberries, sliced

• Confectioners' sugar, for dusting

1. Preheat the oven to 350° F. On a nongreased baking sheet, bake the puff pastry squares until golden brown and puffed, at least 30 minutes. Allow to cool.

2. To assemble the napoleons: Cut the puff pastry squares in half horizontally (separating the tops and bottoms). Place 1 of the cut puff pastry squares on a plate. Top with cream or custard and sliced strawberries. Add a second layer of puff pastry square, cream, and sliced strawberries, and top with a third puff pastry square. Dust the top of each napoleon with confectioners' sugar. **Serves 10.**

THE ART OF GIVING

Purim Inspirations

page 283

THE ARCHITECT
{ Truffles }

Vertically stacked boxes create a dramatic look and visual interest. Nestle color-coordinated truffles, candy, scented tea lights, and potpourri inside gift boxes. Stack on top of an 8x10-inch picture frame or mirrored charger plate and tie with a ribbon.

page 282

THE MINIMALIST
{ Toffee Brittle }

Sometimes less is more. Pair deliciousness with simplicity with just a few ingredients and very little preparation time to create the perfect toffee brittle. A single bite of toffee crunch delivers delectable taste and texture that will delight its recipients.

page 284

THE FASHIONISTA
{ Dark Chocolate Cupcakes }

A good chocolate cake recipe is a timeless classic and an open canvas for your imagination. Transform it into cupcakes that are fabulous and chic by adorning them with edible pearls and French dragees. Cupcakes have always charmed children—these will delight both children and adults.

DELICATE
Toffee Brittle

LUXURIOUS *Truffles*

DRAMATIC *Chocolate Cupcakes*

Toffee Brittle

TOFFEE **BRITTLE** *is a fun and easy confection to make. It's an inspired union of creamy chocolate and crunchy nuts, and you can't eat just one. The smaller pieces are also delicious served on ice cream.*

After experimenting with many toffee recipes, I learned the following about making a successful brittle: it's super easy, but the proper technique is essential. A candy thermometer is a must; the first time I made brittle, I thought I could get away with using my meat thermometer. But I thought wrong. I also learned that spreading the toffee layer superthin gives you a more delicate, tastier, and crunchier brittle.

The only way to prevent the chocolate and toffee layers from separating is to absorb all the excess grease from the toffee layer before spreading the chocolate on top. Just pat the surface of the toffee with a paper towel, and the chocolate will be able to adhere to the toffee layer.

This recipe was adapted from a recipe in Food & Wine Magazine. The original recipe called for butter—which you can certainly use if you choose to make it dairy. It also called for chocolate chips, which I've substituted for chopped pareve chocolate. When using pareve chocolate, I prefer to use good-quality baking chocolate like Scharffen Berger. A full line of Scharffen Berger chocolate is available at the Kitchen Clique.

note: The toffee brittle will stay fresh in the refrigerator in an airtight container for up to ten days.

16 OZ. (2 cups) trans-fat-free margarine

2 CUPS sugar

½ TSP. kosher salt

2½ CUPS toasted nuts (any combination of pistachios, peanuts, almonds, hazelnuts, etc.), finely chopped

2 CUPS baking chocolate, finely chopped

• Coarse sea salt, for sprinkling

1. Grease or spray two 9x13-inch foil pans or baking sheets with nonstick cooking spray. In a heavy saucepan, melt the margarine, sugar, and salt, whisking until smooth. Bring the mixture to a boil over medium–high heat. Boil for 8 minutes, stirring occasionally, and then for 5–8 minutes longer, stirring constantly, until the mixture is an amber color and a candy thermometer registers 300° F when inserted in the center. (Watch the toffee mixture carefully during the last few minutes and stir constantly to prevent it from burning.) Immediately stir in 2 cups of the chopped nuts.

2. Carefully pour the hot toffee into the center of the foil pans or baking sheets. With a spatula, spread the toffee into a thin, flat layer. Allow the toffee to cool for 1 minute, then pat the surface with a paper towel to soak up any excess grease. Sprinkle the chopped chocolate over the top of the toffee. Let the chocolate melt for about 4 minutes, then spread the chocolate evenly over the toffee with a spatula.

3. Allow the toffee brittle to cool for 10 minutes. Sprinkle with the coarse sea salt and the remaining ½ cup of chopped nuts. Freeze the toffee until the chocolate firms up, about 30 minutes. Remove from the freezer and break up into the desired-size pieces. **Serves 8.**

Praline Truffles

1 BAR (15 oz.) pareve baking chocolate

1 CAN (11 oz.) Baker's Choice praline paste

1 TBSP. rum, amaretto, or coffee dissolved in several drops of boiling water

DECORATIONS AND COATINGS

- Ready-made fondant flowers or ready-made icing (I use Wilton's)

- Baker's Choice almond (or other nut flavor) crunch

- Colored sugar

- Confectioners' sugar

1. In the top of a double boiler, melt the chocolate. Add the praline paste and mix gently until melted and evenly incorporated. Remove from the heat. Stir in either the rum, amaretto, or dissolved coffee. Pour into molds or mini cups, or place in the refrigerator to harden for making truffle balls.

2. If using molds or mini cups, place the filled molds or mini cups in the freezer until the truffles are hardened, about 20 minutes. Remove from the freezer and decorate the tops with ready-made fondant flowers or use the ready-made icing to decorate with flowers, leaves, stars, etc. Allow the icing to harden, then transfer to an airtight container. Refrigerate until ready to package or serve. Serve at room temperature.

3. To prepare truffle balls: Refrigerate the truffle mixture until the chocolate is firm yet pliable, about 30 minutes. Line a baking sheet with waxed paper. With a small melon baller, drop small rounded balls of the truffle mixture onto the prepared baking sheet. You may need to roll them slightly between your palms to achieve a perfect round shape. Roll the truffle balls in chopped nuts, colored sugar, or confectioners' sugar to coat. Freeze until firm, about 20 minutes, then store in an airtight container. Refrigerate until ready to package or serve. **Yields 25 large or 50 small truffles.**

Dark Chocolate Cupcakes with Espresso Frosting

DARK, **RICH,** *and moist is how a good chocolate cake should be. I know I can trust this chocolate cake recipe—given to me by Michelle, who loves baking easy, fabulous cakes—to meet these requirements.*

This recipe is a one-bowl cake and is likely to become a favorite staple in your home. Using coconut milk instead of water adds an extra measure of richness. And because of my love of cinnamon, I tend to get heavy-handed with this spice and add it to most of my cakes. It's optional in this recipe, but do give it a try. For a touch of sophistication and fragrant appeal, add several dashes of nutmeg to the batter.

I prefer to use Noblesse chocolate for this frosting recipe. It has a firmer texture than other chocolates, which gives the frosting more body. For a variation, doesn't peanut butter frosting sound incredible? If it sounds good to you, frost the cupcakes with the Peanut Butter Mousse from page 328 instead of the espresso frosting.

note: *If you are making a dark chocolate Bundt cake instead of cupcakes, see page 312 for the glaze recipe.*

1½ CUPS oil

1⅞ CUPS sugar

3 eggs

¾ CUP coconut milk

¾ CUP orange juice

1½ TSP. vanilla extract

2¼ CUPS all-purpose flour

9 TBSP. cocoa powder

1 TSP. baking powder

1½ TSP. baking soda

½ TSP. cinnamon (optional)

PINCH salt

ESPRESSO FROSTING

8 OZ. (1 cup) trans-fat-free margarine

1 TBSP. coconut milk

7 OZ. (2 bars) 55% cocoa Noblesse bittersweet chocolate, melted

1 TSP. vanilla extract

1½ CUPS confectioners' sugar

1–2 TSP. espresso powder, dissolved in several drops of boiling water

1. Preheat the oven to 350° F. Place cupcake foils in a muffin tin. Spray the top of the tin with nonstick flour-and-oil combination baking spray to prevent the cupcakes from sticking to the tin, or for a large Bundt cake, spray a Bundt pan with the nonstick spray.

2. In the large bowl of an electric mixer, or with a hand mixer, cream the oil and sugar. Add the eggs, coconut milk, orange juice, and vanilla and beat on medium speed for 2 minutes. Add the flour, cocoa, baking powder, baking soda, cinnamon, and salt and beat for an additional 2 minutes.

3. Fill the cupcake foils three-quarters full (the batter will rise substantially) or pour the batter into the Bundt pan. Bake until a toothpick inserted in the center comes out clean, 25 minutes for the cupcakes or 1 hour for the Bundt cake. Do not overbake. Cool in the pan for 10 minutes, then remove to a wire rack to cool completely. **Yields 1 Bundt cake or 24 cupcakes.**

4. To prepare the espresso frosting: In the bowl of an electric mixer, beat the margarine and coconut milk until creamy. Beat in the melted chocolate. Add the vanilla extract, confectioners' sugar, and dissolved espresso and beat until creamy. Pipe or spread frosting on top of each cupcake. **Yields icing for 24 cupcakes.**

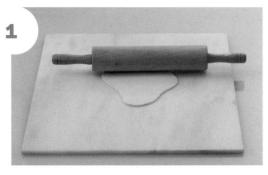

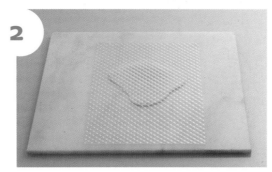

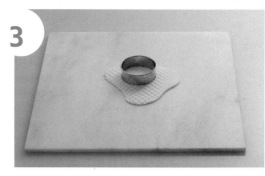

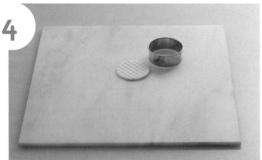

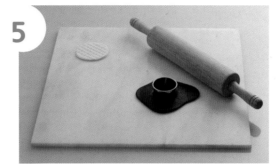

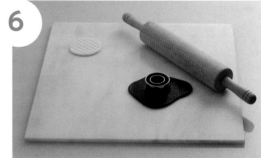

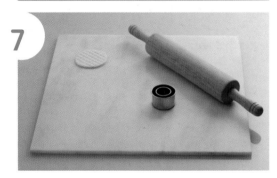

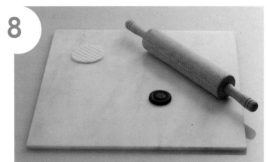

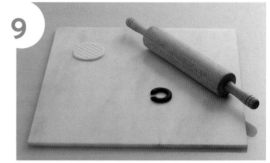

Quilted Fondant for Cupcakes

WHEN I *spotted the quilted mold used for these cupcakes at the Peppermill, I had the flash of inspiration that produced these deceivingly intricate cupcakes. Even if you've never worked with fondant, you will find it super simple to make these quilted fondant cupcake tops, especially since you don't have to drape the sides. I bought some ready-made fondant and broke the rules: to make it pliable, fondant is kneaded like you would knead dough; instead, I placed it in the microwave for just ten seconds. The texture was perfect, and it was easy to roll out. Always keep fondant tightly covered with plastic wrap since it dries out quickly. To get the fondant to adhere to the cupcake, spread a thin layer of icing on top of the cupcake before adding the fondant.*

TO MAKE THE QUILTED CUPCAKE TOPS YOU WILL NEED:

- A quilted mold
- Rolling pin
- Store-bought black or dark brown fondant
- Store-bought white fondant
- Round molds in various sizes

Nectarine and Plum Crostata

CROSTATA IS *an Italian baked pie or tart. It is known to the French as a "galette." These tarts can be sweet or savory and consist of either fresh fruits or vegetables encased in a delicate crust. The free-form nature of the dough will add a rustic charm to any meal, be it casual or elegant.*

Use the season's best produce as your muse. Most fruits work well for this pie and can easily be tucked into the rich, buttery crust. If you're serving this pie at a formal meal, you can add red currants and a bunch of fresh berries as a garnish.

This recipe is simple to make. There is no need to peel the fruit, and it doesn't require any special pans or equipment. You can prepare the dough up to two days in advance and keep it chilled in the refrigerator. The final sprinkling of turbinado sugar over the egg-washed crust gives this flaky, buttery crust an enhanced texture.

alternative: Before baking, sprinkle the top of the crostata with the nutmeg struesel topping from page 352.

CRUST

2 CUPS all-purpose flour

¼ TSP. salt

3 TBSP. sugar

14 TBSP. trans-fat-free margarine, cut into ½-inch cubes

2–4 TBSP. ice water (or more as needed)

¼ CUP apricot preserves

¼ CUP ground almonds

1 egg, beaten

12 TBSP. turbinado sugar, for sprinkling

FRUIT FILLING

4 nectarines, sliced

3 plums, sliced

⅓ CUP PLUS 2 TBSP. sugar

1 TSP. grated lemon zest

1 TBSP. all-purpose flour

½ TSP. cinnamon

GARNISH

- Red currants, mint leaves, and fresh berries, to garnish

---

1. To prepare the crust: blend the flour, salt, and sugar in a food processor. Add the margarine and blend, pulsing, until the mixture is crumbly. Slowly add 2 tablespoons of ice water and mix just until the dough begins to stick together. If needed, add more ice water, about 2–4 tablespoons. Gather the dough and wrap it in plastic wrap. Chill for 45 minutes.

2. Remove the dough from the refrigerator and allow it to soften slightly at room temperature. Transfer the dough to parchment paper and roll out the dough until it is 14 inches in diameter. Transfer the dough with the parchment paper onto a baking sheet. Chill for 10 minutes.

3. In the meantime, prepare the filling: In a medium bowl, toss the nectarine and plum slices with the sugar, lemon zest, flour, and cinnamon.

4. Preheat the oven to 375° F. Spread the apricot preserves and ground almonds over the center of the chilled dough, leaving a 3-4 inch border. Arrange the fruit slices in concentric circles on top of the preserves and ground almonds, so that they are overlapping a bit. Using a spatula to help you, fold the plain crust border over the fruit slices, pleating it to make a circle and pinching to seal any cracks in the dough.

5. Brush the top of the crust with the beaten egg. Sprinkle the crust and fruit center with the turbinado sugar. Transfer the crostata, together with the parchment paper, to a baking sheet. Bake until the crust is golden and the fruit filling is bubbling, 45–50 minutes. Remove from the oven.

6. Slide a long, thin spatula between the parchment paper and the crostata and transfer the crostata to a cooling rack. Allow to cool for at least 20 minutes. Cut into wedges and serve warm or at room temperature, garnished with the red currants, mint leaves, and fresh berries. **Serves 6-8.**

Moscato d'Asti Apricot Compote

20 apricots or small plums, halved and pitted

2 CUPS Moscato d'Asti

2 CUPS water

6–8 TBSP. honey

1 lemon, juiced and zested

1 cinnamon stick

1 sprig thyme (optional)

OPTIONAL GARNISHES

- Whipped cream
- Sugar-coated thyme
- Lemon zest strips
- Cinnamon sticks

INITIALLY I *considered including here my mother's recipe for plum compote, which is a permanent staple in my parents' home. But as many times as I (and others) have tried, it never comes out quite as good as when my mother makes it. So this foolproof recipe has taken its place instead.*

No special touch is needed here. The plums or apricots are steeped in Moscato d'Asti, adding a celebratory touch. This soft, rich compote with its aromatic syrup is also extremely easy to make. You don't even have to peel the fruits. If you are using plums for this recipe, you can reduce the honey since they are naturally less tart than apricots.

note: To coat the rim of a glass with sugar, place a folded wet paper towel on a plate. Turn the glass upside down and press onto the wet paper towel, then immediately press the glass upside down in a bowl of sugar and twist to coat the rim evenly.

1. To prepare the compote: In a medium saucepan, bring all the ingredients to a boil on high heat. Immediately reduce the heat to low and simmer gently, covered, until the fruits are tender, 25 minutes. Allow to cool. Remove the cinnamon stick and thyme sprig and refrigerate.

2. To prepare the sugar-coated thyme: Dip a thyme sprig in water, then immediately coat with sugar. Allow to dry in the refrigerator for several minutes.

3. Serve the compote cold with the garnishes of your choice. **Serves 8.**

Blueberry Lemon Biscuit Pie

6 CUPS fresh blueberries

1 lemon, juiced

1 TSP. lemon zest

¾ CUP sugar

3 TBSP. all-purpose flour

BISCUIT TOPPING

1¾ CUPS all-purpose flour

4 TSP. baking powder

6 TBSP. PLUS 2 TSP. sugar

5 TBSP. trans-fat-free margarine

1 CUP coconut milk

½ TSP. cinnamon

THIS IS *a pleasing way to enjoy antioxidant-rich blueberries. Blueberry pie is a timeless favorite that always gets rave reviews, and the biscuit topping makes it easy as...well, easy as pie.*

The biscuit topping in this recipe is a thick batter that's dropped onto the fruit filling in spoonfuls so that the syrup peeks out and bubbles through the crust. You can bake this pie in a large glass oven-to-table baking dish, or, for a nice plating option, scoop individual portions into glass stemware, ramekins, or crocks.

1. In a round 9-inch Pyrex dish or rectangular 8x10-inch baking dish, toss the blueberries with the lemon juice and zest. Sprinkle with the sugar and flour. Set aside.

2. To prepare the biscuit topping: In a medium bowl, combine the flour, baking powder, and the 6 tablespoons of sugar. Add the margarine and combine until the mixture is crumbly. Make a well in the center of the dough and pour in the coconut milk. Stir quickly until the mixture is just moistened. You should have a thick, wet batter. Cover and allow the batter to stand for 15 minutes.

3. Preheat the oven to 375° F. Drop spoonfuls of the batter onto the blueberries—it's fine to leave small holes for the berries to peek through. In a small bowl, combine the cinnamon and the 2 teaspoons of sugar and sprinkle on the biscuit batter and blueberries.

4. Bake until the top is golden brown and crisp, and a toothpick or fork inserted in the center of the topping comes out clean, at least 55 minutes. Allow to cool until just warm before serving. **Serves 8.**

Fruit Tartare

1 CUP orange juice

2 TBSP. fresh lemon juice

2 TBSP. Grand Marnier, Cointreau, or other orange-flavored liqueur

2 TBSP. honey

9 kiwis, peeled and diced

2 mangos, peeled and diced

20 oz. strawberries, diced

• Fresh mint, cut chiffonade

• Store-bought raspberry sauce, to garnish

THIS FRUIT tartare contains all the essential components of a flawless recipe: healthy, quick, artfully presented, and so refreshing. Reconsidering the composition of a recipe adds drama and differentiation. Here the ingredients of a traditional fruit salad are stacked one atop the other, purely for aesthetic appeal.

It has become a habit in many cultures to serve fruit as dessert. Occasionally I also serve fruit at the start of a meal. Consuming fruits is vital to maintaining a healthy lifestyle, and when you eat them it does make a difference. In fact, Maimonides advises eating fruit at the beginning of every meal to detoxify your system.

The mint chiffonade adds a crisp flavor and cheers up the dish. The French word chiffonade means "made of rags." Chiffonade is a French method for slicing herbs into long, thin ribbons. This technique is more aesthetically appealing when sprinkling herbs like mint or parsley on your dish.

note: To chiffonade, stack and roll a pile of herbs, then slice into thin strands.

1. In a small bowl, combine the orange and lemon juices, liqueur, and honey. Divide the mixture into three equal portions. Combine one portion with the kiwis, one with the mangos, and one with the strawberries.

2. Place a round mold 3 inches wide and 1¾ inches high in the center of a plate. Spoon 4 tablespoons of diced kiwi into the bottom of the mold. Gently tap down the fruit to make sure it is evenly packed so the stack holds its shape. Repeat with a layer of diced mangos and then one of diced strawberries, tapping down until the mold is filled. Remove the mold from the fruit salad by gently lifting it straight up to keep the stack intact.

3. Transfer the mold to another plate and repeat until you have one fruit salad per person.

4. Sprinkle the mint chiffonade on top of each fruit salad, drizzle the plates with the store-bought raspberry sauce, and serve immediately. **Serves 6.**

Pareve Cheese Mousse with White Viennese Crunch

8 oz. (1 cup) non-dairy whip topping

2 CONTAINERS (8 oz. each) Tofutti cream cheese

½ CUP sugar

1 TBSP. vanilla sugar

4 eggs

1 TBSP. lemon juice

2 store-bought 9-inch chocolate pie crusts

14 PIECES white Viennese crunch, chopped

EVER SINCE *I tasted white Viennese crunch, I knew I HAD to find the perfect dessert to pair it with, one that wasn't too rich that it would be overpowering together with the crunch. Then I tasted Judy S.'s delicate cheese mousse, and a match was made. The recipe found its way into my permanent repertoire, and I'm sure you'll agree that this is a perfect pairing.*

tip: To chop the Viennese crunch, place it in a double plastic bag and chop with a meat tenderizer.

1. Preheat the oven to 350° F. In the bowl of an electric mixer, beat the whip topping until peaks form. Beat in the Tofutti cream cheese on medium speed. Gradually add the sugar and vanilla sugar, then the eggs, one at a time, and finally the lemon juice, continuing to beat on medium speed until combined.

2. Pour the mixture into the pie crusts and bake until set, about 45 minutes. Allow to cool for 5 minutes, then top with the chopped Viennese crunch. Cool completely. Refrigerate overnight before serving. **Serves 16.**

Ginger Carrot Cake with Lime Cream Cheese Frosting (Pareve)

2 CUPS carrot, finely grated

1 CUP all-purpose flour

1 CUP sugar

2 eggs

1 TSP. baking soda

½ TSP. salt

½ CUP oil

¼ TSP. ginger

1 TSP. cinnamon

FROSTING

6 OZ. (¾ of a container) Tofutti cream cheese

1 TSP. lime juice

¼ TSP. vanilla extract

¾ CUP confectioners' sugar

OPTIONAL GARNISH

- Store-bought orange sauce

1. Preheat the oven to 350° F. In the bowl of an electric mixer, combine the grated carrot, flour, sugar, eggs, baking soda, salt, oil, ginger, and cinnamon.

2. Pour the batter into a baking pan and bake until a toothpick inserted in the center comes out clean, about 1 hour and 10 minutes. Allow to cool.

3. Prepare the frosting: In the bowl of an electric mixer, beat the pareve cream cheese, lime juice, vanilla extract, and confectioners' sugar. Spread over the cake and refrigerate until set. Spread a thin layer of orange sauce on top, if desired. Serve at room temperature. **Serves 8.**

CALLING ALL *carrot pastry lovers AND cynics: meet the reincarnated carrot cake. I'm very particular about carrot cakes, and even the ones I've tasted in restaurants have proved disappointing. This cake is moist and not cloyingly sweet. The spices are subtle, and the silky crown of the pareve cream cheese frosting makes the yumminess complete.*

There are two ways you can serve this cake. The simpler way is to bake it in a 9-inch round pan and serve in slices. Or you can double the recipe, bake it in a 9x13-inch foil pan, and cut out individual servings of round cakes with a stainless-steel ring mold.

This recipe was given to me by Dini R., who serves this as a sweet side dish to accompany her main dishes.

Balsamic Grilled Peaches with Basil-Pistachio Ice Cream on Cinnamon Skewers

FOR **A** *sweet treat alfresco, you can experiment with a variety of fruit on the grill. Grilling is an art that has expanded way beyond the familiar territory of barbecued meats—everything from vegetables, pastas, breads, and cakes have become common fare on the grill.*

When choosing your fruit for this dish, go for firmer pieces and feel free to garnish with something that has a contrasting texture and temperature, such as ice cream or whipped cream. Alternatively, keep it simple and serve with just the balsamic brown sugar glaze. There's no need to prepare the ice cream from scratch—just add basil and pistachio nuts to store-bought vanilla ice cream the day before your barbecue.

GRILLED PEACHES

- 6 large ripe peaches
- 12 cinnamon sticks
- 6 TBSP. trans-fat-free margarine
- ½ CUP brown sugar
- ⅓ CUP balsamic vinegar
- ½ TSP. ground cinnamon

BASIL PISTACHIO ICE CREAM

- 10 frozen basil cubes or 10 tsp. fresh basil, minced
- ½ CUP shelled pistachio nuts
- 3 CUPS vanilla ice cream, melted
- • Gingersnaps or coconut cookies, crushed

1. To prepare the basil-pistachio ice cream: In a bowl, stir the basil and pistachio nuts into the vanilla ice cream. Freeze for 24 hours.

2. To prepare the grilled peaches: Rinse the peaches and pat dry. Cut each peach in half along the crease and discard the pit. With a metal skewer, pierce through the center of each peach half. Place a cinnamon stick through the holes in the peach halves.

3. In a saucepan over high heat, combine the margarine, brown sugar, balsamic vinegar, and cinnamon. Cook until thick and syrupy, about 4–5 minutes.

4. Heat the grill to high and oil the grate. Grill the peaches until they start to brown and soften, 3–4 minutes per side, basting the peaches with the balsamic brown sugar syrup throughout.

5. To serve, spoon the remainder of the syrup on the grilled peaches and sprinkle the crushed cookies over the center of the peach halves. Place a scoop of the ice cream on the side and serve immediately. **Serves 6.**

Five-Minute Apple Crumb Cake

WHEN I complimented S. Safrin on her delicious apple cake, she laughed and said, "Do you know how long it takes me to make that cake? Five minutes." And that's how the title for this recipe was born.

When I retested this recipe in my own kitchen, it was my very first time baking with ready-made apple pie filling. Well, I will never pass judgment on pie fillings again! And it tastes even better the next day.

alternative: Use blueberry filling or another pie filling of your choice.

1 CAN (28 oz.) apple pie filling

DOUGH

3½ CUPS all-purpose flour

3½ TSP. baking powder

1 CUP sugar

1 TSP. vanilla extract

1 TBSP. fresh lemon juice

2 eggs

1 CUP oil

1. Preheat the oven to 350° F. Combine all the dough ingredients. Divide the dough in half. Spread one half of the dough evenly over the bottom of a 10x15-inch baking sheet. Gently spread the apple pie filling over the dough layer.

2. Grate the remaining half of the dough through a hand grater and sprinkle on top of the apple pie filling. Bake until the top is crisp and golden, about 1½ hours. **Serves 10.**

Hazelnut Chocolate Mousse with Chocolate-Dipped Potato Chips

7 oz. (2 bars) good-quality bittersweet chocolate

6 large eggs

4 Tbsp. sugar

2 Tbsp. hazelnut liquor

4 oz. (½ cup) non-dairy whip topping

CHOCOLATE-DIPPED POTATO CHIPS

• Salted potato chips

10 oz. chocolate chips, melted

1. To prepare the mousse: Melt the chocolate over a double boiler. Remove from the heat. Whisk in the eggs, sugar, and hazelnut liquor. Pour the mousse into 8 mini mousse cups or 4 martini glasses. Refrigerate until the mousse sets.

2. In the bowl of an electric mixer or with a hand mixer, beat the whip topping until firm and peaks form. Add a generous dollop of cream to each mousse cup. Refrigerate until ready to serve.

3. Prepare the chocolate-dipped potato chips: Dip half of a potato chip into the melted chocolate chips. Allow to harden on a sheet of parchment paper. Garnish each mousse serving with a chocolate-dipped potato chip and serve immediately. **Serves 4–8.**

SOMETIMES THE *most important ingredient is the one you leave out. Here the margarine is left out to make an incredibly dense, extravagantly indulgent dessert. Among the few ingredients, the chocolate is clearly the star and, without the margarine, there is little added fat.*

You can serve this mousse in mini dessert cups for a perfectly portioned sweet ending or double the recipe and serve in martini glasses. The mousse is kept refrigerated—not frozen—to maintain its creamy, rich texture.

This is the quickest mousse you'll ever make—and sure to become part of your cooking repertoire.

tip: Prepare a large batch of the chocolate-dipped potato chips so you can serve a bowl heaped with these delightful chips in the center of the table, or serve extra chips on the side with the mousse.

Ice Bowls

FOR A *show-stopping dessert,
serve your choice of ice cream,
sorbet, or sherbet—or portions of all
three—in an ice bowl. Ice bowls are
perfect for entertaining a small in-
timate group (realistically, who has
time to make that many ice bowls?).
The addition of a mint leaf and a
store-bought flaky dough cookie twist
completes this fabulous look.*

*Along with baking and cooking
with your children, you can now add
arts and crafts to your kitchen agenda.
Have your children help you prepare
these ice bowls—they'll be enthusi-
astic about the project and enjoy see-
ing the results (adapted from Martha
Stewart).*

*tip: Take the cartons out of the bowls
in advance, running the ice bowls under
cold water if you need help to release
the cartons. Return the ice bowls to the
freezer until ready to serve. This will
save you time when you are busy entertaining.*

1. Rinse four empty half-gallon cartons and four 1-quart cartons. Cut the tops off the half-gallon cartons, 5 inches up from the base. Cut the tops off the 1-quart cartons, 3 inches up from the base.

2. Place the smaller cartons in the center of the larger cartons. Keeping the top edges of both cartons flush, pierce each pair of cartons through both sides with a metal skewer (the metal will make piercing the car-tons easier), no more than 1 inch from the top. Remove the metal skewer and insert a wooden skewer through the holes.

3. Pour water into the space between the two cartons until the water level is just below the skewer. Freeze for at least 2 days. Remove the cartons from the ice bowls, running them under cold water to help you release the bowls. Freeze until ready to serve.

4. To serve, remove the bowls from the freezer. Place a twice-folded paper towel underneath the bowls to absorb the melting water. Place 3 scoops of the desired dessert into the bowls. Garnish with a mint leaf and a store-bought flaky dough cookie twist. **Yields 4.**

YES, THAT'S A REAL STRAWBERRY! As a food stylist, there are myriad elements that must be taken into consideration to make sure that the food you see in these photographs is beautiful, believable, and multidimensional. The magical appeal, taste, and aroma that you would get from the actual dish must be translated into a single visual image. In short, I strive to make the food come alive on the page.

For this photograph, after shopping in several specialty fruit stores, I chose as many large, plump strawberries as I could find. I cleaned and rinsed them and then started the selection process. One was gorgeous, but it was too perfect and wouldn't look authentic: all the seeds were a uniform yellow color. Others were either too short, asymmetrical, or not vibrant enough. Notice how this strawberry has a variety of seed colors? This was the hero. Photogenic enough to be photographed, yet authentic enough to entice and convince you it's real.

Needless to say, you won't have to worry about your strawberries, salmon fillet, or slice of pie looking perfect. Food that's presented in real life is a lot more forgiving than the camera lens. The camera doesn't lie and every detail is magnified. And you get to eat your creation immediately, without worrying that it will melt, wilt, or oxidize under harsh studio lighting.

The recipe for this charming little morsel of Basil Granita is on page 318.

Crepes Suzette

CHEF MARK GREEN *from Glatt a la Carte has created a menu of vibrant fusions and flavors that will keep the customers coming back for more. These crepes are one of his specialties.*

alternative: Fill the crepes with store-bought spreadable chocolate and drizzle with caramel sauce, chocolate syrup, and chopped nuts. Serve with ice cream on the side.

CREPES

1 large egg

1 TBSP. sugar

16 OZ. (2 cups) non-dairy whip topping

¼ TSP. vanilla extract

2 CUPS all-purpose flour

ORANGE SAUCE

½ CUP fresh orange juice

4 TBSP. light corn syrup

⅔ CUP confectioners' sugar

2 oranges, zested

GARNISHES

• Confectioners' sugar

• Orange segments

• Ice cream

• Blueberries

1. To prepare the crepes: In a large mixing bowl, with a hand mixer, beat the egg until frothy. Add the sugar and beat until evenly incorporated. Beat in the whip topping and vanilla. Slowly add the flour and continue to beat until you achieve a light ribbon effect

2. Spray a skillet with nonstick cooking spray and heat over low heat. When the pan is hot, pour about ¼ cup of the batter into the skillet. Tilt the pan in a circular motion so that the batter coats the surface of the skillet evenly. Fry until lightly golden, 1–2 minutes per side.

3. To prepare the orange sauce: In a saucepan over medium–high heat, combine the orange juice, corn syrup, and confectioners' sugar. Cook until the sauce is reduced by half, 3–4 minutes. Stir in the orange zest and remove from the heat.

4. To serve, fold a crepe in half to form a semicircle, then fold in half again to form a triangle. Arrange three folded crepes on a plate and spoon a generous amount of orange sauce over them. Dust with confectioners' sugar, place orange segments on top, and add a scoop of your choice of ice cream and blueberries on the side. Serve while the crepes and sauce are warm. **Serves 8.**

Warm Chocolate Soufflé with a Hint of Chili

8 oz. (1 cup) trans-fat-free margarine

7 oz. (2 bars) good-quality bittersweet chocolate (I use Rosemarie)

5 eggs

1 egg yolk

1 CUP sugar

⅛ TSP. chili powder

2 TBSP. all-purpose flour

PINCH salt

- Confectioners' sugar, for dusting

GARNISHES

- Ice cream
- Berries

I **LOVE UNIQUE** recipes, but I draw the line at recipes that seem too gimmicky. So if you're thinking, "Really? Chili in a chocolate soufflé cake?" I must tell you this recipe is no gimmick. It may seem counterintuitive, but the chili adds an unexpected depth of flavor, creating an aura of mystery that your taste buds try to decipher. Still, if you're not convinced about the chili, by all means leave it out. It would be a shame to deprive yourself of such goodness.

What makes this soufflé a huge success is that the batter is allowed to sit in the refrigerator for at least 3 hours, allowing the eggs to deflate. This method yields a denser, gooier soufflé.

For some reason, soufflés have earned the reputation of being hard to prepare. Don't believe the rumors! Chocoholics beware—soufflé doesn't get any easier or more delicious than this.

dairy option: Substitute butter for the margarine.

1. In a double boiler, melt the margarine and chocolate over medium heat. In the bowl of an electric mixer, or with a hand mixer, beat the eggs, egg yolk, and sugar. Add the melted chocolate to the egg mixture, then beat in the chili, flour, and salt. Refrigerate for 3–8 hours.

2. Remove the soufflé mixture from the refrigerator 30 minutes before baking and let stand at room temperature. Preheat the oven to 450° F. Spray 8 ramekins with nonstick cooking spray. Fill the ramekins with the soufflé mixture and bake until a crust forms on top and the sides are cake-like and the center is gooey, 10–12 minutes. Remove from the oven. Dust the tops of the soufflés with the confectioners' sugar. Serve warm with ice cream and berries on the side. **Serves 8.**

Sea Salt Caramel Bundt Cake

¾ CUP caramel chips

⅞ CUP coconut milk

4 eggs

1¾ cups sugar

¾ CUP oil

1 PKG. (2.8 oz.) instant caramel pudding or instant vanilla pudding

1½ TSP. vanilla extract

1 CUP orange juice

3 TSP. baking powder

2½ CUPS all-purpose flour

⅛ TSP. sea salt

GLAZE

½ CUP brown sugar

¼ CUP orange juice

2 CUPS confectioners' sugar

1 TSP. vanilla extract

• Sea salt, for sprinkling

CAN YOU ever have enough recipes for quick one-bowl cakes? This Bundt cake recipe, and the three that follow, are easy, one-bowl Bundt cakes that are made from scratch (no cake mix!). If you are one of the many cooks who prefer cooking to baking, and avoid the precise, tedious science baking usually requires, these four recipes will quickly become part of your permanent repertoire. No need to break out your Kitchen Aid—a hand mixer works fine.

The cakes will bake equally nicely in a tube pan, but I prefer to use a 12-cup Bundt pan since it gives you pretty ridges. Not only does a Bundt cake look more inviting than a flat cake, but the hole in the center allows for even baking. To prevent your cake from sticking to the pan, spray the Bundt pan liberally with a nonstick baking spray with flour.

The sweet caramel flavors in this cake are greatly accented by the hint of sea salt. If you especially love the combination of sweet and salty, add a sprinkling of sea salt over the icing while it's still moist. And if you're serving the cake at an affair and want to up the "fancy" for this dessert, you can rename it "Fleur de Sel Caramel Cake." Although the recipe title has an avant garde ring to it, the cake is a classic all-time favorite.

1. Preheat the oven to 350° F. In a small saucepan, melt the caramel chips with the coconut milk over medium heat, stirring constantly. Allow to cool for several minutes.

2. In the bowl of an electric mixer or with a hand mixer, beat the eggs and sugar. Add the oil, caramel pudding or vanilla pudding, vanilla extract, orange juice, baking powder, flour, salt, and the melted caramel chips and coconut milk mixture. Beat for 1–2 minutes, until just well combined.

3. Spray a Bundt pan liberally with nonstick flour-and-oil combination baking spray. Pour the batter into the Bundt pan and bake for 1 hour. Do not overbake. Allow to cool for 10–15 minutes before releasing the cake from the Bundt pan. Cool the cake for at least 1 hour before glazing.

4. To prepare the glaze: In a small saucepan, heat the brown sugar and orange juice over medium heat until the sugar melts. Allow to cool for several minutes. Pour the mixture into a bowl. Add the confectioners' sugar and vanilla extract and whisk until smooth. Drizzle immediately over the cake. Sprinkle the sea salt on the icing, if desired. **Serves 10–12.**

Cointreau Mocha Cake

IF YOU *enjoy cake-mix liquor cakes, you'll love this easy, one-bowl, "from scratch" cake minus the preservatives. You can serve this cake to young children, since the alcohol evaporates during the long baking process and all that's left is the flavor of the Cointreau. If you don't have Cointreau liquor on hand, any orange-flavored or chocolate liquor will do.*

This cake boasts an icing with perfect consistency. I like it when icing is thick so that there's a stark color contrast between the cake and the glaze, giving it a prettier presentation. Many icing recipes call for oil or for too much liquid, which yields a thin icing that fades into the cake. Even adding a drop more liquid than necessary affects its success. The key is to use hot water and to immediately drizzle the icing over the cake before it hardens.

2 CUPS sugar

1 CUP oil

5 eggs

2 TBSP. coffee, dissolved in 2 Tbsp. hot water

2 TSP. vanilla extract

¾ CUP orange juice

¼ CUP Cointreau

2 CUPS all-purpose flour

2 TSP. baking powder

⅓ CUP cocoa powder

PINCH salt

GLAZE

1¼ CUPS confectioners' sugar

1 TSP. vanilla extract

2 TBSP. hot water

1. Preheat the oven to 350° F. Generously spray a 12-cup Bundt pan with nonstick flour-and-oil combination baking spray. In the bowl of an electric mixer or with a hand mixer, cream the sugar and oil. Add the eggs, one at a time, beating well after each addition. Beat in the dissolved coffee, vanilla extract, orange juice, and Cointreau. Slowly add the flour, baking powder, cocoa powder, and salt.

2. Pour the batter into the greased Bundt pan and bake for 50 minutes. Allow to cool for 10–15 minutes before releasing the cake from the pan. Transfer the cake to a wire rack and allow to cool.

3. To prepare the glaze: In a bowl, whisk all the glaze ingredients together until smooth. Immediately drizzle the icing over the cooled cake and allow to harden before slicing. **Serves 10–12.**

Chocolate Chip Blueberry Amaretto Cake

A **PINCH OF** *salt may seem insignificant, but the impact is large. Salt is the flavor catalyst that heightens and enhances sweet flavorings, so don't consider leaving it out. In fact, I often add salt to a sweet recipe of my own accord.*

When preparing this cake, the chocolate chips and blueberries are combined with the batter, but during baking they rise to the top to form a crunchy topping. A good dose of confectioners' sugar sprinkled on top of the cake will pretty it up.

As moms, we want to not only shower our children with calories, but to make every calorie worthwhile. I've therefore completely eliminated non-dairy creamer as a pareve milk option in most of my recipes, and use coconut milk instead for much healthier and just as flavorful results. The taste of the coconut milk is extremely subtle, so it works very well as a milk substitute.

note: If you choose to prepare this recipe as muffins, reserve the chocolate chips to sprinkle on top of the muffins before baking. Bake for 25 minutes.

4 eggs

2 CUPS sugar

1 CUP oil

½ CUP coconut milk

½ CUP orange juice

¼ CUP vodka

¼ CUP amaretto

2 CUPS all-purpose flour

PINCH salt

1 PKG. (3.4 oz.) instant vanilla pudding

2 TSP. baking powder

8 OZ. chocolate chips

6 OZ. blueberries

• Confectioners' sugar

1. Preheat the oven to 350° F. Generously spray a 12-cup Bundt pan with nonstick flour-and-oil combination baking spray. Use only a classic Bundt pan, not one that comes in novelty shapes like a rose or sunflower; the chocolate chips will stick to the grooves and ridges of an intricately designed Bundt pan. In the bowl of an electric mixer or with a hand mixer, cream the sugar and oil. Beat in the eggs, one at a time, then add the coconut milk, orange juice, vodka, and amaretto and beat to combine.

2. Slowly add the flour, salt, vanilla pudding, and baking powder and beat until well combined, about 1 minute. Add the chocolate chips. Fold the blueberries into the batter by hand.

3. Pour the batter into the greased Bundt pan and bake for 1 hour. Do not overbake. Allow to cool for 10–15 minutes before releasing the cake from the Bundt pan. Sprinkle the top of the cake with confectioners' sugar. **Serves 10–12.**

Fudge Marble Bundt Cake

1 CUP oil

2 CUPS sugar

6 eggs

1 TSP. pure vanilla extract

PINCH salt

1 TSP. baking powder

2 CUPS all-purpose flour

¾ CUP chocolate syrup

• Confectioners' sugar (optional)

MY FAMILY *first enjoyed this heavenly cake at Chanie L.'s house. It was my daughter who several months later reminded me to get the recipe. I'm glad she did. I've baked this easy one-bowl cake with my children many Fridays since. It's not just a breakfast cake, it's more of a breakfast-lunch-dinner cake, because by the time Shabbos morning comes around, there's hardly any left!*

note: *High-fructose corn syrup (HFCS) is found in a wide range of foods and beverages, including soda, cereal, and ketchup. HFCS is a lot more harmful than regular table sugar, and just by reading the labels, you'll know which products have it. Since HFSC is detrimental to our children's growing bodies, I use Nesquik chocolate syrup for this recipe since it doesn't contain HFSC.*

1. Preheat the oven to 350° F. In the bowl of an electric mixer or with a hand mixer, cream the oil and sugar. Add the eggs one at a time, beating after each addition, then beat in the vanilla and salt. Add the baking powder, then gradually add the flour and beat until the mixture is well combined.

2. Reserve 1 cup of the batter and pour the remainder into a liberally greased Bundt pan. Beat the reserved batter with the chocolate syrup for 30–60 seconds, then pour the chocolate syrup mixture on top of the batter already in the pan. Gently draw swirls through the batter with a table knife or skewer to create a marble effect. Don't overmix because it will lessen the marble effect.

3. Bake for 55–60 minutes. Transfer to a wire rack and cool for 10 minutes. Turn the cake out of the pan and allow to cool completely. Sprinkle with confectioners' sugar if desired. Keep the cake airtight at room temperature. **Serves 12.**

Apple Rose Custard Turnovers

1 CUP sugar

1 CUP ground walnuts

1 TBSP. cinnamon

12 puff pastry dough squares

1 egg white

1 CUP store-bought custard (I like Baker's Choice)

APPLE ROSES

10 Granny Smith apples

• Nut-flavored liquor

• Red crystal sugar

> **THE EXQUISITE** *effect of the red-tipped roses is produced by sprinkling very thin slices of apple with red sugar crystals to tint the edges red. You form the apple slices into a rose and place it in a puff pastry dough shell together with nuts, cinnamon, and custard. The red crystal sugar can be found at the Peppermill.*
>
> *Credit for this recipe goes to Rivky Eisenberg of the Viennese Table.*

1. To prepare the apple roses: Preheat the oven to 350° F. Peel the apples, cut them in half, and carefully core them. Lay them cut-side down and slice very thinly. Keeping each apple half together (don't separate the slices), transfer the halves to a cookie sheet. Brush the apple slices with nut-flavored liquor and sprinkle generously with red crystal sugar to coat the outer edges. Bake until the apples are soft and pliable, but not mushy, about 20 minutes. Allow to cool.

2. Raise the oven temperature to 400° F. In a mixing bowl, combine the sugar, ground walnuts, and cinnamon. Line muffin tins with the puff pastry squares. The squares will be a bit larger than the tins and will spread out over the top of the pan. (Depending on the size of the squares, they may overhang so much that you won't be able to bake 12 in one pan; you may have to place the pastry shells in alternating muffin cups so they don't overlap one another.)

3. Brush the squares with the egg white. Spoon a generous amount of the nut mixture into each shell, spreading over the bottoms and side. Cut squares of parchment paper and place inside the shells on top of the nut mixture. Fill the squares with pie weights or dry beans to keep the dough from puffing up. Bake until golden, 15–18 minutes. Remove the pie weights and parchment paper. Carefully remove the shells from the muffin tin and allow to cool.

4. Spoon 1 tablespoon of custard into each shell, spreading it over the nuts. Take one slice of apple and roll it as tightly as you can, keeping the pink tips at the top. This will be the center of the rose. Roll another apple slice around the center slice, and continue to wrap slice after slice of apple around the center, overlapping slightly, until the rose fits perfectly into the shell. Place the rose in the shell on top of the custard and gently spread out the top to resemble petals. The apple roses will keep fresh for up to two days in the refrigerator. Do not freeze. **Yields 12 turnovers.**

Basil Granita & Grape-Lime Granita

HAVE **YOU** *ever been wary of trying a new food item, only to discover that you're captivated by the taste? The first time I offered my family and friends basil granita, I got looks of uncertainty. But after one bite, the flavor dances on your taste buds.*

This basil granita calls for store-bought frozen basil cubes, so it takes minutes to prepare. The basil granita is delicious enough on its own, but you can serve it with other flavored granitas if you'd like to replicate the look in this photograph. I've also included a quick recipe for grape-lime granita here—no peeling of fruits required.

to prepare the zest curls: *Peel the zest from oranges, grapefruits, limes, and lemons with a potato peeler. Cut into thin rectangular strips, trimming the sides, tops, and bottoms. Wrap the zest strips tightly around a pencil and freeze for several hours until firm. Use as a garnish for granita.*

to prepare the basil granita strawberries: *Trim the tops and bottoms of several very large strawberries to make them flat and even. Scoop out the center of each strawberry and fill with basil granita. Garnish with mint leaves and serve.*

BASIL GRANITA

¾ CUP sugar

1 CUP water

1 CUP fresh lemon juice

1 TSP. lemon zest

9 frozen basil cubes

GRAPE-LIME GRANITA

1 CUP water

¾ CUP sugar

2 CUPS grape juice

1 lime, juiced and zested

1. To prepare the basil granita: In a medium saucepan, combine the sugar and water and cook over medium–high heat, stirring constantly, until the sugar has dissolved. Stir in the lemon juice and zest. Add the basil cubes and stir until they are dissolved.

2. Pour the mixture into a large pan and freeze. After 30 minutes, remove the mixture from the freezer and, using a fork, scrape the granita into flakes. Return to the freezer. Repeat every 30 minutes until there is no more liquid and all you have are fine, fluffy crystals.

3. To prepare the grape-lime granita: In a medium saucepan, heat all the ingredients until the sugar has dissolved and the ingredients are combined. Pour the mixture into a large pan and proceed with the same directions as the basil granita. **Serves 4.**

Chocolate Bundlettes with Mocha Fondue

18 Tbsp. trans-fat-free margarine

⅞ cup sugar

7 oz. (2 bars) good-quality pareve bittersweet chocolate

½ cup all-purpose flour

3 large eggs, beaten

½ cup vanilla ice cream, melted

MOCHA CREAM

7 oz. (2 bars) good-quality pareve bittersweet chocolate

8 oz. (1 cup) non-dairy whip topping

1 tsp. coffee, dissolved in several drops of hot water

½ tsp. vanilla extract

3–6 Tbsp. confectioners' sugar, to taste, plus extra for dusting

SOME **DESSERTS** are conversation pieces. This recipe is adapted from one of my favorite 8-inch round chocolate cake recipes, but instead of using water in the recipe, I replaced it with melted vanilla ice cream and reduced the amount of sugar. It was one of those fun, "let's see what happens" food experiments gone way better than expected. The ice cream makes the cake super silky, and it melts in your mouth. (You can also use this method for most cakes that call for water or juice in the ingredients. Use your favorite flavor of ice cream.)

To take the fun even further, you fill the centers with mocha cream and serve short wooden skewers of marshmallows and fruit for individual fondues. After filling the centers of the cakes, you'll notice that the chocolate starts seeping out from underneath the cakes so that they somewhat resemble deconstructed chocolate soufflés. If you prefer to keep the chocolate cream from seeping out, place a mini shot glass in the center of the mini Bundt cake and fill the glass with the mocha cream for dipping.

The mocha cream completes the fondue theme, but it's optional. These cakes are divine all by themselves, or try them served warm with ice cream.

1. Preheat the oven to 350° F. In a double boiler, melt the margarine and sugar. Add the chocolate and cook until the chocolate is melted. Stir to combine, then allow to cool.

2. In a medium bowl, beat the flour and eggs with a hand mixer for 1 minute. Add the chocolate and margarine mixture, then beat in the melted ice cream until smooth, for 1 minute.

3. Generously grease a 6-cup bundlette pan. Divide the batter equally among the 6 bundlettes and bake for 40–45 minutes. Allow to cool for 20 minutes. Gently turn out the cakes from the pan onto a flat surface.

4. To prepare the mocha cream: In a saucepan over low–medium heat, combine the chocolate, whip topping, coffee, vanilla, and confectioners' sugar, stirring constantly until the chocolate is melted and the mixture is evenly combined. Reduce the heat and keep the sauce warm over low heat.

5. Dust the cakes with confectioners' sugar. Pour the mocha cream into the center of each cake, or into a mini shot glass placed in the center of each cake, and serve warm. (You may have some mocha cream left over.) Fondue dipping ideas: Serve your mini Bundts and mocha cream sauce with your choice of kiwis, pineapple slices, bananas, pretzels, marshmallows, berries, strawberries, grapes, dried apricots, large nuts, or thick-cut potato chips for dipping into the mocha cream. **Serves 6.**

Healthy Moist Carrot-Orange Muffins

1 CUP whole wheat flour

1 CUP all-purpose flour

1 LB. (16-oz. bag) fresh carrots, finely grated

1 CUP sugar or sugar substitute

¾ CUP oil

¼ CUP fresh orange juice

1 orange, zested

4 eggs

2 TBSP. lemon juice

1 TSP. baking powder

1 TSP. baking soda

1 TSP. vanilla extract

½ TSP. cinnamon

½ TSP. salt

THESE MUFFINS *contain the sweet goodness of freshly grated carrots, unlike so many other carrot muffin recipes that call for a jar of baby food, which imparts a slight bitterness. Grating the carrots does require a bit more effort, but it's well worth it. When your children insist on ice cream or sweets for breakfast, these carrot muffins may work as a reasonable substitute for satisfying a sweet tooth. Keep the muffins tightly covered to maintain moistness.*

note: It's best to bake these muffins directly in a muffin pan. Using disposable cupcake holders will not yield uniform-looking muffins. Carrot curlers to garnish the muffins can be found at the Peppermill.

1. Preheat the oven to 350° F. In the bowl of an electric mixer or with a hand mixer, beat the whole wheat flour, all-purpose flour, grated carrots, sugar, oil, orange juice, orange zest, eggs, lemon juice, baking powder, baking soda, vanilla extract, cinnamon, and salt. Pour the batter into 2 generously greased muffin tins (enough to make 12 muffins), filling the cups two-thirds full.

2. Bake until a toothpick inserted in the center of a muffin comes out clean, 22–25 minutes. Do not overbake. Turn out the muffins from the pan and allow to cool on a wire rack. Store in an airtight container for maximum freshness. **Yields 12 muffins.**

Ice Cream Razzle

8 oz. chocolate

1 CUP peanut butter

2¼ CUPS frosted flakes (not crushed)

1 CUP slivered toasted almonds

1 GALLON vanilla ice cream, thawed for easy mixing

4 9-inch chocolate pie crusts (optional)

GARNISH

• Drizzled melted chocolate and toasted slivered almonds

• Chocolate curls

• Nut crunch (Baker's Choice)

• Wafer cigars and fresh fruit

THIS WAS *the very first dessert Esty served us soon after she got married. She served the ice cream in chocolate pie crusts topped with chocolate curls on a mirrored charger plate. It was festive and yummy, and when Esty told me how easy it was to prepare, I was even more impressed. Even as a newlywed, she had mastered the art of savvy entertaining, transforming a fuss-free dish into a memorable dessert.*

This recipe yields enough to fill four store-bought graham cracker pie crusts and is kept frozen, making it super practical for a large party. Or serve this dessert scooped individually in glassware. Baker's Choice offers a wide variety of delicious nut and candy toppings that you can use as a garnish.

1. In a double boiler, melt the chocolate and peanut butter over low heat. Stir in the frosted flakes and toasted almonds. Allow to cool.

2. Combine the mixture with the vanilla ice cream. Pour the ice cream into the pie crusts or into containers (if you are serving in individual glassware) and freeze. To serve, garnish with your choice of melted chocolate and slivered almonds, chocolate curls, nut crunch, or wafer cigars and fresh fruit. **Serves 16–32.**

Fruit Soup Salad with Toasted Pine Nuts and Craisins

1 CUP pomegranate seeds

½ CUP Craisins

1 lime, juiced

2 PKG. strawberry Jell-O mix, dissolved in 3½ cups hot water

GARNISHES
- Toasted pine nuts
- Mint leaves

FRUIT (6 CUPS)
- Strawberries, quartered
- Blueberries
- Pineapple, peeled and diced
- Kiwis, peeled and diced
- Cherries, halved and pitted
- Mango, peeled and diced

ACROSS BETWEEN *a fruit salad and fruit soup, this recipe combines the characteristics of both. It's quick, refreshing, and great for any time of the year as a snack or dessert. And it's popular with all ages, including children.*

Don't skip the pomegranate seeds in this recipe—they do make a difference. The lime juice cuts the sweetness, so if you prefer your fruit salad more tart than sweet, just add more lime juice. Allow the flavors to mingle in the refrigerator for several hours before serving.

1. In a large container, combine the 6 cups of fruit and the pomegranate seeds. Stir in the Craisins, lime juice, and dissolved strawberry Jell-O. Cover tightly and refrigerate for at least 6 hours.

2. To serve, scoop the salad into bowls and garnish with the toasted pine nuts and mint leaves. **Serves 10.**

Peanut Butter Mousse Vol-au-Vents

PEANUT BUTTER MOUSSE

1 CUP creamy peanut butter

4 OZ. (½ cup) non-dairy whip topping

½ CUP coconut milk

¾ CUP confectioners' sugar

1 CONTAINER (8 oz.) Tofutti cream cheese

½ TBSP. vanilla extract

VOL-AU-VENTS

6 Pepperidge Farm puff pastry shells

4 oz. chocolate, melted

• Store-bought toasted nuts, chopped (I like Baker's Choice)

• Store-bought berry sauce, to garnish

AS **IF** *this peanut butter mousse isn't amazing enough straight off the spoon, I've added a sweet twist on vol-au-vents that will do this dessert justice. A vol-au-vent is a puff pastry shell that resembles a pot with a lid. Vol-au-vent means "windblown," which refers to the surprising lightness of the pastry. Vol-au-vents can accommodate all types of fillings, but they are usually savory. The uniqueness of this vol-au-vent presentation is the chocolate-and-nut-dipped edges that cradle the creamy peanut butter mousse.*

The mousse contains a high proportion of peanut butter, which results in an intense peanut butter flavor. For other creative serving options, serve the mousse in mini parfait or martini glasses topped with chopped nuts and a dollop of strawberry jam for a fabulous deconstruction of the classic PB&J. This mousse also makes for a nice frosting on cupcakes or a delicious filling for store-bought cannoli wrappers.

even simpler: *Skip the vol-au-vent presentation and prepare the mousse as a filling for a pie. This recipe will yield enough mousse to fill one 9-inch graham cracker pie crust. Top with Baker's Choice toasted nut crunch and refrigerate until ready to serve.*

1. To prepare the peanut butter mousse: In the bowl of an electric mixer or with a hand mixer, beat the peanut butter, whip topping, coconut milk, confectioners' sugar, pareve cream cheese, and vanilla. Refrigerate until ready to serve.

2. To prepare the vol-au-vents: Preheat the oven to 350° F. Remove the lids from the puff pastry shells. On a baking sheet, bake the shells and lids until golden brown, about 20 minutes. Remove from the oven and allow to cool.

3. Melt the chocolate in a double boiler. Dip the edges of the vol-au-vents in the chocolate and then immediately dip in the chopped nuts. Allow to cool and harden at room temperature.

4. To assemble, bring the mousse to room temperature. Spoon two heaping scoops of peanut butter mousse into each vol-au-vent. To garnish, prop up the lids of the vol-au-vents against the sides of the pastry and drizzle the berry sauce onto the plate. To make the teardrop design, place round drops of the berry sauce on each plate and, with a toothpick, spread a corner to create a teardrop. **Serves 6.**

Spiced Mocha Mousse with Viennese Crunch

CRUST

3 CUPS graham cracker crumbs

½ CUP brown sugar

6 OZ. (¾ cup) trans-fat-free margarine, melted

½ TSP. cinnamon

WHIP TOPPING

16 OZ. (2 cups) non-dairy whip topping

1 TBSP. coffee, dissolved in several drops of hot water

½ TSP. vanilla extract

14 Viennese crunch bars, chopped

MOUSSE LAYER

7 OZ. (2 bars) good-quality pareve semisweet or bittersweet chocolate

16 OZ. (2 cups) trans-fat-free margarine

1 CUP sugar

2 TBSP. coffee, dissolved in several drops of hot water

1 TSP. vanilla extract

1 TSP. cinnamon

1 TSP. ginger

1 TSP. nutmeg

8 eggs, lightly beaten

IT'S **HARD** to forget the look of pure bliss on my then-two-year-old daughter's face when she ran into the arms of Minnie Mouse at Magic Kingdom and wouldn't let go. She talked about it for weeks, saying, "I love Minnie Mouse, but why doesn't she talk?!" This dessert will conjure up that same childlike euphoria.

There is something about this chocolate mousse that, no matter how many times you prepare it, still has the allure of that very first bite. This rich and silky dessert lends itself splendidly to gentle spicing with a hint of coffee to deepen the flavor.

Most mousse recipes call for raw eggs. Since some people are wary of eating raw eggs, the eggs in this recipe are cooked for thirty seconds to eliminate the risk.

The chocolate you choose is very important. Use a good-quality semisweet or bittersweet chocolate that you would eat out of the wrapper. My personal favorite is Rosemarie.

even simpler: Skip the crust preparation and buy ready-made ones. This recipe will yield enough filling for two 9-inch graham cracker pie crusts.

1. To prepare the crust: Preheat the oven to 350° F. In a bowl, combine the crust ingredients and press onto the bottom of a 9x13-inch foil pan. Bake until lightly browned, 8–10 minutes. Allow to cool.

2. To prepare the mousse: In the top of a double boiler, combine the chocolate, margarine, sugar, coffee, vanilla, cinnamon, ginger, and nutmeg. Heat over simmering water, stirring constantly, until the chocolate is completely melted.

3. Add the lightly beaten eggs, stir for 30 seconds, then remove from the heat. With a mixer, beat the mousse mixture on low speed for 1 minute to make sure the eggs are evenly incorporated. Pour the mixture into the pie crust and spread over the surface of the crust. Allow to cool for several minutes. Freeze until firm.

4. To prepare the whip topping: In the bowl of an electric mixer, beat the whip topping until peaks start to form. Add the dissolved coffee and vanilla and continue to beat until the peaks are stiff. Spread the topping evenly over the mousse layer and freeze until set. Once the whip topping is set, sprinkle with the chopped Viennese crunch. Freeze until ready to serve.

5. To serve, remove the mousse from the freezer and let it thaw for several minutes. Cut 16 round mousse portions using a 2¼-inch ring mold. Take a large round mug or glass that's at least 1–2 inches wider in diameter than the ring mold and place it face down in the center of a medium-sized white plate. Gently tap cocoa powder through a sieve to almost completely cover the edges of the mug and lightly cover the rim of the plate. Remove the mug or glass and place a serving of mousse in the center of the plate. Repeat for the remaining portions of mousse. After slicing the mousse, let it stand at room temperature for 10–15 minutes before serving so the texture is creamy and not too firm. **Serves 16.**

Profiteroles with Chocolate Rum Sauce

PÂTE À CHOUX

6 TBSP. trans-fat-free margarine

¾ CUP coconut milk

PINCH salt

¾ CUP all-purpose flour

3 eggs

CHOCOLATE RUM SAUCE

½ CUP sugar

8 OZ. (1 cup) non-dairy whip topping or heavy cream

7 OZ. (2 bars) good-quality chocolate, finely chopped

1 TSP. vanilla extract

1 TBSP. rum

• Ice cream of your choice

PROFITEROLES ARE *a classic rustic French dessert made from pâte à choux, a precooked dough that's also used to make éclairs. The profiteroles are filled with the ice cream of your choice and topped with a homemade chocolate sauce. Despite their grandiose name, they are quite simple to prepare.*

The dough puffs freeze really well, so if a craving strikes, just pop the frozen puffs into the oven at 350° F for several minutes to defrost while you assemble the rest of the ingredients.

dairy option: *Substitute butter for the margarine and milk for the coconut milk.*

1. To prepare the profiteroles: Preheat the oven to 425° F. In a medium saucepan, bring the margarine, coconut milk, and salt to a boil over high heat. Stir constantly until the margarine is completely melted. Reduce the heat to medium–low. Add the flour, beating with a wooden spoon until the mixture is combined and forms a dough. Remove from the heat and allow to cool for 4-5 minutes.

2. Transfer the dough to the bowl of an electric mixer and beat in the eggs. Line a baking sheet with parchment paper. With a pastry bag or Ziploc bag with the corner snipped off, pipe 18–20 mounds of dough 1½ inches apart onto the prepared baking sheet. Bake until golden, 22-25 minutes. Remove from the oven and prick the side of each profiterole to release the steam. Allow to cool.

3. To prepare the chocolate rum sauce: In a saucepan, heat the sugar over medium heat, stirring constantly, until it begins to caramelize. Whisk in the whip topping or cream and the chocolate until the chocolate is melted. Stir in the vanilla and rum. Cover and keep warm.

4. To serve the profiteroles, slice them in half horizontally and fill with a scoop of ice cream. Drizzle with a generous helping of warm chocolate rum sauce. **Serves 6.**

Blood Orange Mint Sorbet

1 CUP sugar

½ CUP water

2 blood oranges, rind removed and sliced into strips

¾ CUP packed fresh mint leaves

1 TBSP. lemon juice

3 CUPS blood orange juice (from about 10 oranges)

ORANGE SHELLS

6 blood oranges

• Mint leaves, to garnish

YEARS AGO, *serving sorbet in fruit shells was all the rage. The very first dessert I ever prepared was lemon and orange sorbet served in hollowed-out lemons and oranges. This version is a bit more current and every bit as refreshing. Regular orang-es will work, although you won't get the same intense, glorious color. Make sure to use freshly squeezed juice for better taste.*

There's no need for an ice cream maker to create this sorbet. You can simply blend it in a food processor.

note: *Citrus fruits that are kept at room temperature will yield more juice than chilled fruits.*

1. In a small saucepan, combine the sugar, water, strips of orange rind, and mint leaves. Bring to a boil over medium heat. Lower the heat and simmer, stirring occasionally, until the sugar has dissolved, 5 minutes. Remove from the heat and allow the syrup to cool for 20 minutes.

2. Discard the orange rind and mint leaves. Stir the lemon and orange juices into the syrup. Freeze for at least 8 hours, until very firm.

3. To prepare the orange shells: Cut the oranges in half. Scoop out the flesh and press out the juice through a sieve or juicer. Scoop out the remaining pulp and freeze until ready to fill.

4. Remove the sorbet from the freezer and puree in a food processor for 5 minutes until very creamy and smooth. Scoop into orange shells and freeze until ready to serve. Garnish with mint leaves before serving. **Serves 6.**

Warm Deep-Dish Giant Chocolate Chip Cookie Torte

2 CUPS oil

1 CUP sugar

2 CUPS brown sugar

1 TBSP. pure vanilla extract

4 eggs

4 CUPS all-purpose flour

4 TSP. baking powder

1 TSP. salt

1 PKG. (10 oz.) chocolate chips

• Store-bought vanilla ice cream

SHOSHANA R. *treated my family to the most incredible chocolate chip cookies...and the recipe! The original recipe called for shortening, but because the ingredients are so well balanced, it doesn't miss a beat with oil. I'm convinced this is the best chocolate chip cookie recipe I've ever tasted. But how do you transform an already great chocolate chip cookie into a full-blown dessert? Make it more than an inch thick, of course! And...serve it warm with ice cream.*

note: *This recipe yields two 9-inch round cakes. You can serve the second one as a breakfast cake.*

1. Preheat the oven to 350° F. In the bowl of an electric mixer, or with a hand mixer, beat the oil, sugar, brown sugar, vanilla, eggs, flour, baking powder, and salt on medium speed until well combined, about 2–3 minutes. Add the chocolate chips and combine.

2. Pour the batter into two 9-inch round baking pans and bake, uncovered, for 55–60 minutes. Serve warm with a scoop of vanilla ice cream on the side.

3. To reheat, warm the torte, tightly covered, in a preheated 200° F oven for no longer than 1 hour. **Serves 16.**

Lemon Meringue Pie

THIS RECIPE *is from my "oldie but goodie" archive. It was given to me by my friend E. Soibleman. She is one of the most real people I know, and her cooking is fabulous without being frivolous. All the recipes she shares with me somehow manage to reflect both her personality and her cooking skills. Like this dessert. It's unpretentious and utterly delicious. E. S. never cared much for lemon meringue pie until she stumbled on this recipe.*

note: When you top the lemon filling with the meringue, the filling should still be piping hot. This will prevent the meringue from weeping and separating from the filling.

1 CUP sugar

¼ CUP cornstarch

¼ TSP. salt

1½ CUPS cold water

2 lemons, juiced and zested

4 egg yolks

1 TBSP. trans-fat-free margarine

1 9-inch frozen deep-dish pastry shell, baked

MERINGUE

4 egg whites

¼ TSP. cream of tartar

¾ CUP sugar

1. To prepare the lemon filling: Preheat the oven to 350° F. In a medium saucepan, whisk together the sugar, cornstarch, and salt. Stir in the water, lemon juice, and lemon zest, then whisk until smooth. Cook over medium–high heat, stirring constantly, until the mixture comes to a boil.

2. In a bowl, beat the egg yolks. Gradually whisk in ½ cup of the hot sugar and lemon mixture to temper the eggs. Whisk the egg yolk mixture back into the remaining sugar and lemon mixture. Add the margarine and bring to a boil, stirring constantly. Cook until thick, about 1 minute. Remove from the heat and pour the hot filling into the baked pie crust.

3. To prepare the meringue: In a large bowl, whip the egg whites and cream of tartar until foamy. Gradually add the sugar, whipping well after each addition, and continue to whip until very stiff peaks form. Spread the meringue over the hot lemon filling so that it completely covers the filling, sealing the edges at the crust. Bake for 15–20 minutes. Cool at room temperature for 1 hour. Refrigerate for 6 hours before serving. **Serves 8.**

Tangerine Glazed Apple Apricot Strudel

THIS IS *my mother-in-law's signature side dish. Whenever we eat at her home for a Shabbos or holiday meal, this dish stays very close to my plate. Not your typical apple strudel, this one is glazed with fresh tangerine juice. You can also glaze the strudel with fresh orange or clementine juice.*

If you are serving this dish for dessert, dust the top of the strudel with confectioners' sugar and serve with whipped cream or ice cream.

note: Slice the strudel after it has chilled in the refrigerator for several hours to yield neat slices. Reheat as needed.

1 SHEET (8-9 oz.) frozen puff pastry

• Oil

¼ CUP bread crumbs

¾ CUP sugar

6 large Cortland apples, peeled, cored, and thinly sliced

1 lemon, juiced

• Cinnamon

2 TSP. vanilla sugar

15 oz. apricot preserves

1 CUP fresh tangerine juice

1. Preheat the oven to 350° F. Unfold the pastry sheet into a 16x13-inch rectangle and place it on a lightly floured surface with the short side facing you. Brush with a light layer of oil. Sprinkle the bread crumbs and ¼ cup of the sugar evenly over the surface of the dough.

2. In a large bowl, toss the apple slices with the remaining ½ cup of sugar, lemon juice, cinnamon, vanilla sugar, and apricot preserves until well combined. Spread the apple mixture evenly over the dough, leaving a 1-inch border around the edges. Roll the dough jelly-roll style and place, seam-side down, on a baking sheet. Tuck the ends of the roll under and seal. Lightly oil the top of the roll and bake, uncovered, for 30 minutes.

3. Remove the strudel from the oven and pour the tangerine juice over the top. Cover and bake until golden brown, for 1 hour and 15 minutes longer. Allow to cool for 30 minutes at room temperature. Serve warm. **Serves 6.**

Bourbon Toasted Pecan Pie

1¾ CUPS pecans

1 TBSP. fresh orange juice

¾ CUP light corn syrup

3 eggs, beaten

½ CUP sugar

½ CUP brown sugar

3 TBSP. trans-fat-free margarine, melted

1½ TSP. vanilla extract

1 TBSP. bourbon

PINCH salt

1 9-inch frozen deep-dish pastry shell

THE ISSUE *I have with pecan pies is that they tend to be overwhelmingly sweet. Using bourbon, light corn syrup, and brown sugar instead of white sugar significantly cuts the sweetness. The bourbon also adds a trace of smokiness and depth of flavor. And, because it's the little details that always matter, toasting the pecans in a little bit of orange juice transforms this pie from good to great.*

dairy option: Substitute butter for the margarine.

tip: To prepare your pecan pie in an oven-to-table 9-inch dish, slightly thaw the frozen pastry shell. Carefully transfer the pastry shell to the oven-to-table dish before baking.

1. Preheat the oven to 350° F. On a baking sheet, toss the pecans with the orange juice and toast until fragrant, 8–10 minutes. Allow to cool.

2. In the bowl of an electric mixer or with a hand mixer, beat the corn syrup, eggs, sugar, brown sugar, margarine, vanilla extract, bourbon, and salt. Combine with the toasted pecans. Pour the mixture into the pastry shell and bake for 1 hour and 10 minutes. Allow to cool for 1½ hours, then refrigerate. **Serves 8.**

Oreo™ Cookie Dough Pie

2 9-inch chocolate pie crusts

3 CONTAINERS (8 oz. each) non-dairy whip topping

1 CUP chocolate chips

¾ CUP brown sugar

1 CUP all-purpose flour

½ TSP. salt

15 Oreo cookies, crushed

GARNISH

- Whipped topping
- Oreo cookies, halved

> **I**F **YOU** *enjoy cookie dough ice cream and get disappointed when all the cookie dough pieces are gone, this recipe is for you. The fat is omitted from the cookie dough mixture, which yields crumbs instead of malleable bits of dough. This way, you get uniform cookie dough flavor until the very last bite—and with less fat, too.*
>
> *For an elegant plating option, press the two pie crusts onto the bottom of a 9x13-inch foil pan. Pour the filling over the crusts. Using a cookie mold, cut the pie into round shapes or squares and serve.*
>
> *dairy option: Substitute heavy cream for the non-dairy whip topping.*

1. In a large bowl, whip the non-dairy topping until stiff peaks form.

2. To prepare the cookie dough crumbs: Melt the chocolate chips over a double boiler or in the microwave. Immediately add the brown sugar, flour, and salt and mix until evenly incorporated and crumbs form. Combine the melted chocolate mixture and the cookie dough crumbs with the whipped topping. Pour the cookie dough filling into the pie crusts and freeze until ready to serve.

3. To serve, garnish with a dollop of whipped topping and half an Oreo cookie. **Serves 16.**

Chocolate Shortcakes with Vanilla Cream and Berries

PREPARE TO *be smitten after just one bite. You simply have to taste this bewitching dessert to appreciate the essence of every memorable morsel. The cookies are also delicious on their own—melt-in-your-mouth, unrivaled chocolate perfection.*

tip: For a prettily edged cookie, use a scallop cutter.

dairy option: Substitute the margarine with butter and the non-dairy whip topping with heavy cream and confectioners' sugar to taste.

CHOCOLATE SHORTCAKES

1¼ CUPS all-purpose flour

½ CUP cocoa powder

½ TSP. baking powder

11 TBSP. trans-fat-free margarine

⅔ CUP light brown sugar

¼ CUP sugar

½ TSP. kosher salt

1 TSP. vanilla extract

2 eggs

VANILLA CREAM

16 OZ. (2 CUPS) non-dairy whip topping

4 TBSP. confectioners' sugar

1 TSP. vanilla extract

GARNISH

- Fresh berries of your choice

- Chocolate shavings (optional)

1. To prepare the shortcake cookies: Preheat the oven to 350° F. In a bowl, combine the flour, cocoa powder, and baking powder and set aside. In the bowl of an electric mixer, cream the margarine. Beat in the light brown sugar, sugar, salt, and vanilla extract. Add the eggs and beat for 2 minutes.

2. Gradually add the dry ingredients. Beat on low speed for several minutes longer, until the flour is fully incorporated into the dough.

3. Roll out the dough. Using a cookie cutter or knife, cut the dough into the desired shapes. Bake on a cookie sheet for 25 minutes. Allow to cool.

4. Prepare the vanilla cream: In the bowl of an electric mixer, whip the non-dairy whip topping until peaks form. Beat in the confectioners' sugar and vanilla until combined.

5. To serve, place a shortcake cookie on a serving plate. Top with the vanilla cream and berries, then sandwich with another shortcake cookie. Add a dollop of cream on top and some more berries. Garnish with chocolate shavings, if desired. **Yields 12 cookies.**

Fruit Salad with Balsamic Strawberry Coulis, Crunchy Nuts, and Pomegranate Seeds

STRAWBERRY COULIS

1 CUP strawberries, fresh or frozen

½ CUP orange juice

½ CUP confectioners' sugar

3 TBSP. sugar

1 TSP. vanilla extract

1 TBSP. lemon or lime juice

1 TBSP. balsamic vinegar

NUT CRUNCH

½ CUP brown sugar

1½ CUPS Rice Krispies

4 OZ. (½ cup) trans-fat-free margarine

1 CUP walnuts, chopped

FRUIT SALAD

2 CUPS kiwis, peeled and diced

2 CUPS strawberries, diced

2 CUPS blueberries

2 CUPS mango, peeled and diced

• Pomegranate seeds, for sprinkling

THE CRUNCHY *nuts, smooth strawberry coulis, and fresh fruit are three components that, combined, build to a lovely fruit salad crescendo. This fruit salad can serve either as a healthful starter course or a light, refreshing dessert. Aim for a combination of at least four different types of fruits.*

tip: For added effect and flavor, sprinkle pomegranate seeds on top of the fruit salad before serving.

1. To prepare the strawberry coulis: In a food processor, puree all the ingredients until smooth. Refrigerate until ready to serve.

2. To prepare the nut crunch: Preheat the oven to 350° F. In a roasting pan, combine the brown sugar, Rice Krispies, margarine, and walnuts and bake, uncovered, for 10 minutes. Remove from the oven and stir well to blend the flavors. Allow to cool. Store in an airtight container until ready to serve.

3. To serve, in a large bowl, combine the fruits. Scoop the fruit salad into individual serving bowls. Spoon the strawberry coulis over the fruit salad, then spoon the nut crunch on top and serve immediately. Any leftover nut crunch can be frozen. **Serves 8-10.**

Pistachio French Toast with Banana Salsa

PISTACHIO PASTE SYRUP

1 CUP pistachios

1 CUP water

1 CUP sugar

¼ vanilla bean

SALSA

1 banana, peeled and diced

1 Meyer lemon, juiced

1 TSP. sugar

5 fresh mint leaves, julienned

FRENCH TOAST

2 eggs

2 TBSP. sugar

½ TSP. vanilla extract

8 SLICES several-days-old rye bread, crust removed

• Oil, for frying

2 OZ. chocolate bar, grated

PARDES HAS *created an inspiring, eclectic menu encompassing casual and elegant cuisine and reinventing the ordinary (think Garlic Fries and Truffle Mayo with House-Made Red Wine Ketchup or Rosemary-Orange Gnocchi with Spicy Smokey Duck Ragout with Olives). The chef and owner of Pardes, Moses Mendel, was kind enough to share the following outrageous dessert recipe with me.*

Meyer lemons, a featured ingredient in this recipe, are sweeter than traditional lemons. If you're unable to locate Meyer lemons, equal quantities of lemon and mandarin orange or tangerine juices yield a flavor similar to that of Meyer lemons.

even simpler: *Skip the preparation for the pistachio paste syrup and substitute with store-bought pistachio paste.*

1. To prepare the pistachio paste syrup: Preheat the oven to 350° F. Spread the pistachios on a baking sheet and toast for 10 minutes. Meanwhile, in a saucepan, combine the water, sugar, and vanilla bean and bring to a boil over high heat. Add the pistachios to the syrup. Reduce the heat to low and simmer for 1 hour, stirring occasionally. Allow the syrup to cool. Puree and set aside.

2. To prepare the banana salsa: In a bowl, combine the diced banana, lemon juice, sugar, and mint leaves. Set aside.

3. To prepare the French toast: In a bowl, whisk together the eggs, sugar, and vanilla to form a batter. Spread 1 tablespoon of the pistachio paste syrup over 4 slices of the bread. Top each of the slices of bread with another slice to make 4 sandwiches. Dip the sandwiches into the egg batter until the bread is soaked through.

4. In a skillet or griddle, heat the oil over medium heat. Fry the sandwiches in the oil until golden brown on both sides. Remove from the skillet and drain on paper towels. Serve warm with the banana salsa and sprinkled with the grated chocolate. **Serves 4.**

Tiramisu with Chocolate Liquor

3 CONTAINERS (8 oz. each) plain Tofutti cream cheese

1½ CUPS confectioners' sugar

1 TSP. vanilla extract

16 OZ. (2 cups) non-dairy whip topping

1 TBSP. coffee, dissolved in several drops of hot water

1½ PKG. ladyfingers (about 54 ladyfingers)

1 TBSP. coffee, dissolved in ¾ cup of boiling water

1 TBSP. sugar

¼ CUP chocolate liquor

• Mini chocolate chips, cocoa powder, and cinnamon (optional), for dusting

THE PAREVE *cream cheese in this recipe yields an almost identical taste to that of dairy tiramisu. This recipe is perfectly easy, and you can make this dessert way in advance and freeze it.*

For this recipe, I prefer to use Biscuits Gardeil ladyfingers. After pouring the coffee mixture onto the ladyfingers, you may notice that the ladyfingers are not completely soaked. That's okay—they will continue to soften over time but won't get soggy.

You can garnish the tiramisu with your choice of strawberries, chocolate curls, cocoa powder, or mini chocolate chips.

dairy option: Substitute heavy cream for the non-dairy whip topping and mascarpone cheese for the Tofutti cream cheese.

1. In the bowl of an electric mixer or with a hand mixer, beat the cream cheese, confectioners' sugar, and vanilla extract on medium–high speed. Remove from the bowl and set aside.

2. Pour the non-dairy whip topping into the mixing bowl and beat on high speed until peaks form, about 5 minutes. Add the first tablespoon of coffee (dissolved in several drops of hot water), fold in the cream cheese mixture, and beat for 1 minute on low speed until evenly combined.

3. Line a 9x13-inch pan with half of the ladyfingers. In a small bowl, combine the second tablespoon of coffee (dissolved in ¾ cup of boiling water) with the sugar and the chocolate liquor. Pour half of the chocolate liquor mixture over the ladyfingers in the pan. Gently spread half of the cream cheese and whip topping mixture over the ladyfingers layer.

4. Add another layer with the remaining ladyfingers. Pour the remaining chocolate liquor mixture over the second layer of ladyfingers and spread with the rest of the whip topping mixture. Freeze until ready to serve.

5. To serve, slice while the tiramisu is still frozen. Allow the slices to thaw for at least 10 minutes and serve immediately. If desired, sprinkle with mini chocolate chips and dust with cocoa powder and cinnamon before serving. **Serves 12.**

Maple Peach Crisp with Nutmeg Streusel

RIPE, JUICY *peaches star in this pie, but you can substitute them with other stone fruits, such as nectarines, apricots, plums, or cherries—or combine several of these fruits together.*

These types of fruits are referred to as "stone fruits" because of their very large, hard seeds. If using peaches, this simple crisp is best made with ripe yellow peaches rather than the pale, sweet versions, since the yellow peaches impart a stronger flavor.

Pure maple syrup, a featured ingredient in this recipe, is made from the sap of maple trees. It is an unrefined, natural sweetener that contains essential minerals, and it has a delightful, authentic caramel flavor that you can't get from imitation maple syrups.

7 CUPS ripe peaches (about 10 large peaches), peeled and diced

¼ CUP packed brown sugar

4 TBSP. pure maple syrup

3 TBSP. all-purpose flour

1 TSP. lemon juice

½ TSP. grated lemon zest

1 TSP. cinnamon

NUTMEG STREUSEL TOPPING

4 OZ. (½ cup) trans-fat-free margarine

1 CUP all-purpose flour

¾ CUP brown sugar

¼ TSP. nutmeg

¼ TSP. cinnamon

1. Preheat the oven to 350° F. In a bowl, toss the diced peaches with the brown sugar, maple syrup, flour, lemon juice, zest, and cinnamon. Pour the peach mixture into 6-ounce ramekins or a 9x13-inch baking dish. Set aside.

2. To prepare the topping: In a bowl, combine the margarine, flour, brown sugar, nutmeg, and cinnamon until the mixture is crumbly. Sprinkle the topping over the peaches. Bake until the topping is crisp and golden, 50 minutes if using ramekins or at least 1 hour if using a baking dish. **Serves 12.**

Double Chocolate Ganache Tart

RICH, SMOOTH, *and dense, this tart is the equivalent of a giant truffle. Despite its grandiose name, few desserts are simpler to prepare.*

It's also extremely versatile: you can add flavored liquors, brandy, orange zest, or coffee to the ganache and use it to fill mini store-bought tartlets. Top with chocolate curls or, for a quicker alternative, see your local supermarket for the full line of Baker's Choice topping options (I especially love to use their chopped nut crunch topping on this tart).

dairy option: *Substitute the whip topping with heavy cream and the pareve chocolate with dairy chocolate.*

note: *For optimal taste, use only good-quality chocolate, not baking chocolate.*

1 9-inch frozen deep-dish pastry shell, baked, or
1 9-inch graham cracker pie crust

CHOCOLATE GANACHE LAYER

8 oz. (1 cup) non-dairy whip topping

8 oz. good-quality bittersweet chocolate, finely chopped

1 TSP. vanilla extract

CHOCOLATE PUDDING LAYER

16 oz. (2 cups) non-dairy whip topping

1 PKG. (2.8 oz.) instant chocolate pudding

1. To prepare the chocolate ganache layer: In a saucepan, bring the whip topping to a rolling boil over medium-high heat. Remove from the heat. In a bowl, pour the whip topping over the chopped chocolate and allow to stand for several minutes. Add the vanilla extract and stir until the chocolate is completely emulsified and the mixture is smooth. Pour into the baked pastry shell or graham cracker pie crust and refrigerate for several hours until firm.

2. To prepare the chocolate pudding layer: In the bowl of an electric mixer, beat the non-dairy whip topping with the pudding mix for 1 minute. Do not overmix. Pour the pudding mixture over the ganache layer. Refrigerate until firm, at least 2 hours longer. **Serves 8.**

Three-Glaze Cinnamon Buns

WAS AT *Michal's home on Purim when she received a delivery from her sister Aviva that consisted of the most amazing pastries, baked by Aviva herself.*

Aviva owns and operates Viva La Bake Shoppe, a gourmet pastry shop located in Cedarhurst, New York. All of Viva La Bake Shoppe's products are made to order. The entire facility is nut-free, allowing even those with nut allergies to enjoy Aviva's treats. These cinnamon buns are just one example of her incredible pastries that ooze with sweet goodness.

even simpler: You can skip the preparation time for the glazes and drizzle the buns with store-bought icings from Baker's Choice instead. Garnish with Baker's Choice chopped toasted nuts, if desired.

DOUGH

- 3 PACKETS (¼ oz. each) dry yeast
- 2 CUPS warm water
- 1 TSP. PLUS 1 CUP sugar
- 8 OZ. (1 CUP) trans-fat-free margarine, melted
- 4 eggs
- ¼ CUP vanilla sugar
- 1 TSP. salt
- 9 CUPS all-purpose flour

FILLING

- 3 CUPS dark brown sugar
- 6 TBSP. cinnamon
- 12 OZ. (1½ CUPS) trans-fat-free margarine, melted

WHITE GLAZE

- 1 CUP confectioners' sugar
- 1 TBSP. hot water

CHOCOLATE GLAZE

- 1 CUP confectioners' sugar
- 2 TBSP. cocoa powder, dissolved in 2 Tbsp. of hot water
- 2 TSP. hot water

CARAMEL GLAZE

- 1 CUP confectioners' sugar
- ¼ CUP dark brown sugar
- 1 TBSP. PLUS 1 TSP. hot water

1. To prepare the dough: In a small bowl, combine the yeast with the water and 1 teaspoon of the sugar. Let stand until bubbles form, about 10 minutes.

2. In the large bowl of an electric mixer, combine 1 cup of the sugar, the melted margarine, eggs, vanilla sugar, salt, and flour. Add the yeast mixture and beat until the dough separates from the sides of the bowl and forms a ball. The dough should be slightly sticky, but not wet. Cover the bowl with plastic wrap and allow to rise for 2 hours at room temperature.

3. Divide the dough evenly into 3 balls. On a floured surface, roll out each ball into a large, thin 18x25-inch rectangle.

4. To prepare the filling: In a small bowl, combine the brown sugar and cinnamon. Spread the melted margarine over the dough, then sprinkle it heavily with the brown sugar and cinnamon mixture. Roll the dough lengthwise jelly-roll style. Cut into 1½-inch slices. Place the slices on a cookie sheet lined with parchment paper, leaving space between the buns to allow them room to expand. Cover and allow to rise for 30 minutes at room temperature.

5. Preheat the oven to 350° F. Bake the buns until the tops begin to brown slightly, 20 minutes. Do not overbake or they will become dry.

6. To prepare the glazes: Whisk together the ingredients for each glaze in three separate bowls. Drizzle immediately over the buns while they are still warm. **Yields 50 buns.**

Powdered Chocolate Wontons with Caramel Sauce

CARAMEL SAUCE

1¼ CUPS sugar

8 OZ. (1 cup) non-dairy whip topping

1 TSP. lemon juice

¼ TSP. vanilla extract

¼–½ CUP coconut milk, to taste

CHOCOLATE WONTONS

16 wonton wrappers

16 SQUARES chocolate

- Peanut oil, for frying
- Confectioners' sugar, for dusting

THE **COMBINATION** of the crispy crunchy wontons, the oozing richness of the chocolate, and the gooey caramel will send you straight to sweet blissdom. And this is one of the easiest desserts you'll ever make—all you have to do is stuff, seal, and fry.

Sometimes I also add a thin slice of banana or a teaspoon of peanut butter or both to the wontons before wrapping. Just place a spoonful of peanut butter in the center of the wonton, press a thin slice of banana on top, then top with the chocolate square. Make sure to use good-quality chocolate like Rosemarie or Torino.

You'll like the accompanying pareve caramel sauce, which doesn't contain corn syrup. Corn syrup can have a mind of its own; without it, the sauce is creamier and doesn't turn into a hard, sticky mess.

dairy option: Use milk chocolate instead of pareve and Baker's Choice dairy caramel sauce instead of the pareve sauce. .

---

1. To prepare the caramel sauce: In a small saucepan, combine the sugar, whip topping, lemon juice, and vanilla extract. Bring to a boil over medium-high heat, stirring constantly until the sugar has dissolved, then stirring occasionally until the bubbles become bigger and the sauce turns a rich amber color. Be careful not to burn the caramel—as soon as it reaches the desired caramel color, remove from the heat.

2. Stir in the desired amount of coconut milk. If you like a thinner sauce, use ½ cup; if you prefer it rich and gooey, use ¼ cup. Set aside.

3. To prepare the wontons: Pour some warm water into a small bowl. On a clean, dry surface, place 1 chocolate square in the center of a wonton wrapper and brush the edges of the wrapper with the water. Bring each corner of the wrapper to the center, allowing them to overlap slightly, and press to seal. Ensure that the seams are tightly sealed.

4. In a frying pan, heat the peanut oil over medium-high heat until hot (approximately 350° F). Fry the wontons until golden brown, 1–2 minutes per side. Remove from the pan and drain on a paper towel.

5. Dust the wontons with powdered sugar and serve warm with the caramel sauce. **Serves 8.**

Apple Cranberry Blueberry Crisp

5 apples (a combination of Cortland, Granny Smith, and McIntosh), peeled, cored, and diced

½ CAN (7 oz.) whole-berry cranberry sauce

½ CAN (14 oz.) blueberry pie filling

6 oz. fresh blueberries

• Lemon or lime zest

CRISP TOPPING

2 CUPS all-purpose flour

2 TSP. baking powder

¾ CUP sugar

½ TSP. cinnamon

1 egg

½ TSP. vanilla

½ CUP oil

1. Preheat the oven to 350° F. In a bowl, combine the diced apples, cranberry sauce, blueberry pie filling, blueberries, and zest. Pour the mixture into ramekins.

2. In a bowl, combine all the ingredients for the crumb topping until crumbly. Spoon 2 heaping tablespoons on top of the fruit filling in each ramekin. Bake until the top is very crisp and crunchy, at least 1 hour. If you are baking one large crisp, bake for at least 30 minutes longer, so the top will become super crisp. Serve warm or at room temperature. You can freeze any leftover topping. **Serves 12–14.**

I KNOW *what you're thinking: Do I really need another apple cranberry crisp recipe? After you taste this crisp, you'll realize this is the only one you need. There are not that many rules when it comes to cooking. And the rules of cooking are meant to be broken, especially when it suits your taste and creativity. But I do have several rules when it comes to apple cranberry crisps. Most important, the crumb topping should be super crispy and not overly sweet—just like in this recipe. No sogginess allowed. Also, I do like oatmeal, but not in my crumb toppings.*

Finally, the most successful apple pie recipes diversify the flavor with a variety of apples. This results in a more rounded combination of sweet, tart, and crisp. The addition of the two types of antioxidant-packed berries is a lovely twist on this old favorite. My daughter's rule for this recipe? It should appear on my table almost every Shabbos—as a side dish. There's still room for dessert...

note: This recipe uses half a can of whole-berry cranberry sauce and half a can of blueberry pie filling. What to do with the rest? Check out the Cranberry Blueberry Orange Chicken on page 146. It's one of those sixty-second pour-and-bake recipes.

Peanut Butter Chocolate Pie

Y**ES, THIS** *tastes just as good as it looks. Divine, actually! And whether you choose the dairy or pareve version of this pie, I'm told it's way better than those famous peanut butter cups. So you'll be glad you saved room for a slice of this pie. The rich luxurious decadence will make you feel relaxed and lighter. After all, STRESSED spelled backward is DESSERTS. Coincidence? I think not.*

note: *I used to prepare this dessert with soy milk. I now use coconut milk as a healthier alternative. Many soy products are being promoted as a healthy dairy-free alternative, and there has been a huge public misconception regarding the virtues of soy products. Many studies show that most unfermented soy is highly toxic. Some examples of unfermented soy products are soy milk, soy infant formula, and soy-based veggie burgers. For a dairy-free healthy alternative, ideally consume only organic, fermented soy products.*

dairy option: *Substitute the Tofutti cream cheese with dairy whipped cream cheese, the coconut milk with milk, and the pareve chocolate with milk chocolate.*

1 9-inch chocolate graham cracker pie crust

• Salted peanuts, chopped

PEANUT BUTTER LAYER

1 CONTAINER (8 oz.) Tofutti cream cheese

1 CUP peanut butter

¼ CUP sugar

1 egg, beaten

¼ TSP. vanilla extract

CHOCOLATE LAYER

1 BAR (3.5 oz.) good-quality pareve chocolate (I like Rosemarie)

1 TBSP. coconut milk

3 TBSP. sugar

¼ TSP. vanilla extract

1 egg, beaten

½ CONTAINER (4 oz.) Tofutti cream cheese

1. Preheat the oven to 300° F. To prepare the peanut butter layer: Beat the pareve cream cheese, peanut butter, sugar, egg, and vanilla. Spread over the bottom of the graham cracker pie crust.

2. To prepare the chocolate layer: In the top of a double boiler or in the microwave, melt the chocolate with the coconut milk. Beat in the sugar, vanilla, egg, and pareve cream cheese. Spread gently over the peanut butter layer.

3. Bake for 45 minutes or until the center is lightly set. Do not overbake. Allow to cool to room temperature.

4. Sprinkle the chopped salted peanuts over the pie. Chill for at least 6 hours before serving. **Serves 8.**

INDEX

A

Aburi Sesame Tuna with Wasabi Garlic Cream 204

AIOLI

Scallion Quinoa Patties with Lemon Garlic Paprika Aioli 10

ALMONDS

Chocolate French Macarons with Caramel Cream 264

Clementine Glazed Chicken and Baby Arugula Salad with
Balsamic-Soy Vinaigrette. 88

Coconut Couscous with Scallion Lime Syrup and Mango 58

Crispy Beef Salad with Warm Peppers and Thai Sweet-
Chili Vinaigrette 110

Fusion Chef Salad with Triple Crunch 114

Ice Cream Razzle 324

Nectarine and Plum Crostata 386

Purple Cabbage and Yellow Bell Pepper Slaw 108

Romaine with Avocado, Cucumber, Mango, and Red Onion
Dressing. 104

Wild Rice Pilaf with Cherries and Almonds. 21

See also nuts

APPETIZERS AND SIDES

Asian Portobello Mushrooms 14

Baked Sweet Potato Fries with Cajun Mayo and Garlic-Basil
Mayo. 24

Bell Pepper Mushroom Crostini 42

Black and Green Olive Tapenade 50

Butcher's Cut with Broccoli Mashed Potatoes 48

Cauliflower Mash. 62

Challah 27

Coconut Couscous with Scallion Lime Syrup and Mango 58

Deli Roll Sushi with Dipping Sauce 12

Garlic Bread with Porcini-Onion Relish. 18

Lemon Artichoke Cream Potato Salad 43

Mexican Chicken-Filled Crepes with Shallot Sauce. 34

Minced Garlic and Rosemary Garlic Pita Crisps. 46

Mini Mushroom Beef Sliders. 66

No-Grease Everything Knots 40

Orzo Salad with Garbanzos, Peppers, and Dill 33

Pastrami Potato Kugelettes. 26

Pesto Chicken or Sweetbreads with Tomato Basil Polenta
Stacks 44

Potato Kugel and Sweet Potato Roulade. 30

Pulled Meat Wontons with Honey Mustard Sauce 56

Roasted Asparagus and String Bean Bundles 63

Roasted Eggplant and Red Pepper Dip 60

Roasted Fingerlings and Brussels Sprouts with Sage Brown
Butter 32

Salmon Tartare 16

Scallion Quinoa Patties with Lemon Garlic Paprika Aioli 10

Skirt Steak Spring Rolls with Corn off the Cob 38

Stuffed Eggplant Canapés with Veal. 22

Tarragon Egg Salad and Guacamole on Wonton Crisps. 54

Teriyaki Sesame Pasta 53

Tomato Basil Salad with a Duo of Vinegars. 52

Tongue Polonaise. 28

Tri-Color Garlic Mashed Potatoes with Caramelized
Shallots. 20

Trio of Spiced Olive Tapas 64

Tuna Tartare 36

Wild Rice Pilaf with Cherries and Almonds. 21

Apple Cranberry Blueberry Crisp. 358

Apple Rose Custard Turnovers 316

APPLES

Apple Cranberry Blueberry Crisp. 358

Apple Rose Custard Turnovers 316

Arugula Waldorf Salad with Maple Walnuts 109

Five-Minute Apple Crumb Cake. 299

Sour Cream Apple Pie with Walnut Streusel. 228

Tangerine Glazed Apple Apricot Strudel 339

Apricot Balsamic Cornish Hens 124

APRICOT JAM

Apricot Balsamic Cornish Hens 124

Coconut Tilapia with Apricot Teriyaki Sauce. 188

Lime Sea Bass with Sweet Chili Apricot Relish. 192

Nectarine and Plum Crostata 286

Tangerine Glazed Apple Apricot Strudel 339

APRICOTS

Apricot Balsamic Cornish Hens 124

Moscato d'Asti Apricot Compote 288

Spring Mix with Candied Hazelnuts and Pecans and
Balsamic-Strawberry Vinaigrette 92

ARTICHOKES

Lemon Artichoke Cream Potato Salad 43

Arugula Waldorf Salad with Maple Walnuts. 109

ARUGULA

Arugula Waldorf Salad with Maple Walnuts 109

Clementine Glazed Chicken and Baby Arugula Salad with
Balsamic-Soy Vinaigrette. 88

Crispy Beef Salad with Warm Peppers and Thai Sweet-
    Chili Vinaigrette 110
Garlic Bread with Porcini-Onion Relish. 18
Asian Portobello Mushrooms 14
Asian Slaw with Chow Mein Noodles and Sesame Dressing 90

ASPARAGUS
Creamy Broccoli Asparagus Soup 84
Halibut in Balsamic Honey Butter Sauce 247
Roasted Asparagus and String Bean Bundles 63
Avocado, Tomato, and Hearts of Palm Salad. 116

AVOCADO
Avocado, Tomato, and Hearts of Palm Salad 116
Creamy Broccoli Asparagus Soup 84
Crispy Sesame Chicken Cutlets with Avocado Hummus . . . 138
Fusion Chef Salad with Triple Crunch in Tortilla Wraps 114
Romaine with Avocado, Cucumber, Mango,
    and Red Onion Dressing 104
Smoked Turkey and Chicken Salad with Creamy Avocado
    Dressing. 100
Tarragon Egg Salad and Guacamole on Wonton Crisps. 54

B

Baby Red Potato Salad with Caesar Dill Dressing. 96
Baked Sweet Potato Fries with Cajun Mayo and Garlic-Basil
    Mayo. 24
Balsamic Duck a l'Orange. 148
Balsamic Grilled Peaches with Basil-Pistachio Ice Cream on
    Cinnamon Skewers 298

BANANAS
Pistachio French Toast with Banana Salsa. 348
Warm Cinnamon Buns with Flambéed Rum Bananas 262

BARS
Better-Than-Snickers Dessert Bars 220
Basil Granita. 318

BASIL
Baked Sweet Potato Fries with Cajun Mayo and Garlic-Basil
    Mayo. 24
Balsamic Grilled Peaches with Basil-Pistachio Ice Cream
    on Cinnamon Skewers 298
Basil Granita 318
Bell Pepper Mushroom Crostini 42
Fettuccine with Pistachio Pesto Alfredo Cream. 224

Grilled Steak with Herb and Garlic Tapenade 170
Mediterranean Olives. 64
No-Grease Everything Knots 40
Panko-Crusted Tomato Basil Chilean Sea Bass 198
Pesto Chicken or Sweetbreads with Tomato Basil Polenta
    Stacks 44
Pistachio-Crusted Salmon with Eggplant Puree. 202
Sun-Dried Tomato and Basil Capons. 130
Tomato Basil Salad with a Duo of Vinegars. 52
Bavarian Strawberries 'n' Cream Napoleon 275
BBQ Tortilla Chip Salad. 98

BARBECUE CHIPS
BBQ Tortilla Chip Salad. 98

BARBECUE SAUCE
Grilled Chicken Satay with Peanut Butter Barbecue Sauce . . . 136
Mini Mushroom Beef Sliders. 66
Pulled Meat Wontons with Honey Mustard Sauce. 56
Rack of Flanken with Cola Marinade and Coffee Barbecue
    Sauce 158
Skirt Steak Spring Rolls with Corn off the Cob 38
Tamari French Roast or Brisket 178

BEANS
Orzo Salad with Garbanzos, Peppers, and Dill 33
Minestrone Soup 83
Tuscan Chicken with Spaghetti. 140

BEEF
Beef Bourguignon. 80
Butcher's Cut with Broccoli Mashed Potatoes 48
Creole Veal Burgers with Remoulade Sauce 160
Crispy Beef Salad with Warm Peppers and Thai Sweet-
    Chili Vinaigrette 110
Filet Mignon au Poivre 174
Garlic Bread with Porcini-Onion Relish. 18
Garlic Teriyaki Roast 166
Grilled Steak with Herb and Garlic
    Tapenade. 170
Lemon-Thyme Delmonico Roast 162
Marinated Cherry-Soy London Broil 164
Mini Mushroom Beef Sliders. 66
New York Strip Steak with Cabernet Merlot Reduction
    Sauce and Crispy Shallots 168
Pasta Bolognese. 156
Pulled Meat Wontons with Honey Mustard Sauce. 56
Rack of Flanken with Cola Marinade and Coffee Barbecue
    Sauce 158

Savory Club Steak with Caramelized Onions 152
Skirt Steak Spring Rolls with Corn off the Cob 38
Smoked Sweet-and-Sour Ribs 167
Tamari French Roast or Brisket 178
Tongue Polonaise 28
Twenty-Garlic-Clove Standing Rib Roast 176
See also corned beef; pastrami
Beef Bourguignon 80
Bell Pepper Mushroom Crostini 42

BERRIES
Chocolate Shortcakes with Vanilla Cream and Berries 344
Easy Cheesecake with Berry Cups 252
Green Tea Lychee Berry Tart 248
Nectarine and Plum Crostata 286
Warm Chocolate Soufflé with a Hint of Chili 308
See also blueberries; strawberries
Best Chicken Soup 76
Better-Than-Snickers Dessert Bars 220

BEVERAGES
Orange Mousse in Phyllo Baskets with Citrus Punchsietta . . . 272
Pomegranate Strawberry Mocktail with Sorbet 270
Strawberries and Cream Smoothies 236
Black and Green Olive Tapenade 50
Blackened Tuna with Tropical Salad and Honey-Lime Dressing . . . 94
Blood Orange Mint Sorbet 334
Blueberry Lemon Biscuit Pie 290

BLUEBERRIES
Apple Cranberry Blueberry Crisp 358
Blueberry Lemon Biscuit Pie 290
Chocolate Chip Blueberry Amaretto Cake 313
Cranberry Blueberry Orange Chicken 146
Crepes Suzette 306
Fruit Salad with Balsamic Strawberry Coulis, Crunchy
Nuts, and Pomegranate Seeds 346
Fruit Salad with Toasted Pine Nuts and Craisins 326
Spring Mix with Candied Hazelnuts and Pecans and
Balsamic-Strawberry Vinaigrette 92
Bourbon Toasted Pecan Pie 340

BREAD
Bell Pepper Mushroom Crostini 42
Challah 27
Garlic Bread with Porcini-Onion Relish 18
Minced Garlic and Rosemary Garlic Pita Crisps 46
No-Grease Everything Knots 40
Pistachio French Toast with Banana Salsa 348

Stuffed French Bread with Spinach, Herbs, and Cheese 227
Three-Glaze Cinnamon Buns 354
Warm Cinnamon Buns with Flambéed Rum Bananas 262

BROCCOLI
Butcher's Cut with Broccoli Mashed Potatoes 48
Cashew Chicken Stir-Fry with Sweet Chili Glaze 142
Creamy Broccoli Asparagus Soup 84
One-Pot Chicken Dinner 128

BRUSSELS SPROUTS
Roasted Fingerlings and Brussels Sprouts with Sage Brown
Butter 32

BURGERS
Creole Veal Burgers with Remoulade Sauce 160
Mini Mushroom Beef Sliders 66
Butcher's Cut with Broccoli Mashed Potatoes 48

BUTTERNUT SQUASH
Cream of Roasted Butternut Squash Soup with Herbes de
Provence Tuiles 70
Vegetable Dumpling Soup 72

C

CABBAGE
Minestrone Soup 83
Purple Cabbage and Yellow Bell Pepper Slaw 108

CAJUN
Baked Sweet Potato Fries with Cajun Mayo and Garlic-Basil
Mayo 24
Creole Veal Burgers with Remoulade Sauce 160
Sixty-Second Cajun Salmon with Dill 182

CAKES
Chocolate Bundlettes with Mocha Fondue 320
Chocolate Chip Blueberry Amaretto Cake 313
Cointreau Mocha Cake 312
Dark Chocolate Cupcakes with Espresso Frosting 284
Easy Cheesecake with Berry Cups 252
Five-Minute Apple Crumb Cake 299
Fudge Marble Bundt Cake 314
Ginger Carrot Cake with Lime Cream Cheese Frosting
(Pareve) 296
Healthy Moist Carrot-Orange Muffins 322
Marscapone Cheese Danishes 254
Mini Cheese Babkas 234

Mini Chocolate Chip Cheesecakes 255
No-Bake Cheesecake Mousse 216
Plum Torte 274
Sea Salt Caramel Bundt Cake 310
Warm Deep-Dish Giant Chocolate Chip Cookie Torte 336
See also pies; tarts

CAPERS
Black and Green Olive Tapenade 50
Mediterranean Olives 64
Sole in Lime Caper Chili Sauce 226
Tarragon Egg Salad and Guacamole on Wonton Crisps 54

CAPONS
Sun-Dried Tomato and Basil Capons 130

CARAMEL
Better-Than-Snickers Dessert Bars .220
Chocolate French Macarons with Caramel Cream 264
Powdered Chocolate Wontons with Caramel Sauce 356
Sea Salt Caramel Bundt Cake 310
Sour Cream Apple Pie with Walnut Streusel 228
Three-Glaze Cinnamon Buns 354
Caramelized Baked Sticky Sesame Chicken 149
Caramelized Pear Spinach Salad with Pomegranate and Pecans .112

CARROTS
Carrot Chips 98
Ginger Carrot Cake with Lime Cream Cheese Frosting
(Pareve) 296
Healthy Moist Carrot-Orange Muffins 322
Cashew Chicken Stir-Fry with Sweet Chili Glaze 142
Cauliflower Mash 62
Challah 27
Cheese Truffles 214

CHEESE
Cheese Truffles 214
Cream of Spinach Soup 222
Fettuccine with Pistachio Pesto Alfredo
Cream 224
Four-Ingredient Fettuccine Alfredo 224
Ginger Carrot Cake with Lime Cream Cheese Frosting
(Pareve) 296
Haloumi Salad with Warm Mushrooms and Teriyaki
Dressing 212
Heirloom Caprese Salad on Rosemary Skewers 246
Linguine with White Wine Cream Sauce and Mushrooms . 240
Mascarpone Cheese Danishes 254
Mini Cheese Babkas 234

Panko Mozzarella Sticks with Red Wine Vinegar Marinara
Sauce 230
Pareve Cheese Mousse with White Viennese Crunch 294
Penne Vodka 256
Slow-Cooked French Onion Soup .250
Stuffed French Bread with Spinach, Herbs, and Cheese 227
See also cheesecake; cream cheese; mozzarella; parmesan

CHEESECAKE
Easy Cheesecake with Berry Cups .252
Mini Chocolate Chip Cheesecakes .255
No-Bake Cheesecake Mousse 216

CHERRIES
Arugula Waldorf Salad with Maple Walnuts 109
Fruit Soup Salad with Toasted Pine Nuts and Craisins 326
Green Tea Lychee Berry Tart 248
Marinated Cherry-Soy London Broil 164
Romaine with Avocado, Cucumber, Mango, and Red Onion
Dressing 104
Wild Rice Pilaf with Cherries and Almonds 21

CHESTNUTS
Roasted Chestnut Pumpkin Soup 74
Chicken Fire Poppers 132

CHICKEN
Apricot Balsamic Cornish Hens 124
Best Chicken Soup 76
Caramelized Baked Sticky Sesame Chicken 149
Cashew Chicken Stir-Fry with Sweet Chili Glaze 142
Chicken Fire Poppers 132
Clementine Glazed Chicken and Baby Arugula Salad with
Balsamic-Soy Vinaigrette 88
Cranberry Blueberry Orange Chicken 146
Crispy Sesame Chicken Cutlets with Avocado Hummus . . . 138
Grilled Chicken Satay with Peanut Butter Barbecue
Sauce 136
Mexican Chicken-Filled Crepes with Shallot Sauce 34
One-Pot Chicken Dinner 128
Pesto Chicken or Sweetbreads with Tomato Basil Polenta
Stacks 44
Roasted Portobello Chicken Salad 118
Savory Chicken with Papaya Salsa 126
Smoked Turkey and Chicken Salad with Creamy Avocado
Dressing 100
Sun-Dried Tomato and Basil Capons 130
Tuscan Chicken with Spaghetti 140
Chilean Sea Bass with Chive Chimichurri 186

CHILI PEPPERS

Crispy Sesame Chicken Cutlets with Avocado Hummus . . . 138

Sole in Lime Caper Chili Sauce 226

CHILI SAUCE

Cashew Chicken Stir-Fry with Sweet Chili Glaze 142

Crispy Beef Salad with Warm Peppers and Thai Sweet-Chili

Vinaigrette 110

Lime Sea Bass with Sweet Chili Apricot Sauce 192

Rack of Flanken with Cola Marinade and Coffee Barbecue

Sauce 158

Savory Chicken with Papaya Salsa 126

Sole in Lime Caper Chili Sauce 226

Tamari French Toast or Brisket 178

CHIMICHURRI

Chilean Sea Bass with Chive Chimichurri 186

CHIVES

Cheese Truffles 214

Chilean Sea Bass with Chive Chimichurri 186

Deli Roll Sushi with Dipping Sauce 12

Grilled Steak with Herb and Garlic Tapenade 170

No-Grease Everything Knots 40

Scallion Quinoa with Lemon Garlic Paprika Aioli 10

Stuffed Eggplant Canapés with Veal 22

Stuffed French Bread with Spinach, Herbs, and Cheese 227

Two-Toned Gefilte Fish Gift Squares 208

Chocolate Bundlettes with Mocha Fondue 320

Chocolate Chip Blueberry Amaretto Cake 313

Chocolate Chunk Pudding Cookies 244

Chocolate Toffee Torte 260

Chocolate French Macarons with Caramel Cream 264

Chocolate Shortcakes with Vanilla Cream and Berries 344

CHOCOLATE

Better-Than-Snickers Dessert Bars 220

Chocolate Bundlettes with Mocha Fondue 320

Chocolate Chip Blueberry Amaretto Cake 313

Chocolate Chunk Pudding Cookies 244

Chocolate French Macarons with Caramel Cream 264

Chocolate Shortcakes with Vanilla Cream and Berries 344

Chocolate Toffee Torte 260

Dark Chocolate Cupcakes with Espresso Frosting 284

Double Chocolate Ganache Tart 353

Fudge Marble Bundt Cake 314

Hazelnut Chocolate Mousse with Chocolate-Dipped Potato

Chips 300

Ice Cream Razzle 324

Mini Chocolate Chip Cheesecakes 255

Oreo Cookie Dough Pie 342

Peanut Butter Chocolate Pie 360

Powdered Chocolate Wontons with Caramel Sauce 356

Praline Truffles 283

Profiteroles with Chocolate Rum Sauce 332

Three-Glaze Cinnamon Buns 354

Tiramisu with Chocolate Liquor 350

Toffee Brittle 282

Warm Chocolate Soufflé with a Hint of Chili 308

Warm Deep-Dish Giant Chocolate Chip Cookie Torte 336

CINNAMON

Balsamic Grilled Peaches with Basil-Pistachio Ice Cream

on Cinnamon Skewers 298

Moscato d'Asti Apricot Compote 288

Pomegranate Strawberry Mocktail with Sorbet 270

Three-Glaze Cinnamon Buns 354

Warm Cinnamon Buns with Flambéed Rum Bananas 262

CITRUS FRUITS. *See* lemons; limes; oranges

Clementine Glazed Chicken and Baby Arugula Salad with

Balsamic-Soy Vinaigrette 88

Coconut Couscous with Scallion Lime Syrup and Mango 58

Coconut Tilapia with Apricot Teriyaki Sauce 188

COCONUT

Coconut Couscous with Scallion Lime Syrup and Mango . . . 58

Coconut Tilapia with Apricot Teriyaki Sauce 188

Pomegranate Strawberry Mocktail with

Sorbet 270

COFFEE

Chocolate Bundlettes with Mocha Fondue 320

Cointreau Mocha Cake 312

Dark Chocolate Cupcakes with Espresso Frosting 284

Rack of Flanken with Cola Marinade and Coffee Barbecue

Sauce 158

Spiced Mocha Mousse with Viennese Crunch 330

Cointreau Mocha Cake 312

COLESLAW

Asian Slaw with Chow Mein Noodles and Sesame

Dressing 90

Crispy Kani Slaw with Spicy Mayo 97

Purple Cabbage and Yellow Bell Pepper Slaw 108

COOKIES

Chocolate Chunk Pudding Cookies 244

Chocolate French Macarons with Caramel Cream 264

Chocolate Shortcakes with Vanilla Cream and Berries 344

CORN

Roasted Corn and Sausage Soup 82

Skirt Steak Spring Rolls with Corn off the Cob 38

Smoked Turkey and Chicken Salad with Creamy Avocado

Dressing 100

CORNED BEEF

Roasted Asparagus and String Bean Bundles 63

COUSCOUS

Coconut Couscous with Scallion Lime Syrup and Mango 58

CRAISINS

BBQ Tortilla Chip Salad 98

Caramelized Pear Spinach Salad with Pomegranate and

Pecans 112

Fruit Soup Salad with Toasted Pine Nuts and Craisins 326

Purple Cabbage and Yellow Bell Pepper Slaw 108

Romaine with Avocado, Cucumber, Mango, and Red Onion

Dressing 104

Strawberry Spinach Salad with Yogurt Poppy Seed

Dressing 218

Cranberry Blueberry Orange Chicken .146

CRANBERRY

Apple Cranberry Blueberry Crisp 358

Cranberry Blueberry Orange Chicken .146

Cream of Roasted Butternut Squash Soup with Herbes de

Provence Tuiles 70

Cream of Spinach Soup 222

Creamy Broccoli Asparagus Soup 84

Creamy Roasted Tomato Vodka Soup .238

Creole Veal Burger with Remoulade Sauce 160

CREAM CHEESE

Easy Cheesecake with Berry Cups 252

Ginger Carrot Cake with Lime Cream Cheese Frosting

(Pareve) 296

Mini Cheese Babkas 234

Mini Chocolate Cheesecakes 255

Pareve Cheese Mousse with White Viennese Crunch 294

Crepes Suzette 306

CREPES

Crepes Suzette 306

Mexican Chicken-Filled Crepes with Shallot Sauce 34

CRISPS

Apple Cranberry Blueberry Crisp 358

Maple Peach Crisp with Nutmeg Streusel 352

Crispy Beef Salad with Warm Peppers and Thai Sweet-Chili

Vinaigrette 110

Crispy Kani Slaw with Spicy Mayo 97

CRISPY ONIONS

Orange-Scented Rack of Veal 154

Pesto Caesar Salad with Crispy Onions in Tortilla Bowls 106

Pistachio-Crusted Salmon with Eggplant

Puree 202

Tuna Steaks with Dijon Garlic Sauce .196

Crispy Sesame Chicken Cutlets with Avocado Hummus 138

CUCUMBERS

Crispy Kani Slaw with Spicy Mayo 97

Haloumi Salad with Warm Mushrooms and Teriyaki

Dressing 212

Romaine with Avocado, Cucumber, Mango, and Red Onion

Dressing 104

Tropical Kani Salad with Sriracha Lime

Dressing 120

CUPCAKES

Dark Chocolate Cupcakes with Espresso Frosting 284

Mini Chocolate Chip Cheesecakes 255

Mini Cheese Babkas 234

CUSTARD

Apple Rose Custard Turnovers 316

Bavarian Strawberries 'n' Cream Napoleon 275

Eggnog Crème Brûlée 242

D

DAIRY

Better-Than-Snickers Dessert Bars 220

Cheese Truffles 214

Chocolate Chunk Pudding Cookies 244

Cream of Spinach Soup 222

Creamy Roasted Tomato Vodka Soup 238

Easy Cheesecake with Berry Cups 252

Eggnog Crème Brûlée 242

Fettuccine with Pistachio Pesto Alfredo Cream 224

Four-Ingredient Fettuccine Alfredo 224

Green Tea Lychee Berry Tart 248

Halibut in Balsamic Honey Butter Sauce 247

Haloumi Salad with Warm Mushrooms and Teriyaki

Dressing 212

Heirloom Caprese Salad on Rosemary Skewers 246

Key Lime Pie with Pecan Crust 232

Linguine with White Wine Cream Sauce and Mushrooms . . .240
Mascarpone Cheese Danishes. 254
Mini Cheese Babkas 234
Mini Chocolate Chip Cheesecakes .255
No-Bake Cheesecake Mousse 216
Panko Mozzarella Sticks with Red Wine Vinegar Marinara
    Sauce 230
Penne Vodka 256
Slow-Cooked French Onion Soup .250
Sole in Lime Caper Chili Sauce 226
Sour Cream Apple Pie with Walnut Streusel. 228
Strawberries and Cream Smoothies 236
Strawberry Spinach Salad with Yogurt Poppy Seed
    Dressing. 218
Stuffed French Bread with Spinach, Herbs, and Cheese. 227

DANISHES

Mascarpone Cheese Danishes. 254
Dark Chocolate Cupcakes with Espresso Frosting. 284
Deli Roll Sushi with Dipping Sauce. 12

DESSERTS

Apple Cranberry Blueberry Crisp. 358
Apple Rose Custard Turnovers 316
Balsamic Grilled Peaches with Basil-Pistachio Ice Cream
    on Cinnamon Skewers 298
Basil Granita 318
Bavarian Strawberries 'n' Cream Napoleon. 275
Better-Than-Snickers Dessert Bars 220
Blood Orange Mint Sorbet. 334
Blueberry Lemon Biscuit Pie 290
Bourbon Toasted Pecan Pie. 340
Chocolate Bundlettes with Mocha Fondue 320
Chocolate Chip Blueberry Amaretto Cake. 313
Chocolate Chunk Pudding Cookies 244
Chocolate French Macarons with Caramel Cream 264
Chocolate Shortcakes with Vanilla Cream and Berries. 344
Chocolate Toffee Torte 260
Cointreau Mocha Cake. 312
Crepes Suzette 306
Dark Chocolate Cupcakes with Espresso Frosting. 284
Double Chocolate Ganache Tart 353
Easy Cheesecake with Berry Cups. 252
Eggnog Crème Brûlée. 242
Five-Minute Apple Crumb Cake. 299
Fruit Salad with Balsamic Strawberry Coulis, Crunchy Nuts,
    and Pomegranate Seeds. 346

Fruit Soup Salad with Toasted Pine Nuts and Craisins 326
Fruit Tartare. 292
Fudge Marble Bundt Cake 314
Ginger Carrot Cake with Lime Cream Cheese Frosting
    (Pareve) 296
Grape-Lime Granita. 318
Green Tea Lychee Berry Tart 248
Hazelnut Chocolate Mousse with Chocolate-Dipped
    Potato Chips 300
Healthy Moist Carrot-Orange Muffins. 322
Ice Bowls 302
Ice Cream Razzle 324
Key Lime Pie with Pecan Crust 232
Lemon Meringue Pie. 338
Maple Peach Crisp with Nutmeg Streusel 352
Mascarpone Cheese Danishes. 254
Mini Cheese Babkas 234
Mini Chocolate Chip Cheesecakes 255
Moscato d'Asti Apricot Compote 288
Nectarine and Plum Crostata 286
No-Bake Cheesecake Mousse 216
Orange Mousse in Phyllo Baskets with Citrus Punchsietta . . .272
Oreo Cookie Dough Pie 342
Pareve Cheese Mousse with White Viennese Crunch. 294
Peanut Butter Chocolate Pie 360
Peanut Butter Mousse Vol-au-Vents 328
Pistachio French Toast with Banana Salsa 348
Plum Torte 274
Pomegranate Strawberry Mocktail with Sorbet 270
Powdered Chocolate Wontons with Caramel Sauce. 356
Praline Truffles 283
Pretzel-Crusted Lemon Lime Pie 268
Profiteroles with Chocolate Rum Sauce 332
Quilted Fondant for Cupcakes 285
Sea Salt Caramel Bundt Cake 310
Sorbet and Ice Cream Sandwich Trifle 266
Sour Cream Apple Pie with Walnut Streusel. 228
Spiced Mocha Mousse with Viennese Crunch. 330
Tangerine Glazed Apple Apricot Strudel 339
Three-Glaze Cinnamon Buns 354
Tiramisu with Chocolate Liquor 350
Toffee Brittle 282
Warm Chocolate Soufflé with a Hint of Chili 308
Warm Cinnamon Buns with Flambéed Rum Bananas 262
Warm Deep-Dish Giant Chocolate Chip Cookie Torte. 336

DILL

Baby Red Potato Salad with Caesar Dill Dressing 96

Citrus Dill Olives. 64

Orzo Salad with Garbanzos, Peppers, and Dill 33

Sixty-Second Cajun Salmon with Dill 182

DIPS

Aburi Sesame Tuna with Wasabi Garlic Cream 204

Baked Sweet Potato Fries with Cajun Mayo and Garlic-Basil
Mayo. 24

Black and Green Olive Tapenade 50

Crispy Sesame Chicken Cutlets with Avocado
Hummus 138

Roasted Eggplant and Red Pepper Dip 60

Savory Chicken with Papaya Salsa. 126

Smoked Turkey and Chicken Salad with Creamy Avocado
Dressing. 100

See also dressings; sauces

Double Chocolate Ganache Tart. 353

DRESSINGS

Asian Slaw with Chow Mein Noodles and Sesame
Dressing. 90

Baby Red Potato Salad with Caesar Dill Dressing 96

BBQ Tortilla Chip Salad. 98

Blackened Tuna with Tropical Salad and Honey-Lime
Dressing. 94

Crispy Kani Slaw with Spicy Mayo. 97

Haloumi Salad with Warm Mushrooms and Teriyaki
Dressing. 212

Lemon Artichoke Cream Potato Salad 43

Romaine with Avocado, Cucumber, Mango, and Red Onion
Dressing. 104

Smoked Turkey and Chicken Salad with Creamy Avocado
Dressing. 100

Strawberry Spinach Salad with Yogurt Poppy Seed
Dressing 218

Tropical Kani Salad with Sriracha Lime Dressing 120

See also vinaigrettes

DUCK

Balsamic Duck a l'Orange 148

Pomegranate Honey Glazed Duck Breast with Sesame
Roasted Sweet Potatoes. 134

DUMPLINGS

Vegetable Dumpling Soup. 72

E

Easy Cheesecake with Berry Cups. 252

EGG ROLLS

Skirt Steak Spring Rolls with Corn off the Cob 38

Eggnog Crème Brûlée 242

EGGPLANT

Eggplant Canapés with Veal 22

Pistachio-Crusted Salmon with Eggplant Puree. 202

Roasted Eggplant and Red Pepper Dip 60

EGGS

Tarragon Egg Salad and Guacamole on Wonton Crisps. 54

F

Fettuccine with Pistachio Pesto Alfredo Cream 224

Filet Mignon au Poivre. 174

FINGERLINGS

Roasted Fingerlings and Brussels Sprouts with Sage Brown
Butter 32

FISH

Aburi Sesame Tuna with Wasabi Garlic Cream 204

Blackened Tuna with Tropical Salad and Honey-Lime
Dressing. 94

Chilean Sea Bass with Chive Chimichurri. 186

Coconut Tilapia with Apricot Teriyaki Sauce. 188

Crispy Kani Slaw with Spicy Mayo. 97

Halibut in Balsamic Honey Butter Sauce 247

Lime Sea Bass with Sweet Chili Apricot Relish. 192

Panko-Crusted Tomato Basil Chilean Sea Bass 198

Pistachio-Crusted Salmon with Eggplant Puree. 202

Poached Sweet and Tangy Salmon 206

Sake-Glazed Salmon with Shitake and Portobello
Mushrooms. 184

Salmon Tartare 16

Sixty-Second Cajun Salmon with Dill 182

Sole in Lime Caper Chili Sauce 226

Striped Sesame Teriyaki Salmon 194

Sushi Gefilte Fish 190

Sweet Gefilte Fish with Caramelized Tomatoes, Mushrooms,
and Onions 200

Tropical Kani Salad with Sriracha Lime Dressing 120
Tuna Steaks with Dijon Garlic Sauce 196
Tuna Tartare 36
Two-Toned Gefilte Fish Gift Squares 208
Five-Minute Apple Crumb Cake 299

FONDANT
Praline Truffles 283
Quilted Fondant for Cupcakes 285
Four-Ingredient Fettuccine Alfredo 224

FROSTING
Dark Chocolate Cupcakes with Espresso Frosting 284
Ginger Carrot Cake with Lime Cream Cheese Frosting
(Pareve) 296
See also glazes
Fruit Salad with Balsamic Strawberry Coulis, Crunchy Nuts,
and Pomegranate Seeds 346
Fruit Soup Salad with Toasted Pine Nuts and Craisins 326
Fruit Tartare 292
FRUIT. *See* apples; apricots; berries; blueberries; cherries;
cranberry; kiwi; lemons; limes; lychees; mango; olives; oranges;
papaya; peaches; pears; plums; pomegranate; strawberries

FRUIT SALAD
Fruit Salad with Balsamic Strawberry Coulis, Crunchy Nuts,
and Pomegranate Seeds 346
Fruit Soup Salad with Toasted Pine Nuts and Craisins 326
Fruit Tartare 292
Fudge Marble Bundt Cake 314
Fusion Chef Salad with Triple Crunch in Tortilla Wraps 114

G

GANACHE
Double Chocolate Ganache Tart 353

GARBANZOS
Minestrone Soup 83
Orzo Salad with Garbanzos, Peppers, and Dill 33
Garlic Bread with Porcini-Onion Relish 18
Garlic Teriyaki Roast 166

GARLIC
Aburi Sesame Tuna with Wasabi Garlic Cream 204
Baked Sweet Potato Fries with Cajun Mayo and Garlic-Basil
Mayo 24
Garlic Bread with Porcini-Onion Relish 18

Garlic Teriyaki Roast 166
Grilled Steak with Herb and Garlic Tapenade 170
Minced Garlic and Rosemary Garlic Pita Crisps 46
No-Grease Everything Knots 40
Savory Garlic Olives 64
Scallion Quinoa Patties with Lemon Garlic Paprika Aioli 10
Tri-Color Garlic Mashed Potatoes with Caramelized
Shallots 20
Tuna Steaks with Dijon Garlic Sauce 196
Twenty-Garlic-Clove Standing Rib Roast 176

GEFILTE FISH
Sushi Gefilte Fish 190
Sweet Gefilte Fish with Caramelized Tomatoes, Mushrooms,
and Onions 200
Two-Toned Gefilte Fish Gift Squares 208
Ginger Carrot Cake with Lime Cream Cheese Frosting
(Pareve) 296

GLAZES
Cointreau Mocha Cake 312
Sea Salt Caramel Bundt Cake 310
Three-Glaze Cinnamon Buns 354
See also frosting
Grape-Lime Granita 318

GRANITA
Basil Granita 318
Grape-Lime Granita 318
Green Tea Lychee Berry Tart 248
Grilled Chicken Satay with Peanut Butter Barbecue Sauce 136
Grilled Steak with Herb and Garlic Tapenade 170

GUACAMOLE
Tarragon Egg Salad and Guacamole on Wonton Crisps 54

H

Halibut in Balsamic Honey Butter Sauce .247
Haloumi Salad with Warm Mushrooms and Teriyaki
Dressing 212
Hazelnut Chocolate Mousse with Chocolate-Dipped
Potato Chips 300

HAZELNUTS
Garlic Bread with Porcini-Onion Relish 18
Hazelnut Chocolate Mousse with Chocolate-Dipped
Potato Chips 300

Spring Mix with Candied Hazelnuts and Pecans and Balsamic-Strawberry Vinaigrette 92

Healthy Moist Carrot-Orange Muffins 322

HEARTS OF PALM

Avocado, Tomato, and Hearts of Palm Salad 116

Heirloom Caprese Salad on Rosemary Skewers 246

HERBS. *See* basil; chives; parsley; rosemary; sage; thyme

HONEY

Blackened Tuna with Tropical Salad and Honey-Lime Dressing 94

Halibut in Balsamic Honey Butter Sauce 247

Pomegranate Honey Glazed Duck Breast with Sesame Roasted Sweet Potatoes 134

Pulled Meat Wontons with Honey Mustard Sauce 56

HORSERADISH

Coconut Tilapia with Apricot Teriyaki Sauce 188

Pickled Dark Turkey Roast with Brown Sugar Horseradish Sauce 144

Sushi Gefilte Fish 190

Twenty-Garlic-Clove Standing Rib Roast 176

HUMMUS

Crispy Sesame Chicken Cutlets with Avocado Hummus 138

I

Ice Bowls 302

Ice Cream Razzle 324

ICE CREAM

Balsamic Grilled Peaches with Basil-Pistachio Ice Cream on Cinnamon Skewers 298

Chocolate Bundlettes with Mocha Fondue 320

Crepes Suzette 306

Ice Cream Razzle 324

Profiteroles with Chocolate Rum Sauce 332

Sorbet and Ice Cream Sandwich Trifle 266

Warm Chocolate Soufflé with a Hint of Chili 308

Warm Cinnamon Buns with Flambéed Rum Bananas 262

Warm Deep-Dish Giant Chocolate Chip Cookie Torte 336

ICING. *See* glazes; frosting

J

JALAPENO

Best Chicken Soup 76

Blackened Tuna with Tropical Salad and Honey-Lime Dressing 94

Tuna Tartare 36

K

KANI

Crispy Kani Slaw with Spicy Mayo 97

Tropical Kani Salad with Sriracha Lime Dressing 120

Key Lime Pie with Pecan Crust 232

KIWI

Fruit Salad with Balsamic Strawberry Coulis, Crunchy Nuts, and Pomegranate Seeds 340

Fruit Soup Salad with Toasted Pine Nuts and Craisins 326

Fruit Tartare 292

KUGEL

Pastrami Potato Kugelettes 26

Potato Kugel and Sweet Potato Roulade 30

L

LAMB

Rack of Lamb with Orange Mustard Rosemary Sauce 172

LEEKS

Best Chicken Soup 76

Vegetable Dumpling Soup 72

Lemon Artichoke Cream Potato Salad 43

Lemon Meringue Pie 338

LEMONS

Blueberry Lemon Biscuit Pie 290

Lemon Artichoke Cream Potato Salad 43

Lemon Meringue Pie 338

Lemon-Thyme Delmonico Roast 162

Pretzel-Crusted Lemon Lime Pie 268

Scallion Quinoa Patties with Lemon Garlic Paprika Aioli 10

Lemon-Thyme Delmonico Roast 162

LETTUCE

BBQ Tortilla Chip Salad. 98

Fusion Chef Salad with Triple Crunch in Tortilla Wraps 114

Haloumi Salad with Warm Mushrooms and Teriyaki
Dressing. 212

Pesto Caesar Salad with Crispy Onions in Tortilla Bowls. . . .106

Romaine with Avocado, Cucumber, Mango, and Red Onion
Dressing. 104

Smoked Turkey and Chicken Salad with Creamy Avocado
Dressing. 100

Terra Stix, Mushroom, and Bell Pepper Salad 102

Lime Sea Bass with Sweet Chili Apricot Relish 192

LIMES

Blackened Tuna with Tropical Salad and Honey-Lime
Dressing. 94

Coconut Couscous with Scallion Lime Syrup and Mango 58

Ginger Carrot Cake with Lime Cream Cheese Frosting
(Pareve) 296

Key Lime Pie with Pecan Crust 232

Lime Sea Bass with Sweet Chili Apricot Relish 192

Pretzel-Crusted Lemon Lime Pie 268

Sole in Lime Caper Chili Sauce 226

Tropical Kani Salad with Sriracha Lime Dressing 120

Linguine with White Wine Cream Sauce and Mushrooms 240

LYCHEES

Green Tea Lychee Berry Tart. 248

M

MANGO

Blackened Tuna with Tropical Salad and Honey-Lime
Dressing. 94

Coconut Couscous with Scallion Lime Syrup and Mango 58

Fruit Salad with Balsamic Strawberry Coulis, Crunchy Nuts,
and Pomegranate Seeds. 346

Fruit Soup Salad with Toasted Pine Nuts and Craisins 326

Fruit Tartare. 292

Romaine with Avocado, Cucumber, Mango, and Red Onion
Dressing. 104

Strawberry Spinach Salad with Yogurt Poppy Seed
Dressing. 218

Tropical Kani Salad with Sriracha Lime Dressing 120

Maple Peach Crisp with Nutmeg Streusel 352

Marinated Cherry-Soy London Broil 164

Mascarpone Cheese Danishes 254

MAYONNAISE

Baked Sweet Potato Fries with Cajun Mayo and Garlic-Basil
Mayo. 24

Crispy Kani Slaw with Spicy Mayo. 97

MEAT. *See beef; lamb; veal*

Mexican Chicken-Filled Crepes with Shallot Sauce 34

Minced Garlic and Rosemary Garlic Pita Crisps 46

Minestrone Soup 83

Mini Mushroom Beef Sliders 66

Mini Cheese Babkas. 234

Mini Chocolate Chip Cheesecakes. 255

MINT

Blood Orange Mint Sorbet. 334

Fruit Tartare. 292

Green Tea Lychee Berry Tart. 248

Pistachio French Toast with Banana Salsa 348

Pomegranate Strawberry Mocktail with Sorbet 270

MOCHA

Chocolate Bundlettes with Mocha Fondue 320

Cointreau Mocha Cake. 312

Spiced Mocha Mousse with Viennese Crunch. 330

Moscato d'Asti Apricot Compote. 288

MOUSSE

Hazelnut Chocolate Mousse with Chocolate-Dipped
Potato Chips 300

No-Bake Cheesecake Mousse 216

Orange Mousse in Phyllo Baskets with Citrus Punchsietta . . .272

Pareve Cheese Mousse with White Viennese Crunch 294

Peanut Butter Mousse Vol-au-Vents 328

Spiced Mocha Mousse with Viennese Crunch. 330

MOZZARELLA

Heirloom Caprese Salad on Rosemary Skewers. 246

Panko Mozzarella Sticks with Red Wine Vinegar Marinara
Sauce 230

Stuffed French Bread with Spinach, Herbs, and Cheese. 227

MUFFINS

Healthy Moist Carrot-Orange Muffins. 322

MUSHROOMS

Asian Portobello Mushrooms 14

Bell Pepper Mushroom Crostini 42

Garlic Bread with Porcini-Onion Relish. 18

Haloumi Salad with Warm Mushrooms and Teriyaki
  Dressing.. 212
Linguine with White Wine Cream Sauce and
  Mushrooms...240
Mini Mushroom Beef Sliders.............................66
Roasted Portobello Chicken Salad.....................118
Roasted Portobello Mushroom Soup 78
Sake-Glazed Salmon with Shitake and Portobello
  Mushrooms.. 184
Sweet Gefilte Fish with Caramelized Tomatoes, Mushrooms,
  and Onions 200
Terra Stix, Mushroom, and Bell Pepper Salad.......... 102

MUSTARD
Pulled Meat Wontons with Honey Mustard Sauce..........56
Rack of Lamb with Orange Mustard Rosemary
  Sauce 172
Striped Sesame Teriyaki Salmon 194
Tuna Steaks with Dijon Garlic Sauce.................. 196

N

Nectarine and Plum Crostata 286
New York Strip Steak with Cabernet Merlot Reduction Sauce
  and Crispy Shallots 168
No-Bake Cheesecake Mousse 216
No Grease Everything Knots 40

NOODLES
Asian Slaw with Chow Mein Noodles and Sesame
  Dressing..90
Best Chicken Soup..................................... 76
Fusion Chef Salad with Triple Crunch in Tortilla
  Wraps..114

NUTS
Cashew Chicken Stir-Fry with Sweet Chili
  Glaze.. 142
Fruit Salad with Balsamic Strawberry Coulis, Crunchy Nuts,
  and Pomegranate Seeds................................346
Peanut Butter Mousse Vol-au-Vents 328
Toffee Brittle 282
See also almonds; chestnuts; hazelnuts; peanuts; pecans; pine
  nuts; pistachios; walnuts

O

OLIVES
Black and Green Olive Tapenade 50
Orzo Salad with Garbanzos, Peppers, and Dill 33
Trio of Spiced Olive Tapas 64
Tuscan Chicken with Spaghetti........................140
One-Pot Chicken Dinner................................ 128

ONIONS
Garlic Bread with Porcini-Onion Relish................ 18
Orange-Scented Rack of Veal 154
Pesto Caesar Salad with Crispy Onions in Tortilla Bowls....106
Pistachio-Crusted Salmon with Eggplant Puree...........202
Romaine with Avocado, Cucumber, Mango, and Red Onion
  Dressing...104
Savory Club Steak with Caramelized Onions 152
Slow-Cooked French Onion Soup 250
Sweet Gefilte Fish with Caramelized Tomatoes, Mushrooms,
  and Onions 200
Tuna Steaks with Dijon Garlic Sauce.................. 196
See also crispy onions; red onions
Orange Mousse in Phyllo Baskets with Citrus Punchsietta 272

ORANGES
Balsamic Duck a l'Orange 148
Blood Orange Mint Sorbet.............................334
Citrus Dill Olives...................................64
Clementine Glazed Chicken and Baby Arugula Salad with
  Balsamic-Soy Vinaigrette.............................88
Cranberry Blueberry Orange Chicken................... 146
Crepes Suzette 306
Healthy Moist Carrot-Orange Muffins..................322
Orange Mousse in Phyllo Baskets with Citrus Punchsietta ...272
Orange-Scented Rack of Veal 154
Rack of Lamb with Orange Mustard Rosemary Sauce 172
Orange-Scented Rack of Veal 154
Oreo Cookie Dough Pie................................342
Orzo Salad with Garbanzos, Peppers, and Dill 33

P

Panko-Crusted Tomato Basil Chilean Sea Bass............... 198

Panko Mozzarella Sticks with Red Wine Vinegar Marinara
    Sauce. 230

PANKO CRUMBS
    Crispy Sesame Chicken Cutlets with Avocado Hummus . . . 138
    Panko-Crusted Tomato Basil Chilean Sea Bass 198
    Panko Mozzarella Sticks with Red Wine Vinegar Marinara
        Sauce 230

PAPAYA
    Savory Chicken with Papaya Salsa. 126
Pareve Cheese Mousse with White Viennese Crunch 294

PARMESAN
    Fettuccine with Pistachio Pesto Alfredo Cream. 224
    Four-Ingredient Fettuccine Alfredo 224
    Linguine with White Wine Cream Sauce and Mushrooms . . .240
    Penne Vodka 256

PARSLEY
    Asian Portobello Mushrooms 14
    Best Chicken Soup. 76
    No-Grease Everything Knots 40
    Roasted Portobello Mushroom Soup 78
Pasta Bolognese 156

PASTA
    Fettuccine with Pistachio Pesto Alfredo Cream. 224
    Four-Ingredient Fettuccine Alfredo 224
    Linguine with White Wine Cream Sauce and Mushrooms . . .240
    Minestrone Soup 83
    Orzo Salad with Garbanzos, Peppers, and Dill 33
    Pasta Bolognese. 156
    Penne Vodka 256
    Teriyaki Sesame Pasta 53
    Tuscan Chicken with Spaghetti. 140

PASTRAMI
    Beef Bourguignon. 80
    Deli Roll Sushi with Dipping Sauce 12
    Fusion Chef Salad with Triple Crunch in Tortilla Wraps 114
    Garlic Bread with Porcini-Onion Relish. 18
    Pastrami Potato Kugelettes 26
    Pulled Meat Wontons with Honey Mustard Sauce. 56
    Roasted Asparagus and String Bean Bundles 63
Pastrami Potato Kugelettes 26

PASTRY
    Apple Rose Custard Turnovers. 316
    Bavarian Strawberries 'n' Cream Napoleon. 275
    Mascarpone Cheese Danishes. .254
    Nectarine and Plum Crostata 286

Orange Mousse in Phyllo Baskets with Citrus Punchsietta . . .272
Peanut Butter Mousse Vol-au-Vents 328
Powdered Chocolate Wontons with Caramel Sauce. 356
Profiteroles with Chocolate Rum Sauce 332
Tangerine Glazed Apple Apricot Strudel 339

PEACHES
    Balsamic Grilled Peaches with Basil-Pistachio Ice Cream
        on Cinnamon Skewers 298
    Maple Peach Crisp with Nutmeg Streusel 352
Peanut Butter Chocolate Pie 360
Peanut Butter Mousse Vol-au-Vents. 328

PEANUT BUTTER
    Grilled Chicken Satay with Peanut Butter Barbecue
        Sauce 136
    Ice Cream Razzle 324
    Peanut Butter Chocolate Pie 360
    Peanut Butter Mousse Vol-au-Vents 328

PEANUTS
    Better-Than-Snickers Dessert Bars 220
    Peanut Butter Chocolate Pie 360
    Terra Stix, Mushroom, and Bell Pepper Salad 102

PEARS
    Caramelized Pear Spinach Salad with Pomegranate and
        Pecans 112

PECANS
    Bourbon Toasted Pecan Pie. 340
    Caramelized Pear Spinach Salad with Pomegranate and
        Pecans 112
    Cheese Truffles. 214
    Key Lime Pie with Pecan Crust .232
    Spring Mix with Candied Hazelnuts and Pecans and Balsamic-
        Strawberry Vinaigrette. 92
    Terra Stix, Mushroom, and Bell Pepper Salad 102
    Warm Cinnamon Buns with Flambéed Rum Bananas 262
Penne Vodka 256

PEPPERS
    Bell Pepper Mushroom Crostini .42
    Best Chicken Soup. 76
    Crispy Beef Salad with Warm Peppers and Thai Sweet-Chili
        Vinaigrette. 110
    Orzo Salad with Garbanzos, Peppers, and Dill 33
    Purple Cabbage and Yellow Bell Pepper Slaw. 108
    Roasted Eggplant and Red Pepper Dip 60
    Terra Stix, Mushroom, and Bell Pepper Salad 102
Pesto Caesar Salad with Crispy Onions in Tortilla Bowls 106

Pesto Chicken or Sweetbreads with Tomato Basil Polenta
Stacks 44

PESTO
Chilean Sea Bass with Chive Chimichurri. 186
Fettuccine with Pistachio Pesto Alfredo Cream 224
Pesto Caesar Salad with Crispy Onions in Tortilla Bowls 106
Pesto Chicken or Sweetbreads with Tomato Basil Polenta
Stacks 44

Pickled Dark Turkey Roast with Brown Sugar Horseradish
Sauce. 144

PIE
Blueberry Lemon Biscuit Pie 290
Bourbon Toasted Pecan Pie. 340
Chocolate Toffee Torte 260
Ice Cream Razzle 324
Key Lime Pie with Pecan Crust 232
Lemon Meringue Pie. 338
Oreo Cookie Dough Pie 342
Pareve Cheese Mousse with White Viennese Crunch. 294
Peanut Butter Chocolate Pie 360
Pretzel-Crusted Lemon Lime Pie 268
Sour Cream Apple Pie with Walnut Streusel. 228
Spiced Mocha Mousse with Viennese Crunch. 330
See also tarts

PINE NUTS
Cream of Spinach Soup. 222
Crispy Beef Salad with Warm Peppers and Thai Sweet-Chili
Vinaigrette. 110
Fettuccine with Pistachio Pesto Alfredo
Cream. 224
Fruit Soup Salad with Toasted Pine Nuts and Craisins 326
Pesto Chicken or Sweetbreads with Tomato Basil Polenta
Stacks. 44
Roasted Portobello Chicken Salad 118

PILAF
Wild Rice Pilaf with Cherries and Almonds. 21
Pistachio-Crusted Salmon with Eggplant
Puree 202
Pistachio French Toast with Banana Salsa 348

PISTACHIOS
Balsamic Grilled Peaches with Basil-Pistachio
Ice Cream on Cinnamon Skewers 298
Fettuccine with Pistachio Pesto Alfredo
Cream. 224
Pistachio French Toast with Banana Salsa. 348

Pistachio-Crusted Salmon with Eggplant
Puree. 202
Strawberry Spinach Salad with Yogurt Poppy Seed Dressing 218

PITA
Minced Garlic and Rosemary Garlic Pita Crisps. 46
Plum Torte 274

PLUMS
Moscato d'Asti Apricot Compote 288
Nectarine and Plum Crostata 286
Plum Torte 274
Poached Sweet and Tangy Salmon. 206

POLENTA
Pesto Chicken or Sweetbreads with Tomato Basil Polenta
Stacks 44
Pomegranate Honey Glazed Duck Breast with Sesame Roasted
Sweet Potatoes. 134
Pomegranate Strawberry Mocktail with Sorbet 270

POMEGRANATE
Caramelized Pear Spinach Salad with Pomegranate and
Pecans 112
Clementine Glazed Chicken and Baby Arugula Salad with
Balsamic-Soy Vinaigrette. 88
Fruit Salad with Balsamic Strawberry Coulis, Crunchy Nuts,
and Pomegranate Seeds. 346
Fruit Soup Salad with Toasted Pine Nuts and Craisins 326
Lime Sea Bass with Sweet Chili Apricot Relish 192
Pomegranate Honey Glazed Duck Breast with Sesame
Roasted Sweet Potatoes. 134
Pomegranate Strawberry Mocktail with Sorbet 270

POPPY SEEDS
Strawberry Spinach Salad with Yogurt Poppy
Seed Dressing. 218

POTATO CHIPS
Hazelnut Chocolate Mousse with Chocolate-Dipped
Potato Chips 300
Potato Kugel and Sweet Potato Roulade. 30

POTATOES
Baby Red Potato Salad with Caesar Dill Dressing 96
Butcher's Cut with Broccoli Mashed Potatoes 48
Hazelnut Chocolate Mousse with Chocolate-Dipped
Potato Chips 300
Lemon Artichoke Cream Potato Salad 43
One-Pot Chicken Dinner 128
Pastrami Potato Kugelettes 26
Potato Kugel and Sweet Potato Roulade. 30

Roasted Fingerlings and Brussels Sprouts with Sage Brown
    Butter 32
Square French Fries 186
Tri-Color Garlic Mashed Potatoes with Caramelized
    Shallots 20

POULTRY. *See chicken; duck; turkey*
Powdered Chocolate Wontons with Caramel Sauce 356
Praline Truffles 283
Pretzel-Crusted Lemon Lime Pie 268
Profiteroles with Chocolate Rum Sauce 332
Pulled Meat Wontons with Honey Mustard Sauce 56

PUMPKIN
Roasted Chestnut Pumpkin Soup 74
Vegetable Dumpling Soup 72
Purple Cabbage and Yellow Bell Pepper Slaw 108

Q

Quilted Fondant for Cupcakes 285

QUINOA
Scallion Quinoa Patties with Lemon Garlic Paprika Aioli 10

R

Rack of Flanken with Cola Marinade and Coffee Barbecue
    Sauce 158
Rack of Lamb with Orange Mustard Rosemary Sauce 172

RED ONIONS
Asian Slaw with Chow Mein Noodles and Sesame Dressing . 90
Avocado, Tomato, and Hearts of Palm Salad 116
Blackened Tuna with Tropical Salad and Honey-Lime
    Dressing 94
Clementine Glazed Chicken and Baby Arugula with Balsamic-
    Soy Vinaigrette 88
Coconut Couscous with Scallion Lime Syrup and Mango 58
Fusion Chef Salad with Triple Crunch in Tortilla Wraps 114
Haloumi Salad with Warm Mushrooms and Teriyaki
    Dressing 212
Orzo Salad with Garbanzos, Peppers, and Dill 33
Roasted Eggplant and Red Pepper Dip 60

Romaine with Avocado, Cucumber, Mango, and Red Onion
    Dressing 104
Tarragon Egg Salad and Guacamole on Wonton Crisps 54
Tomato Basil Salad with a Duo of Vinegars 52

RED WINE
Beef Bourguignon 80
New York Strip Steak with Cabernet Merlot Reduction
    Sauce and Crispy Shallots 168
Slow-Cooked French Onion Soup 250

RELISH
Garlic Bread with Porcini-Onion Relish 18
Lime Sea Bass with Sweet Chili Apricot Relish 192

REMOULADE SAUCE
Creole Veal Burger with Remoulade Sauce 160

RICE
Deli Roll Sushi with Dipping Sauce 12
Sushi Gefilte Fish 190
Wild Rice Pilaf with Cherries and Almonds 21
Roasted Asparagus and String Bean Bundles 63
Roasted Chestnut Pumpkin Soup 74
Roasted Corn and Sausage Soup 82
Roasted Eggplant and Red Pepper Dip 60
Roasted Fingerlings and Brussels Sprouts with Sage Brown
    Butter 32
Roasted Portobello Chicken Salad 118
Roasted Portobello Mushroom Soup 78
Romaine with Avocado, Cucumber, Mango, and Red Onion
    Dressing 104

ROSEMARY
Grilled Steak with Herb and Garlic Tapenade 170
Heirloom Caprese Salad on Rosemary Skewers 246
Minced Garlic and Rosemary Garlic Pita Crisps 46
Mini Mushroom Beef Sliders 66
Rack of Lamb with Orange Mustard Rosemary Sauce 172

ROULADE
Potato Kugel and Sweet Potato Roulade 30

S

SAGE
Roasted Fingerlings and Brussels Sprouts with Sage Brown
    Butter 32
Sake-Glazed Salmon with Shitake and Portobello Mushrooms . 184

SALAD

Arugula Waldorf Salad with Maple Walnuts 109

Asian Slaw with Chow Mein Noodles and Sesame
Dressing. 90

Avocado, Tomato, and Hearts of Palm Salad 116

Baby Red Potato Salad with Caesar Dill Dressing 96

BBQ Tortilla Chip Salad. 98

Blackened Tuna with Tropical Salad and Honey-Lime
Dressing 94

Caramelized Pear Spinach Salad with Pomegranate and
Pecans 112

Clementine Glazed Chicken and Baby Arugula Salad with
Balsamic-Soy Vinaigrette. 88

Crispy Beef Salad with Warm Peppers and Thai Sweet-Chili
Vinaigrette. 110

Crispy Kani Slaw with Spicy Mayo. .97

Fusion Chef Salad with Triple Crunch in Tortilla Wraps 114

Haloumi Salad with Warm Mushrooms and Teriyaki
Dressing. 212

Heirloom Caprese Salad on Rosemary Skewers. 246

Lemon Artichoke Cream Potato Salad 43

Orzo Salad with Garbanzos, Peppers, and Dill 33

Pesto Caesar Salad with Crispy Onions in Tortilla Bowls. . . .106

Purple Cabbage and Yellow Bell Pepper Slaw. 108

Roasted Portobello Chicken Salad 118

Romaine with Avocado, Cucumber, Mango, and
Red Onion Dressing 104

Smoked Turkey and Chicken Salad with Creamy Avocado
Dressing. 100

Spring Mix with Candied Hazelnuts and Pecans and Balsamic-
Strawberry Vinaigrette. 92

Strawberry Spinach Salad with Yogurt Poppy Seed
Dressing. 218

Tarragon Egg Salad and Guacamole on Wonton Crisps. 54

Terra Stix, Mushroom, and Bell Pepper Salad 102

Tomato Basil Salad with a Duo of Vinegars. 52

Tropical Kani Salad with Sriracha Lime Dressing 120

Salmon Tartare 16

SALMON

Pistachio-Crusted Salmon with Eggplant Puree. 202

Poached Sweet and Tangy Salmon 206

Sake-Glazed Salmon with Shitake and Portobello
Mushrooms. 184

Salmon Tartare 16

Sixty-Second Cajun Salmon with Dill 182

Striped Sesame Teriyaki Salmon 194

Two-Toned Gefilte Fish Gift Squares. 208

SALSA

Pistachio French Toast with Banana Salsa. 348

Savory Chicken with Papaya Salsa. 126

SAUCES

Chicken Fire Poppers. 132

Chocolate Bundlettes with Mocha Fondue 320

Coconut Tilapia with Apricot Teriyaki Sauce. 188

Creole Veal Burgers with Remoulade Sauce 160

Crepes Suzette 306

Deli Roll Sushi with Dipping Sauce 12

Filet Mignon au Poivre 174

Fruit Salad with Balsamic Strawberry Coulis, Crunchy
Nuts, and Pomegranate Seeds 346

Grilled Chicken Satay with Peanut Butter Barbecue
Sauce 136

Halibut in Balsamic Honey Butter Sauce 247

Lime Sea Bass with Sweet Chili Apricot Relish. 192

Linguine with White Wine Cream Sauce and
Mushrooms. 240

Marinated Cherry-Soy London Broil 164

Mexican Chicken-Filled Crepes with Shallot Sauce. 34

New York Strip Steak with Carbernet Merlot Reduction
Sauce and Crispy Shallots 168

Panko Mozzarella Sticks with Red Wine Vinegar Marinara
Sauce 230

Pesto Chicken or Sweetbreads with Tomato-Basil Polenta
Stacks 44

Pickled Dark Turkey Roast with Brown Sugar Horseradish
Sauce 144

Powdered Chocolate Wontons with Caramel Sauce. 356

Profiteroles with Chocolate Rum Sauce 332

Pulled Meat Wontons with Honey Mustard Sauce. 56

Rack of Flanken with Cola Marinade and Coffee Barbecue
Sauce 158

Rack of Lamb with Orange Mustard Rosemary Sauce 172

Roasted Asparagus and String Bean Bundles 63

Tongue Polonaise. 28

Tuna Steaks with Dijon Garlic Sauce. 196

Warm Cinnamon Buns with Flambéed Rum Bananas 262

SAUERKRAUT

Pulled Meat Wontons with Honey Mustard Sauce. 56

SAUSAGES

Roasted Corn and Sausage Soup 82

Savory Chicken with Papaya Salsa 126
Savory Club Steak with Caramelized Onions. 152
Scallion Quinoa Patties with Lemon Garlic Paprika Aioli 10

SCALLIONS

Asian Slaw with Chow Mein Noodles and Sesame
 Dressing. 90
Blackened Tuna with Tropical Salad and Honey-Lime
 Dressing. 94
Coconut Couscous with Scallion Lime Syrup and Mango 58
Purple Cabbage and Yellow Bell Pepper Slaw. 108
Scallion Quinoa Patties with Lemon Garlic Paprika Aioli 10

SEA BASS

Chilean Sea Bass with Chive Chimichurri. 186
Lime Sea Bass with Sweet Chili Apricot Relish. 192
Panko-Crusted Tomato Basil Chilean Sea Bass 198
Sea Salt Caramel Bundt Cake 310

SESAME

Aburi Sesame Tuna with Wasabi Garlic Cream 204
Asian Slaw with Chow Mein Noodles and Sesame
 Dressing. 90
Caramelized Baked Sticky Sesame Chicken 149
Crispy Sesame Chicken Cutlets with Avocado Hummus . . . 138
Pomegranate Honey Glazed Duck Breast with Sesame
 Roasted Sweet Potatoes. 134
Striped Sesame Teriyaki Salmon 194
Teriyaki Sesame Pasta 53

SESAME SEEDS

Aburi Sesame Tuna with Wasabi Garlic Cream 204
Asian Slaw with Chow Mein Noodles and Sesame
 Dressing. 90
Caramelized Baked Sticky Sesame Chicken 149
Challah 27
Cheese Truffles. 214
Clementine Glazed Chicken and Baby Arugula Salad with
 Balsamic-Soy Vinaigrette. 88
Crispy Sesame Chicken Cutlets with Avocado
 Hummus 138
Crispy Kani Slaw with Spicy Mayo. 97
Deli Roll Sushi with Dipping Sauce 12
Fusion Chef Salad with Triple Crunch in Tortilla Wraps 114
No Grease Everything Knots. 40
Purple Cabbage and Yellow Bell Pepper Slaw. 108
Roasted Asparagus and String Bean Bundles. 63
Striped Sesame Teriyaki Salmon 194
Tuna Steaks with Dijon Garlic Sauce. 196

SHALLOTS

Bell Pepper Mushroom Crostini 42
Filet Mignon au Poivre 174
Mexican Chicken-Filled Crepes with Shallot Sauce. 34
New York Strip Steak with Cabernet Merlot Reduction
 Sauce and Crispy Shallots 168
Tri-Color Garlic Mashed Potatoes with Caramelized
 Shallots. 20
Wild Rice Pilaf with Cherries and Almonds. 21

SIDE DISHES. *See appetizers and sides*

Sixty-Second Cajun Salmon with Dill 182

SKEWERS

Balsamic Grilled Peaches with Basil-Pistachio Ice Cream
 on Cinnamon Skewers 298
Grilled Chicken Satay with Peanut Butter Barbecue Sauce . . . 136
Heirloom Caprese Salad on Rosemary Skewers. 246
Sixty-Second Cajun Salmon with Dill 182
Skirt Steak Spring Rolls with Corn off the Cob 38
Slow-Cooked French Onion Soup. 250
Smoked Turkey and Chicken Salad with Creamy Avocado
 Dressing. 100
Sole in Lime Caper Chili Sauce 226
Sorbet and Ice Cream Sandwich Trifle 266

SORBET

Blood Orange Mint Sorbet. 334
Pomegranate Strawberry Mocktail with Sorbet. 270
Sorbet and Ice Cream Sandwich Trifle 266

SOUFFLÉ

Warm Chocolate Soufflé with a Hint of Chili 308

SOUP

Beef Bourguignon. 80
Best Chicken Soup. 76
Cream of Roasted Butternut Squash Soup with Herbes de
 Provence Tuiles. 70
Cream of Spinach Soup. 222
Creamy Broccoli Asparagus Soup 84
Creamy Roasted Tomato Vodka Soup 238
Minestrone Soup 83
Roasted Chestnut Pumpkin Soup. 74
Roasted Corn and Sausage Soup 82
Roasted Portobello Mushroom Soup 78
Slow-Cooked French Onion Soup 250
Vegetable Dumpling Soup. 72
Sour Cream Apple Pie with Walnut Streusel. 228
Spiced Mocha Mousse with Viennese Crunch. 330

SPINACH

Caramelized Pear Spinach Salad with Pomegranate and
Pecans 112

Cream of Spinach Soup. 222

Minestrone Soup 83

Strawberry Spinach Salad with Yogurt Poppy Seed
Dressing. 218

Stuffed French Bread with Spinach, Herbs, and Cheese. 227

SPREADS. *See* dips

Spring Mix with Candied Hazelnuts and Pecans and Balsamic-
Strawberry Vinaigrette 92

SPRING ROLLS

Skirt Steak Spring Rolls with Corn off the Cob 38

SQUASH

Cream of Roasted Butternut Squash Soup with Herbes de
Provence Tuiles. 70

Roasted Pattypans and Squash. 174

Vegetable Dumpling Soup 72

SRIRACHA SAUCE

Tropical Kani Salad with Sriracha Lime Dressing 120

Crispy Kani Slaw with Spicy Mayo. 97

STIR-FRY

Cashew Chicken Stir-Fry with Sweet Chili Glaze 142

Strawberries and Cream Smoothies 236

STRAWBERRIES

Basil Granita Strawberries 318

Bavarian Strawberries 'n; Cream Napoleon. 275

Fruit Salad with Balsamic Strawberry Coulis, Crunchy
Nuts, and Pomegranate Seeds 346

Fruit Soup Salad with Toasted Pine Nuts and Craisins 326

Fruit Tartare. 292

Pomegranate Strawberry Mocktail with
Sorbet. 270

Spring Mix with Candied Hazelnuts and Pecans and Balsamic-
Strawberry Vinaigrette. 92

Strawberries and Cream Smoothies 236

Strawberry Spinach Salad with Yogurt Poppy Seed
Dressing. 218

Strawberry Spinach Salad with Yogurt Poppy Seed Dressing . . . 218

STRING BEANS

Roasted Asparagus and String Bean Bundles 63

Striped Sesame Teriyaki Salmon. 194

Stuffed Eggplant Canapés with Veal 22

Stuffed French Bread with Spinach, Herbs, and Cheese. 227

Sun-Dried Tomato and Basil Capons. 130

SUN-DRIED TOMATOES

Mediterranean Olives 64

Sun-Dried Tomato and Basil Capons. 130

Sushi Gefilte Fish. 190

SUSHI

Deli Roll Sushi with Dipping Sauce 12

Sushi Gefilte Fish 190

SWEET CHILI SAUCE

Cashew Chicken Stir-Fry with Sweet Chili Glaze 142

Crispy Beef Salad with Warm Peppers and Thai Sweet-Chili
Vinaigrette. 110

Lime Sea Bass with Sweet Chili Apricot Relish 192

Savory Chicken with Papaya Salsa. 126

Tamari French Roast or Brisket 178

SWEET POTATOES

Baked Sweet Potato Fries with Cajun Mayo and Garlic-Basil
Mayo. 24

Pomegranate Honey Glazed Duck Breast with Sesame
Roasted Sweet Potatoes. 134

Potato Kugel and Sweet Potato Roulade. 30

Smoked Sweet-and-Sour Ribs 167

Sweet Gefilte Fish with Caramelized Tomatoes, Mushrooms,
and Onions. 200

SWEETBREADS

Pesto Chicken or Sweetbreads with Tomato Basil Polenta
Stacks 44

T

Tamari French Roast or Brisket 178

Tangerine Glazed Apple Apricot Strudel. 339

TAPAS

Trio of Spiced Olive Tapas 64

TAPENADE

Black and Green Olive Tapenade .50

Grilled Steak with Herb and Garlic Tapenade 170

Tarragon Egg Salad and Guacamole on Wonton Crisps. 54

TARTARE

Fruit Tartare. 292

Salmon Tartare 16

Tuna Tartare 36

TARTS

Double Chocolate Ganache Tart .353

Green Tea Lychee Berry Tart 248
Nectarine and Plum Crostata 286
See also pies
Teriyaki Sesame Pasta 53

TERIYAKI
Coconut Tilapia with Apricot Teriyaki Sauce 188
Haloumi Salad with Warm Mushrooms and Teriyaki
Dressing 212
Striped Sesame Teriyaki Salmon 194
Teriyaki Sesame Pasta 53
Terra Stix, Mushroom, and Bell Pepper Salad 102
Three-Glaze Cinnamon Buns 354

THYME
Black and Green Olive Tapenade 50
Lemon-Thyme Delmonico Roast 162
Moscato d'Asti Apricto Compote 288
Roasted Portobello Mushroom Soup 78

TILAPIA
Coconut Tilapia with Apricot Teriyaki Sauce 188
Tiramisu with Chocolate Liquor 350
Toffee Brittle 282
Tomato Basil Salad with a Duo of Vinegars 52

TOMATOES
Avocado, Tomato, and Hearts of Palm Salad 116
BBQ Tortilla Chip Salad 98
Creamy Roasted Tomato Vodka Soup 238
Fusion Chef Salad with Triple Crunch in Tortilla
Wraps 114
Haloumi Salad with Warm Mushrooms and Teriyaki
Dressing 212
Heirloom Caprese Salad on Rosemary Skewers 246
Panko-Crusted Tomato Basil Chilean Sea Bass 198
Penne Vodka 256
Pesto Chicken or Sweetbreads with Tomato Basil Polenta
Stacks 44
Smoked Turkey and Chicken Salad with Creamy Avocado
Dressing 100
Sun-Dried Tomato and Basil Capons 130
Sweet Gefilte Fish with Caramelized Tomatoes, Mushrooms,
and Onions 200
Tomato Basil Salad with a Duo of Vinegars 52
Tongue Polonaise 28

TORTE. *See* pie

TORTILLA CHIPS
BBQ Tortilla Chip Salad 98

TORTILLAS
Fusion Chef Salad with Triple Crunch in Tortilla Wraps 114
Pesto Caesar Salad with Crispy Onions in Tortilla Bowls 106
Tri-Color Garlic Mashed Potatoes with
Caramelized Shallots 20

TRIFLE
Sorbet and Ice Cream Sandwich Trifle 266
Trio of Spiced Olive Tapas 64
Tropical Kani Salad with Sriracha Lime Dressing 120

TRUFFLES
Cheese Truffles 214
Praline Truffles 283
Tuna Steaks with Dijon Garlic Sauce 196
Tuna Tartare 36

TUNA
Aburi Sesame Tuna with Wasabi Garlic Cream 204
Blackened Tuna with Tropical Salad and Honey-Lime
Dressing 94
Tuna Steaks with Dijon Garlic Sauce 196
Tuna Tartare 36

TURKEY
Best Chicken Soup 76
Deli Roll Sushi with Dipping Sauce 12
Fusion Chef Salad with Triple Crunch in Tortilla Wraps 114
Pickled Dark Turkey Roast with Brown Sugar Horseradish
Sauce 144
Pulled Meat Wontons with Honey Mustard Sauce 56
Smoked Turkey and Chicken Salad with Creamy Warm
Avocado Dressing 100
Tuscan Chicken with Spaghetti 140
Twenty-Garlic-Clove Standing Rib Roast 176
Two-Toned Gefilte Fish Gift Squares 208

V

VEAL
Creole Veal Burgers with Remoulade Sauce 160
Orange-Scented Rack of Veal 154
Stuffed Eggplant Canapés with Veal 22
Vegetable Dumpling Soup 72

VIENNESE CRUNCH
Pareve Cheese Mousse with White Viennese Crunch 294
Spiced Mocha Mousse with Viennese Crunch 330

VINAIGRETTES

Clementine Glazed Chicken and Baby Arugula Salad with
Balsamic-Soy Vinaigrette.............................88

Crispy Beef Salad with Warm Peppers and Thai Sweet-Chili
Vinaigrette................................. 110

Spring Mix with Candied Hazelnuts and Pecans and Balsamic-
Strawberry Vinaigrette...............................92

See also dressings

W

WALNUTS

Apple Rose Custard Turnovers........................... 316

Arugula Waldorf Salad with Maple Walnuts 109

Chilean Sea Bass with Chive Chimichurri.................186

Fruit Salad with Balsamic Strawberry Coulis, Crunchy
Nuts, and Pomegranate Seeds........................346

Pesto Chicken or Sweetbreads with Tomato Basil Polenta
Stacks...44

Sour Cream Apple Pie with Walnut Streusel...............228

Warm Chocolate Soufflé with a Hint of Chili.................308

Warm Cinnamon Buns with Flambéed Rum Bananas..........262

Warm Deep-Dish Giant Chocolate Chip Cookie Torte........336

WASABI

Aburi Sesame Tuna with Wasabi Garlic
Cream.. 204

Sushi Gefilte Fish 190

WHITE WINE

Garlic Bread with Porcini-Onion Relish..................... 18

Haloumi Salad with Warm Mushrooms and Teriyaki
Dressing...212

Linguine with White Wine Cream Sauce and
Mushrooms...240

Moscato d'Asti Apricot Compote 288

Savory Rib Steak with Caramelized Onions............... 152

Wild Rice Pilaf with Cherries and Almonds.................. 21

WINE. *See* red wine; white wine

WONTONS

Cream of Roasted Butternut Sqash Soup with Herbes de
Provence Tuiles......................................70

Powdered Chocolate Wontons with Caramel Sauce........356

Pulled Meat Wontons with Honey Mustard Sauce..........56

Tarragon Egg Salad and Guacamole on Wonton Crisps......54

Y

YOGURT

Strawberry Spinach Salad with Yogurt Poppy Seed
Dressing...218

Strawberries and Cream Smoothies 236

Z

ZUCCHINI

Best Chicken Soup....................................... 76

Roasted Pattypans and Squash......................... 174

Vegetable Dumpling Soup............................... 72